AF428431

Shattered and Becoming

Shattered and Becoming:
A Teacher's Journey Between Policy and Purpose

Andrew D. L. Goff

GOLD THREAD PRESS
An imprint of Heartset & Mindset LLC
heartsetandmindset.org
© 2026 Heartset & Mindset LLC

Published by Gold Thread Press
An imprint of Heartset & Mindset LLC

ISBN (Hardcover): 979-8-9944249-3-3
ISBN (Paperback): 979-8-9944249-1-9
ISBN (eBook): 979-8-9944249-2-6

Library of Congress Control Number: 2026902459
Printed in the United States of America

For every student I have had the privilege to teach, young children and adult learners alike, who have shaped my growth as a leader.

CONTENTS

AUTHOR'S NOTE

This memoir is a personal account based on my experiences, reflections, and memories during my time as an early childhood educator. Although the events are drawn from real-life circumstances, I have changed or combined certain names, identifying details, locations, timelines, and organizational titles to protect the privacy of individuals and institutions. However, some individuals may recognize aspects of themselves or others. These similarities reflect my effort to portray real experiences while safeguarding individual privacy through altered identifying details.

Conversations, emails, and text message exchanges referenced in this memoir are based on my personal recollections and paraphrased for narrative clarity. Composite characters and reconstructed dialogues have been used to reflect the essence of real situations while respecting individual privacy.

This book is not intended to serve as an official or authorized account of any institution, school district, or organization. The views expressed in this book are solely mine and do not represent the official policies, positions, or opinions of any employer, public agency, or educational entity, past or present.

INTRODUCTION

This is a story of becoming. Not through ease, but through tension. Not because everything went right, but because some things went heartbreakingly wrong. It is not simply a story about teaching. It is about identity and the search for wholeness inside systems that often reward fragmentation.

The journey that led to this book began with my first memoir, *Love Is a Classroom*. Although the two books are different in scope and tone, this one would not exist without the first. *Love Is a Classroom* started as something private. It was where I went to grieve and make sense of experiences I could not yet name. Entry by entry, I wrote through confusion, trying to understand what had happened and how it had affected me.

Over time, the writing shifted. It no longer spoke only from my perspective. When I shared pieces aloud, others recognized their own experiences in my words. What began as private reflection became something shared. Those early events pulled me apart and then helped put me back together. They showed me that the most personal moments often reveal something collective.

This book continues that arc by examining lessons about leadership, responsibility, and integrity that apply far beyond education. It is not only a record of what I lived through, but an account of how I now understand those moments with more clarity, distance, and compassion. Though you will meet people in these pages whose decisions and actions caused real harm, I ask that you resist the urge to villainize them. I believe, as I hope you will, that the teachers or administrators in this story were doing the best they could with the tools, support, and self-awareness they had at the time. Their missteps were real, and the impact on me was real, yet harm can exist without intent. That is one of the central tensions this story holds.

I offer this story as both a mirror and a window. A mirror for those who have felt silenced, confused, or discouraged by institutional expectations that do not match the realities of human connection. A window into what authentic leadership requires when the systems around us resist it. It is for anyone who has ever asked, "Is it me?" or "How do I lead with integrity in a place that rewards compliance over relationships?"

Throughout this journey, I found compassion for others and, eventually, for myself. Forgiveness did not arrive as a single moment. It unfolded slowly, revealed in small insights that emerged over time. If you have experienced something similar, I hope you hear this clearly: you do not need to rush toward resolution. You do not need perfect language to be allowed to speak. You do not need to hold your truth quietly to protect others' comfort.

Before you step into the first chapter, I will offer this. The epilogue brings the story together in a way I could only see with distance. It is brief, yet it carries the clearest expression of what this journey taught me about teaching, leadership, and becoming a professional in any capacity. My hope is that the chapters leading up to it make that final reflection more meaningful, because this book is an invitation to speak honestly, reflect deeply, and heal on your own terms. My identity took shape through classroom experiences, conflict, grief, and values that pushed me toward clarity. The stories in these pages show where that shift began and how the struggle itself became the heart of the work.

***

This story picks up where *Love Is a Classroom* left off. As I entered my second year at Vista Elementary, I imagined things would feel lighter and steadier. Instead, it felt as if I was returning to uncertainty all over again.

My classroom at Vista, room 125, was down two teaching assistants. The previous team had moved into other roles at the school, roles that better aligned with their long-term goals. I was happy for them, truly, but their absence left me anxious. The search for replacements began as soon as the school year ended. By midsummer, three candidates had walked in and out of Kris's office, the highly respected and deeply principled school principal. None had been the right fit.

"They must speak Spanish," Kris reminded the hiring committee, her voice calm but resolute. The district's Binding Compliance Order required that children of families whose native language was not English be offered equitable access to instruction in their home language. This qualification was nonnegotiable.

I sat on the committee, watching each candidate closely, not just for credentials but also for presence. I was looking for intuition, the rare kind of patience and energy that could hold space for three- and four-year-olds navigating big needs inside tiny bodies. Then Cecilia walked in.

She had an unteachable warmth and a kind of wisdom that didn't need to be spoken. Maybe it came from raising three children or from her mother's home-based childcare program. Or maybe it was simply who she was. Within minutes, I knew. Cecilia didn't just meet the requirement; she set a new standard, one that led to her being hired midsummer.

The school year began with just the two of us. We still hadn't found a second assistant who met the district's criteria, and now I carried an additional benchmark in my mind. It was the one Cecilia had set for what was possible. Within days, she had already built trust with every family in the room. It was uncanny. I watched how parents exhaled when they spoke with her and how quickly they relaxed in her presence. They trusted her the way you trust someone who has held your newborn or stood beside you in a hospital waiting room. In a way, we were doing just that. We were sharing life's most precious moments with the families of our students.

Three weeks into the school year, room 125 wasn't perfect, but compared to the chaotic start the year before, it felt like progress. When Lillie finally joined our team, everything shifted again. She was young, in her early twenties, and brought a completely different energy to the classroom. She met the Spanish requirement. She had no children, few life obligations, and limited classroom experience. At first, I didn't know what to make of her. She had firm boundaries, something Cecilia and I hadn't yet mastered. She didn't take the job home with her or carry it in her body the way we did. Sometimes, that frustrated me, but I also admired her for it.

What mattered most was that Lillie loved the kids, especially the ones who needed extra support. She showed up for them every day. Within a week, the three of us had built something meaningful: a classroom community rooted in trust, joy, and connection. My knowledge of the curriculum and passion for inclusion gave shape to our days. By mid-fall, both our morning and afternoon groups had become the kind of community I'd always striven to create.

Then there was the other side of my job, the part that had made me question my integrity ever since Jovan Allen's Individual Education Program meeting in January of the previous year. Every meeting with special education administrators reminded me that, to the district, policies and compliance often mattered more than children and families. As Thanksgiving approached, the tension between the joy I found in the classroom and the frustration I felt toward the system became more difficult to manage. It was like trying to inflate a balloon that was already stretched to its limits. Each breath felt risky.

I loved our classroom. I loved the relationships we were building. I also knew how fragile it all was, how easily it could be interrupted by decisions made far from room 125. That fragility made the job hard to tolerate at times. Deep inside, I wanted something more. Not just for myself, but for every individual trying to do this work in a system that often forgets its purpose.

A week before Thanksgiving, I received an unexpected opportunity that would allow me to act on the very impulse I had been carrying for years: the desire to influence the policies and practices of special education from the inside.

And so began the next chapter of my life.

CHAPTER 1

THE APPLICATION

———

The rush of excitement hit me before I could even exhale, but it was quickly blunted by a familiar wave of hesitation. I stared at the open email, my mind racing. Around the corner, Natalie, my wife, was in the bedroom nursing our two-month-old, Itzel, to sleep. Citlali, our three-year-old, was already down for the night, her soft snoring filling the silence of our three-bedroom duplex. As I examined the subject line of the email, I asked myself, *Do I wait until tomorrow, when everyone is well-rested, to tell Natalie?*

Sensations stirred my stomach, tickled my sides, and squeezed my throat. I read the email again, slowly this time, savoring each word. Then I clicked on the first link. The details were almost too good to be true: a full scholarship for a doctorate in early childhood special education leadership. Five slots. A dream opportunity that couldn't have come at a more complicated time. The deadline was less than two weeks away, the week after Thanksgiving. I needed to tell Natalie or maybe ask her. No, I needed to just tell her. But how?

The frustration of ten and a half years of special education policies rested uncomfortably on my daily routine in the classroom. Before every Individual Education Program meeting in recent years, I couldn't stop replaying the moments when I'd witnessed the school district's failure to treat children and families with basic human dignity and provide the services they were legally entitled to. *The status quo isn't just unacceptable. It's broken. This scholarship is an opportunity,* I told myself. *It is essential if I want to influence anything beyond my classroom walls.*

"I laid her in the crib," Natalie whispered optimistically as she walked into the living room.

Her face was a picture of relief, though it was certain to be short-lived. Itzel wasn't a good sleeper. Acid reflux had turned nights into long stretches of interrupted rest. The spitting up and persistent crying made consistency nearly impossible, which was just one of the factors that complicated my desire.

I was sitting on the edge of the couch, the computer open on my lap. I stared at the email again. I felt like I was Citlali when she held a secret. The words were bubbling up inside me, and I knew that if I didn't say something, I wouldn't sleep. Then again, if I did say something, I probably wouldn't sleep either.

"I'm going to get ready for bed," Natalie said, already halfway down the hall.

I glanced at the corner of my computer screen: 8:14 p.m., November 21. One teaspoon of courage, a full cup of fear, and Natalie's growing maternal exhaustion churned in my stomach. I had to say something.

"Wait," I blurted, my voice thick with nerves but quiet so as not to wake the children. She paused and looked back at me. I took a deep breath. "I got an email this afternoon from the University of Colorado. They're offering five full scholarships for a doctorate in early childhood special education leadership. I . . ."

But I didn't get to finish.

"Are you crazy?" Natalie's voice exploded across the room, as waking the children wasn't a consideration for her at that moment. "We just had a baby! No! Absolutely not!" Each sentence was laced with anger. Her words were punctuated by expletives. "I'm going to sleep."

With that, silence. I felt the air leave the room. The courage I'd scraped together just moments before evaporated as her words echoed in my ears. *Absolutely not.* I couldn't blame her. Her priority has always been family, and I had a difficult time framing the opportunity as something that would benefit all of us.

That night, I drifted in and out of a restless sleep. Itzel awoke crying. I rose from bed and walked her around the dark duplex while Natalie slept, stirring only when Itzel needed to nurse. After two months of this pattern, I was too tired to care. That night, all I could think about were the possibilities I was being asked to forget.

I held Itzel close. Her tiny body was warm and limp against my chest, but my mind was far away. I wanted nothing more than to dwell in that email, to imagine a future where I had a doctorate, where I could influence a change in school districts across the country that had failed so many children with disabilities and their families. I was already living that future in my mind. In the present, I was walking circles in the dark.

What if I go for it anyway?

***

The morning passed in a blur. My mind darted between the joy of possibility and the pull of reality. I floated through my day in room 125, balancing on a tightrope where euphoria and anxiety tugged at opposing sides. I needed a second opinion, fast. The clock was ticking, and if I didn't move, the opportunity would slip through my fingers. I needed three letters of recommendation by the end of the weekend. For something this big, there was only one person I could turn to: Virginia.

I'd met Virginia and her supervisor two years earlier when I was in Denver looking for a job before my family moved there from Tucson. Our first conversation had been casual, strictly business, focused on job opportunities at Rocky Mountain Community College, though none existed. Still, her supervisor added my name to the list of part-time instructors at the college. That spring, I taught my first online class for the college. In no time, Virginia and I developed a relationship of deep respect and camaraderie. We became each other's sounding boards. Our conversations spanned everything from pedagogy to the messiness of life. Virginia had been the director of a private preschool, a role that fascinated me. She found my experience as an early childhood special educator equally compelling. We learned from each other and challenged each other, and most of all, we commiserated with one another about the unique pressures of working with young children and their families. After Cecilia and Lillie left for lunch, I grabbed my phone and dialed her number.

"Hey, friend, happy Friday!" Virginia's voice was as bright and warm as ever. I could picture her in her office, reclined in her chair, beneath an eight-by-eight-foot patchwork quilt. Each patch had been decorated by a child, parent, or teacher and was gifted to her when she retired from her last childcare program.

"Hey, Virginia. Do you have a few minutes to chat? I've got something I need to process and get off my chest."

"Of course, what's going on?" Her voice dropped, sensing the dilemma in mine.

"I got an email yesterday. The University of Colorado Denver is offering five scholarships for a doctorate in early childhood special education leadership. I really want to apply, but Natalie . . . she's not exactly thrilled. Let's just say her response was far from the queen's English." I paused, feeling the sting of the conversation from the night prior. "I don't know if I should try to convince her or just wait for a better time in my life. What do you think?"

Virginia took a few seconds, letting the moment settle before answering. "That's a tough one. I know this is huge for you, one of those once-in-a-lifetime things we always talk about. When the right door opens, you can't ignore it. Maybe keep it open without making any promises, you know?"

"Yeah, I know. It's just . . . I've been through so much with the special education system, both here and back in Tucson. I love developing a deeper understanding of the familiar. I feel like I need to do this." The frustration of years fighting for children's rights during and after Individual Education Program meetings and battling bureaucratic nonsense welled up as I spoke.

"Listen," Virginia said tenderly, "you and I, we're lifelong learners. This is your passion. You've got the knowledge and drive to have a significant influence on the way special education works in a district or even the state. You've said it yourself countless times, 'Schools see special education as fixing kids, but kids don't need to be fixed.' You believe that, and it's powerful." She paused for a few seconds. "Let me ask you this: if there aren't any scholarships down the road, would you still want to do it? Would you be okay paying for it yourself?"

Her words hit hard. I hadn't thought that far ahead. "You're right. Of course, I'd want to do it . . . but I don't think I could ever afford it, and who knows if there will be a full scholarship at a university nearby? I'd regret it if I didn't at least try." I paused, the facts of the next hurdle settling in. "But what about Natalie? How do I even begin to convince her?"

"Tell her the same thing you just told me. Be honest. If you don't apply, will you resent her for it? Will that resentment end up causing more damage than the time commitment if you were accepted?"

I got a little defensive, something unfamiliar to our relationship. "Wait, wait. I would never resent her. That's a little too far." I took a moment to collect myself. "Sorry, I mean, I'm so lucky, privileged . . . fortunate to have everything I have now." I thought carefully about my next words. "I suppose I worry she'll resent me if I go for it. Then where does that leave us? I don't know. It's complicated. I need your help."

There was a brief pause on the other end of the line. "You're right, Andrew. It's complicated. But nothing's guaranteed. If—

and that's a big IF—you get accepted, then you can have the conversation again. You can always say no if you decide it's not the right time."

"Yeah, but I've got another issue. The application is due next weekend. And, Virginia, we're driving to Wisconsin on Monday to see my family. The trip is a big undertaking, and it demands my full attention. I need to get the application in before we leave, and I don't know when I will be able to work on it. Can you write me a letter of recommendation by Sunday? If I can get Natalie on board, that is."

"Of course. I'll get it to you by tomorrow afternoon. Even if you don't use it this time, you'll have it for the future. You never know what opportunities are waiting. You don't need a doctorate to have the influence you're thinking about."

Her unwavering support calmed my muscles a little, but my mind was restless. "Thanks, Virginia. And hey, we should get together over winter break."

"Sure. Otherwise, Wednesdays work for me next semester if you want to grab lunch."

"Absolutely . . . but I'll let you know. I've got a lot on my plate, no pun intended. Plus, I've never left the classroom for lunch. I'm a 'working lunch' kind of person."

"I get it. It's good for your mental health to get out of the classroom once in a while. Don't be a stranger."

I ended the call. The afternoon slipped by in a haze of paperwork and classroom events, but the conversation gnawed at me. By the time I was driving home, I had a plan forming in my head. I'd tell Natalie after dinner. Timing was everything, and I needed to get this right. What if she still said no?

I took a deep breath, thinking that the next few hours could change everything.

***

Natalie reluctantly reached the same conclusion Virginia and I had discussed. If she said no, it might have created more stress later than if she agreed. My acceptance into the program was far from guaranteed. I promised her I'd be present for her and the girls whenever they needed me. If I ever became the same absent, stressed-out husband I'd been during the conversational Spanish classes the year before, I would withdraw. Natalie wasn't thrilled, but she understood the significance. It was something I'd pursue eventually, and we both knew there would never be a "right time."

On Sunday, November 24, I submitted my application: three letters of recommendation, a polished résumé reflecting my potential as a leader and researcher, and a carefully crafted letter of intent. As I clicked submit, I told myself, *At least I tried,* though I couldn't help but imagine the possibilities. That night, we packed our bags and prepared for a potentially treacherous road trip to Wisconsin. I pushed the application to the back of my mind.

Over the next few months, I focused on being a present father and husband. Still, the application's status hung in the background. On March 5, having heard nothing, I emailed the admissions office. Two days later, I learned my application had been misfiled with the master's program applicants. The doctoral decisions had already been made in mid-February. It stung. I'd allowed myself to imagine what could be.

As a courtesy, the university moved my application into next year's review pool, but I wasn't ready to let go. I emailed the lead faculty member for the Early Childhood Special Education Department at CU Denver. After several exchanges, I secured an interview, even though they had already accepted their five candidates. Maybe I could take a class or two over the summer, just to get started.

On Monday, March 17, during lunch, I received an email from the admissions office with the subject line: *UCD School of*

Education and Human Development Admissions. However, the children and families were arriving for the afternoon session. I didn't want any bad news to impact my energy in the classroom, so I followed Cecilia and Lillie to greet the children and families.

By 3:00 p.m., the unopened email dominated my thoughts. I hadn't told Cecilia or Lillie about my interests, unsure if I'd even get in. When I finally sat down at my desk, I texted Natalie.

I got an email from CU Denver.

Did you open it? she replied.

Not yet. Phone call? I need to mope with you.

Thumbs up.

I called. She picked up immediately.

"Okay, are you ready for this?" I asked, more to steady myself than anything else. "Here it goes."

Dear Andrew Goff,

> *Congratulations! The faculty members in the School of Education and Human Development's Doctoral Studies program at the University of Colorado Denver have reviewed your application and recommend that you be admitted, effective this summer, to begin the Doctor of Education for Leadership and Educational Equity program in the Early Childhood Special Education concentration area.*

I jumped out of my chair, heart pounding.

"YESSSSSSSSSSSSSSSSSSSSSSSSSSSSS!" I shouted, then quickly lowered my voice. "I got in! I GOT IN FOR THIS YEAR! I can't believe it. I'm the sixth student!"

"Congratulations," Natalie said warmly. Her voice was genuine.

"Thank you. And I promise, if school ever gets in the way of me being a good husband and father, I'll pause and finish at a more appropriate time."

"I know you will." She sounded slightly amused.

"I'll be home in twenty minutes. Should we celebrate tonight or wait four years?"

"The girls and I had a long day. We can celebrate another time. I love you."

"I love you too," I said, hanging up, still in disbelief.

The next morning, I shared the news with Cecilia and Lillie.

"That's great, Andrew!" Cecilia said.

"It'll be amazing for our class," Lillie added.

"I can't imagine how this year could get better . . . but I don't know what I don't know, right?" I laughed, the excitement still fresh in my chest.

I ran down the hallway to room 121 to tell Ana, my closest friend at Vista. She taught in one of the two English Language Development–Spanish classrooms for the Explorer program. As part of the cohort of visiting teachers from Spain, Ana had been recruited under the Binding Compliance Order.

"Congratulations! I'm so happy for you," Ana exclaimed, then her face softened. "Does this mean you're not going to be working here next year?"

"Absolutely not! The program wants me to stay in the classroom. They're flexible about it. Plus, as part of the scholarship, I need to keep working with and advocating for students with disabilities for the next five years."

"I love that!" Ana said, her excitement returning.

I explained more about the program and how Natalie and I had reached an agreement. Ana thought it would be fantastic for our early childhood education team. We all needed something to unite us besides district politics. I began to imagine how I could introduce ideas from the program that would bring us closer together, including the new principal, who was still in the hiring process. It was down to two candidates, and we were all anxious to see who would step into the role.

"It's sad Kris is leaving," Ana said thoughtfully.

I agreed. "She's done so much for me and for our Foundations program."

"Whatever happens, your schoolwork will make your classroom even better."

"That's the hope," I replied, smiling.

Two weeks later, it was officially announced that Jorge Sanchez had been hired as our new principal for the following year. He was currently leading an early childhood–focused school in the district. Initially, our team was excited to have someone who spoke our professional language. As we learned more about him, Ana and Esmeralda, the other English Language Development–Spanish teacher, as well as the two teachers in English Language Development–English Explorer classrooms, began to realize that more than the face in the front office would be changing.

My Foundations classroom wasn't structured like their Explorer classrooms, so I wasn't as concerned. Still, big changes were coming.

CHAPTER 2

CONVERSATIONS

The steady clap of a man's wing-tipped dress shoes echoed down the long, brick-walled corridor connecting the early childhood classrooms to the rest of Vista Elementary. Each step grew louder as they approached room 125, where I was finishing my final lesson plan of the year. My focus drifted from the computer screen to the doorway. The sound paused, then it was replaced by a soft shuffle. An enthusiastic face emerged from the hallway.

The man, likely around five-foot-eight without the shoes, was sharply dressed for a Friday afternoon. His raven-black hair, neatly styled and streaked with gray at the sides, framed a warm smile.

"Andrew?" he asked, his tone inviting.

I rose from my chair. "Mr. Sanchez! It's great to meet you. Please, come in."

"Oh, please call me Jorge," he said, using the Spanish pronunciation. "I've heard so much about you. It's wonderful to finally connect. You're one of the few teachers I haven't met yet." His voice, like his shoes, was smooth, appealing, and precise.

"Nothing too bad, I hope," I quipped.

"Of course not. One of the other early childhood teachers said you have a real impact on kids and families. It's a gift."

Compliments like that didn't come around often. "I just do my best. Last year's class was one of those you never forget."

Jorge's face softened. "Teachers like you make this school one of the best in the district. I'm excited to work with you."

His sincerity caught me off guard. I gestured to the rolling chair behind my desk, but Jorge waved it off and took a seat in one of the tiny blue preschool chairs at the kidney-shaped table. I joined him, careful not to sit at the center of the arc. I didn't want to give off any sense of hierarchy.

"How has your month been, visiting staff and classrooms?" I asked.

"Wonderful." His tone was humble. "I'm thrilled to be joining Vista. The work here is impressive. Tell me about your classroom."

"Our setup's a bit different from other early childhood education classrooms. The district calls it a Foundations classroom. We serve children ages three to five. Lillie and Cecilia, my two teaching assistants, are essential. I couldn't do it without them."

"Teaching assistants?" Jorge's eyebrows dipped. "Oh, you mean paraprofessionals? You have two?"

I nodded. "We usually have up to six kids with developmental delays or disabilities. The district assigns us two teaching assistants—sorry, paras—for that reason. We run a morning and an afternoon class. It's a daily marathon."

"And how many neighborhood kids?"

"Ten," I replied.

"Do they all speak English?"

"About a third started this year speaking only English. Another third spoke both English and Spanish. The rest, mostly Spanish. Some didn't speak much at all when they started, regardless of language."

Jorge scanned the room, clearly picturing the children. "That sounds like a challenge."

"At times, but I've developed endless strategies over the past eleven years that bridge language barriers. Mr. Tom, our speech-language pathologist, was just telling me how far each child has come this year."

"Do you speak Spanish?"

"It's been a journey. I took four semesters in college and a full year of conversational Spanish for teachers last year. I also practice daily with staff, kids, and families. I'm not fluent, but I get by in a preschool classroom."

"Have you taken the Spanish Proficiency Test?"

"No. It never came up."

"You should consider it. It could open doors."

"I'm sure I wouldn't pass, but I think I support English language learners well. I'm also in my second English Language Development Department course and scheduled for a third this summer. We already use most of the strategies from those courses. Things like visual supports, body language, repetition . . . it's good for all the children."

Jorge's expression balanced interest with skepticism and curiosity.

After a few moments of silence, Jorge pivoted topics. "Andrew, I think you'll be happy to hear I'm bringing the curriculum we use at my current school to Vista." His eyes were locked on mine. "It focuses on language, literacy, and self-regulation. It's called Every Early Learner Succeeds."

My stomach turned. *A new curriculum for my room?* I'd heard about a curriculum change, but I was told by the early childhood education team that it only applied to their Explorer classrooms. My students were younger and had significantly more diverse support needs. Plus, we had finally adjusted to our current curriculum.

"Trust me," Jorge said, sensing my reaction, "I think you'll love it. It's structured, builds on kids' experiences and interests, and emphasizes relationships with children and families. I'm already very experienced with the curriculum, so I'll be able to coach everyone."

I nodded, willing myself to stay open. Jorge's confidence softened some of my hesitation. I had learned to adapt before, so maybe I could again.

I shifted in the small blue chair, noticing how Jorge leaned forward, still engaged. "So, Andrew, enough about curriculum for a moment. What are you hoping for next year?"

His question caught me off guard. I hadn't expected to share my wish list so directly. I'd been jotting ideas down all year and adding them to a document on my computer.

"I actually have a list with some ideas," I offered. "Mind if I pull it up?"

"Please," Jorge said.

I stood and walked back to my desk. After grabbing my laptop, I glanced at the clock in the bottom right corner of the screen. 4:36. The workday was over. As I sat back down at the kidney table, I opened the file labeled "Notes for Next Year."

"So," I began, scanning the list, "one thing I'd love to do more of is home visits. We were able to do a few this year, and they made a huge difference. They helped us build relationships with families, especially the ones who were hesitant to engage early on. There's something powerful about sitting in a family's living room and listening."

Jorge held an agreeable grin. "That makes sense. I've always believed in the value of home visits. Definitely something we can look at building into the schedule."

"That would be amazing," I said, feeling a wave of relief. "Even one or two more visits per family could strengthen our classroom community."

I scrolled down. "Another thing, and this is a bigger ask, but it's been on my mind all year. Room 122 has more space, a private bathroom, and direct access to the playground with a wheelchair ramp. For the kids in our class, especially those with mobility support needs, it would make a real difference. I'd appreciate it if you would consider relocating our classroom to that room."

Jorge looked thoughtful. "Is that Ms. Sharon's room?"

"It is," I said. "And I know switching rooms would be a big lift. Perhaps, if it's framed as a way to support children with disabilities, maybe it could be reconsidered. She is empathetic to the challenges room 125 poses for children who need extensive mobility, adaptive, social, and emotional support."

"I see your point," he said. "Let me look into that. The physical space and location really do impact learning, especially with younger children."

I nodded, feeling encouraged. "Those are the big things. Oh, I'd like to involve Mr. Tom in lesson planning. His background as a speech therapist brings a different lens to our classroom. I think it could enrich the community."

Jorge smiled. "I appreciate your initiative. Keep bringing ideas like this forward. It's clear you care deeply about your students. I want you to know that I will always be available to support you however I can. Come to me with any professional concerns, even if they feel personal."

"I'm grateful for your candor," I said, closing my laptop. The conversation had been productive and hopeful. As he stood and stepped toward the door, I felt the weight of it all settling in. A new curriculum, a doctorate program, a shifting school culture—it was a lot.

"Happy birthday, by the way," Jorge said with a warm smile.

"Thank you," I replied, surprised. "How did you know?"

He gestured toward the classroom door. "The whiteboard gave it away."

We both laughed as he exited the room. The sound of his shoes echoed down the hallway, fading into the distance.

I stood alone in the stillness of room 125, the afternoon light catching the edge of the sensory table. My phone buzzed in my pocket.

We love you Daddy. Come home so we can eat cake.

A smile tugged at my cheek. I shut down the computer, flicked off the lights, and walked down the familiar brick corridor. Artwork, stacked on the floor to be sent home, fluttered slightly as I passed.

A new curriculum was coming, yes. But so were many opportunities to grow.

***

The late-evening summer sun cast a warm, fading glow across the Rocky Mountain Community College classroom, painting everything in soft amber as its rays began to retreat. In the corner of the room, Virginia, now promoted from professor to chair of the Early Childhood Education Department, chatted with the guest presenter, a genetic counselor, who was packing up her materials. This was the final night of the summer semester for Early Childhood Education 260: The Exceptional Child, a course I was teaching. For once, Virginia was not the instructor. She was a student in my class. A quiet, almost bittersweet energy floated in the air as students paused at the door to share their appreciation before leaving.

"Thank you for coming and sharing your expertise. Andrew's been bringing in specialists who work with children who have disabilities, and it's been such an eye-opener," I heard Virginia say. Her admiration for my instructional approach was clear.

The genetic counselor smiled, her warmth genuine. I approached them and said, "Thank you, Virginia. I'll admit, I was a bit intimidated being your instructor. I had to step up my game."

We joined in laughter, my own gratitude bubbling to the surface. "Thank you for sharing your experiences working with Chenyl and Jovan," I added, turning to the genetic counselor. I was referring to a family I had worked with during my first year at Vista Elementary who had deeply impacted, and who continued to impact, my life. Jovan had Batten Disease, a neurodegenerative condition. "They completely changed the way I see my responsibilities as a teacher, the way I see families and inclusion. Have you been working with them recently?"

The counselor's expression softened. "I've checked in with Chenyl every few months as Jovan's condition progresses. It's hard for her, but we've built a network of support for her and her younger son Gianni. I do what I can, but ultimately, it's up to the family."

"Thank you," I said quietly, feeling the tenderness of her care. "I know any kind of support means the world to them. It's hard to navigate the resources and policies alone."

Virginia chimed in, demonstrating her newfound knowledge as a graduate of my class. "That seems to be a common theme among all the guest presenters. It's clear the underlying message is that we, as teachers and directors, need to understand the laws, support families, and advocate."

"Precisely," I responded, as the genetic counselor slung her bag over her shoulder. She shared a few parting words with us and exited the room.

Virginia turned to me. "Andrew, this class was something special. I've learned so much from the specialists you brought in, but also from the way you connected it all to the children you've worked with. It's been really powerful."

I smiled, letting her words sink in. "I'm glad it resonated. I didn't want to focus on textbook definitions of disabilities. I felt it was more important to bring in real voices and real stories. Summers are the perfect time for most specialists to share their experiences."

Virginia nodded. "I love how you're never satisfied with doing things the same way twice."

I laughed, a bit embarrassed. "Natalie would disagree. It's not always my best trait. And this was only my second time teaching the course. The first round, in Tucson, wasn't exactly seamless. Honestly, I was learning right alongside all of you this summer."

"You made it look effortless," she said, her voice carrying a touch of adoration. "If I ever need another class, I'm asking for you to be the teacher."

As we walked toward the door, a question she'd posed at the start of the summer returned. "Have you given any more thought to applying for my former associate professor position here? They're still accepting applications. It's an opportunity, and I know you'd be great for it."

Her encouragement tugged at me. We had spoken several times about the value of pursuing opportunities, even when they don't make sense. "It's tempting, but I can't leave my classroom. I would miss the children and the families too much."

"After taking this class, that's understandable. Seems like they and the service providers would miss you too," she said with a smile as we exited the building.

The parking lot outside was vast and quiet, caught between the last stretch of daylight and the onset of artificial light. We lingered on the sidewalk, talking about the new curriculum I had just been trained on. The challenge was exciting, but the uncertainties were undeniable. For the next half hour, we discussed everything from future classes I might teach to concepts I was learning in the two university courses I was taking that summer. We circled back to the question of whether I should consider the associate professor position at Rocky Mountain Community College.

"I've already made the commitment to the school and my colleagues. I know families are counting on our classroom. I've been told it is a fixture of the Vista community," I said at last. "Plus, the university scholarship requires that I work directly with children who have disabilities. With the new curriculum and Jorge's coaching, I think this year's going to push me more than any before. And I'll have support. It gives me a good context for applying the concepts I'm learning. We both know there's nothing better for learning than putting it into practice."

As we finally said our goodbyes, the parking lot lights had fully taken over. I got into my car, ready for my last week of summer break. No teaching. No planning. No learning. Just time to be with Natalie, Citlali, and Itzel.

As I drove home, the future felt promising. Opportunities that had once seemed like a fantasy were suddenly within reach. Still, lurking behind each blessing was the quiet fear of failure—no matter how absurd it seemed.

***

Morning air from the window evaporative cooler swept into our duplex through the playroom. What had started as a guest room had evolved into Itzel's nursery after Citlali's third birthday, then into a playroom and makeshift office during the summer heat. My workspace was a glass-topped rolling desk squeezed into the back half of the closet. The desk was just large enough for my stack of books and my laptop. Toys were spilled across every room in the home, but none as much as in the playroom. Itzel now shared a room with Citlali.

Dawn was emerging through the kitchen window. After pacing the hallway for nearly an hour, trying to coax Itzel back to sleep, I finally felt her body grow heavy in my arms. I gently laid the eleven-month-old in her crib and tiptoed out. Almost immediately, I heard the soft voice that always seemed to stir before the rest of the house.

"Daddy, can I watch TV?"

Citlali stood behind me, eyes wide. I turned. "Morning, sweetheart. It's really early. You should go back to sleep."

"But, Daddy, the sun's awake, so I'm awake."

"Okay, but no screen time. You can listen to a movie until Mommy and I wake up."

She handed me the tablet. "Which one do you want?" I asked, already knowing.

"*Frozen*," she replied, then added, "Daddy, when is Mommy going to wake up?"

"Sweetie, she was up late with Itzel. We need to let her sleep. After *Frozen*, I'll make you breakfast, and we can play." I handed her the tablet.

Citlali turned away from me and took the first step toward her and Itzel's bedroom.

I crouched down and threw my arm around her. "Your sister just fell asleep. Go into the living room. No singing, okay?"

"But, Daddy, Itzel wants to play with me."

"No, my love. Itzel wants to sleep."

Citlali hesitated, then scampered into the living room. I watched her place the tablet on her Dora the Explorer table and retreat to her dress-up pile of clothes in the corner. Near the pile was an end table with a stack of journal articles from my summer classes. They were reminders of a summer spent juggling fatherhood, teaching, and being a student. Soon, I'd trade the community college role for the job I truly loved.

I made my way to the kitchen and glanced at the time on the microwave: 5:18 a.m. Too early for a summer morning.

Back in bed, my mind wouldn't rest. I made a mental checklist for the coming school year and thought about how grateful I was to be working again with Cecilia, Lillie, and Mr. Tom. Jorge had approved two of the three requests I made during our introduction last May. We were scheduled to do home visits the first week, and we were moving to room 122. I was eager to clear out the storage buckets crammed into the other half of the closet in the playroom at home opposite my office. However, after the summer trainings on the Every Early Learner

Succeeds curriculum, I wasn't sure how many of my favorite materials designed to facilitate special education interventions in those buckets could be incorporated into the classroom. It was a concern I had carried through the summer.

Just then, I heard Citlali's voice ring out with the familiar tune from the movie she was watching, *Frozen.*

I bolted upright from my bed. "Citlali! Sweetheart, your sister is sleeping. Please don't sing."

"But, Daddy, Itzel is awake."

Just then, I heard a soft whimper from the children's bedroom.

"Citlali, you woke your sister."

"Can you get her so she can play?"

"She's tired. She needs sleep." I could already predict how the morning was going to go.

I slumped onto the couch and grabbed my journal. Only a few pages remained. Between early morning thought dumps, notes from university courses, and to-do lists for school, I was burning through pages faster than ever. I scribbled:

Back to school next week. The classes this summer were good. They got me thinking more about who I am as a teacher and how I engage with the children, families, Lillie, Cecilia, and Mr. Tom. I look forward to my classes on leadership, including children with disabilities and—

"Daddy, can you go get Itzel now?"

I sat up and inhaled deeply. "If you want to play with Itzel, you can, but stay in her crib with her."

Her face lit up. She danced off, humming "Let It Go" under her breath.

I leaned back on the couch, staring at my notebook. Four more days until school. Waking up with the girls, reserving homework for weekends and evenings, and staying present with the family had been part of the agreement Natalie and I made when I got into the doctoral program. So far, I was holding up my end. What we hadn't discussed was how I'd manage the changes at Vista. That was a conversation Natalie never wanted to have.

CHAPTER 3

ROOM 122

Monday, August 18 arrived with a familiar sense of anticipation. Anticipation for the start of the new school year, but also for the chance to finally test the theories I had immersed myself in through two summer graduate classes. Though these concepts didn't map directly onto daily classroom tasks, they offered new insight into how I saw myself in the work of nurturing young children and their families. Best of all, I'd get to explore this insight in the much-coveted room 122.

The Vista staff gathered in the library, settling into their grade-level teams for our all-staff meeting. The hum of the window air conditioners and lighthearted chatter filled the space with a refreshing energy. The buzz at the start of a school year always had a specific texture: hopeful, a bit chaotic, and alive.

I found my usual seat at the early childhood education table, where the four Explorer classroom teachers—Ana, Cindy, Esmeralda, and Sharon—were already seated. I set my black mailbag down and pulled out a chair beside Ana. Her thin, chocolate-brown hair brushed her shoulders. She looked up with emotion as legible as words. Her face always spoke first, regardless of language.

"Andrew! How did your summer classes end?" she asked, her Spanish accent thick. "You have to share everything you've learned since the Every Early Learner Succeeds training in July."

I smiled, appreciating her curiosity. "It was a lot but really insightful. One of my classes focused on school culture. I ended up writing a paper about the impact Kris had on my classroom and how her leadership showed up in everyday interactions, not just formal decisions. I thought about how she helped families transition from my classroom to all of yours."

Cindy nodded thoughtfully. "That sounds interesting."

"More than I can explain this early in the morning," I joked. "I wrote a paper about how tools like assessments shape the culture of our classrooms. If we set goals as a team this year, I think we should consider things we hadn't before."

Sharon, sitting across from me, tilted her head. She was narrow-framed and middle-aged, and she always tried a bit too hard to fit in. "That's great, Andrew, but with everything you've got going on . . . college classes, your family . . . how do you expect to stay fully present in the classroom? That's going to be a real challenge."

Her words were tinged with condescension. I felt a flicker of irritation but offered a polite smile. "It's definitely a balancing act," I said. "But being in the classroom grounds me. It gives me context. I can see the impact of everything I'm learning, right there with the children."

"Hmm," she replied. "I suppose it's just a matter of priorities."

Ana gave me a look of solidarity. Cindy shifted in her seat. Esmeralda checked her phone, disengaged from the tension.

Cindy broke the silence. "Andrew, what else did you learn about?"

"A lot of perspective-taking," I said. "I had to consider how I would use tools like evaluations and professional development plans in different leadership roles. It made me think about how disconnected some tools can feel from real teaching."

Ana nodded. "Like the Teaching Observation Protocol evaluations. They want us to check boxes and hit benchmarks, but they're not in the classroom with us. They don't see what we see."

I was about to respond when Sharon spoke again. "If you're balancing everything so well, maybe you can share your secret. I could use a tip."

Her voice cut through the conversation, fixed on the expired topic. It was typical of her not to let go once she'd latched onto a personal concern. I took a slow breath, forcing composure. "It's about setting clear boundaries," I said evenly. "And speaking up before something small becomes something bigger."

Esmeralda glanced up and smiled. "I like that, Andrew."

I shifted in my seat, trying to shake off the discomfort.

At exactly 8:00 a.m., Jorge stood at the front of the room. His confident posture radiated the energy of a poised leader. With a bright smile and a PowerPoint backdrop, he called for everyone's attention.

"Good morning, team," he began warmly. His voice cut through the noise. "Before we get down to business, I want to start by thanking you all for welcoming me into the Vista community. I look forward to building on all the incredible work you do."

He gestured to the screen behind him. "I had the privilege of working with a great team here at Vista to complete the school Innovation Plan this past summer." He went on to thank the five individuals in attendance who assisted him. "I want to begin by sharing our new mission, our vision, and our values."

He turned to the screen. "At Vista, we are dedicated to ensuring that every student leaves us not just proficient but empowered. Our mission is to prepare all of our students to be confident, critical thinkers who are ready for the challenges of high school, higher education, and beyond. Our vision is to honor the strengths our students bring while equipping them with the tools to succeed in an ever-changing world. And our values—collaboration, innovation, and equity—guide everything we do."

Jorge paused, scanning the room as he let the words settle. "This mission doesn't happen by accident," he continued. "It happens because of each of you. You are the center of this work. And this morning, I want to talk about one of the ways we're striving to push this mission through our Innovation Plan." He nodded to the tables. "Each table should have five copies. This plan is more than a packet of papers. It represents our shared commitment to student success, from early childhood through fifth grade."

Ana and I exchanged a glance. I couldn't tell what she was thinking, but I was skeptical about how much this document aligned with the shared values our early childhood team had worked to build in the past. Those values hadn't come easily. Over the previous two years, our team had weathered its share of friction and fatigue. Ana had been the peacemaker, always trying to keep everyone working together, while I focused on ensuring that children leaving the Foundations classroom received the support they needed as they transitioned into the Explorer rooms. Sharon preferred to stay within the boundaries of the curriculum, Cindy often stepped in to keep us on track, and Esmeralda, though kind, tended to withdraw when disagreements surfaced. We had struggled to find common ground on how to balance the expectations of Vista's administration, the district's shifting policies, and the needs of families and children. The conflict eventually grew so tense that Kris, our former principal, brought in a district mediator to help us identify shared values and define team norms that could hold us together. Even with that progress, unity still felt fragile.

Jorge continued. "The Innovation Plan emphasizes multiple measures of success. It's designed to align with district and state goals. For us, that means focusing on school culture, achievement, and accountability. We want all students, including our English language learners, to have the tools and support they need to thrive."

What does school culture, achievement, and accountability mean for him? I wondered, flipping through the pages.

Jorge's tone shifted. "I also want to recognize our responsibility under the Binding Compliance Order. This legally binding agreement ensures we provide equitable and effective support for English language learners. Every program, curriculum choice, and decision must reflect our commitment to English acquisition while honoring students' native languages. That starts with our youngest learners."

He paused, looking directly at our table. "Now, I want to recognize a team that doesn't always get the attention it deserves: our early childhood education teachers."

Our team exchanged startled looks, like students caught off guard by a question they didn't expect to answer.

"You are the foundation of everything we do at Vista," Jorge said. "The Innovation Plan starts with your work. The training you did this summer in Every Early Learner Succeeds, and your support for bilingual development, are a testament to your professionalism."

Applause filled the room. Ana, Cindy, Esmeralda, and I smiled politely. Sharon thanked Jorge on behalf of the team. The spotlight, though sincere, didn't distract me from my wonderings about the school values—collaboration, innovation, and equity—and Jorge's definitions of culture, achievement, and accountability.

Jorge wrapped up. "Every Early Learner Succeeds is one piece of the vision. Combined with your expertise, it will give our students what they need to grow socially, linguistically, and academically."

As he moved on to other topics, side chatter consumed our early childhood education team. Gratitude lingered, but so did a subtle sense of what that visibility might mean for our work. The tension from the past two years lurked just below the surface. Eyes from other grade levels pulled at old instincts, Sharon leaning into visibility and the rest of us retreating into caution.

***

To call room 122 spacious would be an understatement. My desk sat against the wall where room 125 would have ended. The walnut-laminated surface was no larger than a cutting board, just enough for my laptop and a ceramic mug from my first year of teaching, which had "Best Teacher Ever" printed in gold cursive. Of all the shirts, ties, and boxes of candy I'd received, nothing matched its quiet validation. At the end of each day, I'd glance at the mug and reassure myself I'd done my best. I swiveled in my desk chair, smiling at what this space made possible. It was two classrooms in one. The space felt open and alive. The possibilities were infinite.

Twenty feet of deep-blue carpet stretched in front of me. Behind me lay another fifteen feet of floor space. Sunlight streamed through a wide corner window, connecting the room to the outside world. On the opposing end of the same wall stood a door that opened directly onto the early childhood playground. It was a literal and symbolic gateway to the Vista community. A passageway between Ana's classroom and mine housed two bathrooms and two closets, each large enough to be its own room.

I'd heard Sharon wasn't happy about her relocation to room 125. Her tone during the morning meeting confirmed what I had suspected since the switch was made official a week earlier. Whatever the politics, Jorge had orchestrated the change, and it felt like a clear win for Lillie, Cecilia, our learners, their families, and me.

"Wow, Andrew! I would have never imagined we'd be in this classroom," Lillie said to me as she and Cecilia walked into room 122 after their lunch break.

"This will be so much better for our students who aren't toilet trained and the children who need mobility support," Cecilia added.

"Right! I'm so excited! Aaaaaand, we have Ana and Maya next door." Maya was Ana's teaching assistant and the mother of a child who had been in my class my first year at Vista.

The anticipation for endless potential bounced between the three of us. Our conversation flowed like a mountain stream running between trees and rocks. Then the stream ended. "I've been thinking about the potential limits on our ability to adapt the curriculum for our learners with additional support needs."

Cecilia and Lillie appeared caught off guard. I continued. "During the staff meeting this morning, Jorge was talking about culture, achievement, and accountability. He explicitly drew attention to the Every Early Learner Succeeds curriculum. I could be wrong, but the dots I'm connecting lead me to believe we're going to have to stick to the script more than we anticipated."

"Like, make the kids fit into the curriculum rather than the curriculum fit the kids?" Lillie said, echoing our past conversations about what it meant to create a truly inclusive classroom, one that honored each child's abilities, interests, experiences, and family culture.

"Pretty much. I'm sure there will be some flexibility, but too much flexibility might deviate from Jorge's definitions of culture, achievement, and accountability."

The conversation ended with the recognition that we could not stew in potential problems. We mapped out the plan for the remainder of the afternoon, committing to a positive attitude.

With Ana as my neighbor, I knew positivity wouldn't be hard to find. After Cecilia and Lillie left, I stepped into her room. Ana stood from her desk. Her eyes were bright.

"Andrew. I'm so excited you are in the room next to us!" she exclaimed with her arms open to welcome me.

"It's hard to believe. I owe it all to Jorge. Swapping rooms took some guts."

Ana didn't respond. We'd spent time together over the summer, not just in curriculum trainings but at family gatherings with Natalie and Sergio, her boyfriend.

"Are you ready for the new curriculum?" she asked, already knowing the answer.

"I'm not sure. I looked at the first unit. Considering the activities and developmental expectations, it's going to be hard to adapt, especially for our students on the autism spectrum or from families who do not live with White American norms. Cecilia, Lillie, and I are frustrated, but I think Jorge knows where we stand. We're hoping he'll be more flexible once he becomes familiar with the Foundations classroom and our work. What about you?"

"I don't think it's good for your class, but Maya and I like it. We'll help you. We can tell Jorge and the early childhood education team that you are doing everything perfectly."

We laughed, and the shared understanding of my challenges softened my concerns. Ana's quiet encouragement had always helped me navigate uncertainty.

"Tell me more about your college classes," she said. "You got interrupted this morning."

"They went well! I got all A's. One focused on technology in leadership roles, which was the class I was talking about in the library. The other was about power and privilege. They gave me a lot to think about."

"What do you mean, 'power,' and . . . what was the other word?"

"Privilege. It's how our traits, characteristics, and experiences influence the opportunities we have in society and how those impact the way we treat people and how we get treated." She looked at me with a puzzled expression. "For example, as a White, native English-speaking man, I have access to things Natalie, as a native Spanish-speaking Mexican woman, doesn't."

Ana nodded, thoughtful.

"Between that and the tech leadership course, I feel armed and dangerous with knowledge," I joked.

She looked more confused than moments earlier, most certainly unfamiliar with the idiom.

"What do you want to do after you finish your degree?"

"If I ever finish . . . I can't imagine leaving the classroom. An associate professor job opened at Rocky Mountain Community College, but I didn't apply. I love teaching young children, and my scholarship requires me to stay in the classroom."

"Good. You can't leave while I'm here," she teased.

"Sí, jefe," I said with a playful salute.

The rest of the day was a whirlwind of preparation. Cecilia, Lillie, and I threw ourselves into setting up the classroom. Room 122 offered more space than we'd ever had. We found homes for our materials easily. Learning centers began to take shape with minimal effort. The start of the year felt uncomplicated and filled with possibility. Co-creating the environment with my classroom team and Ana's steady support made me more excited than I had been in years.

***

The late-afternoon Tuesday sun beat down on the rows of modest homes in the Vista neighborhood. I pulled up to Nelia's house with Cecilia in the passenger seat. It was past assigned work hours, so Lillie didn't join us. Nelia's family lived in a post–World War II bungalow like everyone else in the neighborhood. This was our sixth and final home visit before the start of the school year. Jorge had given us one day for visits, which was acceptable given how much we still had to do to get room 122 ready.

Nelia's mother greeted us at the door with a warm smile. "Come in, come in," she said in Spanish. Between her gestures and my novice Spanish, I could follow most simple statements. Nelia stood just behind her, peeking out shyly.

The living room was serene and tidy, with carefully arranged furniture and family photos lining the walls.

"¿Desean que les traiga un poco de agua para tomar?" Nelia's mother offered as we eyed a place to sit.

"Yes. Thank you," Cecilia and I said. It wasn't thirst but the unspoken courtesy of moments like these that made us say yes to a glass of water. Cecilia settled in the middle of an almond leather love seat. I took the floor beside her.

Nelia perched on the edge of a neighboring chair that matched the couch, gripping a small doll. Her mother handed us glasses of water.

"She loves learning," she said in Spanish. "She's always helping around the house and playing family with her dolls. She's very excited to start school."

I leaned forward, addressing Nelia in Spanish. "What do you want to learn in school this year?"

She glanced at her mother for reassurance, then answered softly but confidently. "I want to be a teacher or doctor."

"That's a great goal," I said, my enthusiasm sincere. "Maybe you can be a teacher or doctor in our classroom."

Her eyes lit up. She jumped up and ran to what I could only assume was her bedroom.

Her mom nodded proudly. "She likes to help people. When her little cousins come over, she always makes sure they're okay if they fall or cry. She's very caring."

I could not understand all the words that followed, so I asked Cecilia to translate. After she did, I turned to her and said, "Sounds like we've got another teacher for the class."

Cecilia laughed softly, looking at Nelia as she returned with a box of toy medical supplies. "We'll have plenty of opportunities for you to be a helper. You'll have lots of new friends."

The conversation shifted to the school year and what Nelia and her family could expect.

"She'll be in the morning class," I explained. "We start at 7:45 and end at 10:30." I described how we'd be using the Every Early Learner Succeeds curriculum, emphasizing learning plans, centers, and play. Her mom listened intently, nodding as I explained how play would help develop Nelia's language and problem-solving skills.

When Nelia heard the word "play," she brightened and described how she liked to be a doctor for her dolls. I assured her mom that we had lots of classroom materials she would enjoy.

"I'm very happy she is in your classroom. We've heard so many good things about it," her mother said, meeting our eyes with calm assurance.

As the visit wrapped up, we thanked her for welcoming us into their home. We took a photo of Nelia, another with her mom, and asked for a picture of their whole family for our first unit: families. She found one for us and walked us to the door. She and Nelia waved through the screen as we stepped back into the late-summer heat.

Back in the car, Cecilia let out a satisfied sigh. "These visits make such a difference. I just love how connected I feel to them before the first day of school."

I nodded. "It gives us more ideas on how to set up the room so the children can engage right away. And I feel way more confident using my Spanish."

"Your Spanish is much better than you think it is."

"If you say so," I said with disbelief.

As I started the engine, I turned to her. "We got six done today. It's too bad we can't do more. Still, I think it's going to be a good year."

At that moment, I truly believed that it would be. Exhausted but inspired, I looked ahead with optimism. *I'll figure out the Every Early Learner Succeeds curriculum like I've figured out every other curriculum*, I told myself, driving home that evening. As long as I had Cecilia and Lillie, things would come together.

***

We started meeting with families in the classroom on Wednesday morning. Grace, Jorge's administrative assistant, would call down to our room when families came to register their children. After completing their paperwork, they were directed to room 122. The process added unpredictability, but it allowed us to meet families on their schedule. Cecilia discovered this approach the year before, and it had worked far better than the system I used my first year at Vista. So here we were again, adapting our plans as we went.

Lillie, Cecilia, and I picked up where we left off on Monday afternoon. The furniture from room 125 filled only half of our new, much larger space. The back half of room 122 felt organized. We had a library with a standing bookshelf and beanbag chairs, a shelf with puzzles, and the blue kidney-shaped table. The front half, however, was undefined, as making it coherent for three-year-olds, especially those new to a classroom, was still a work in progress. We were aligning the free-play centers in the front half with the first unit of the new curriculum's "learning" themes: blocks became a living room, the literacy center a home office, the art center a bedroom, table toys a game room, the science center a laundry room, and dramatic play was the kitchen.

Even so, I wasn't convinced we'd pull it off. I was used to curricula that followed the children's lead. The Every Early Learner Succeeds curriculum required teachers to define every area in advance. Materials stayed put until the unit ended. It felt rigid.

Midmorning, Ernesto arrived with his mother, Gabriela. As Vista's community liaison, Gabriela spent her days moving between the front office and classrooms throughout the school. The two entered room 122 through the front door. Ernesto's eyes widened the moment he stepped inside, as if he had entered another world. The dramatic play area immediately caught his attention. The kitchen was the same size as our circle-time carpet. A white plastic chain signaled it was closed, yet the new layout included an exit on the other side. Ernesto slipped through without hesitation.

"Buenos días, Gabriela," I called from across the room.

"Buenos días, Mr. Andrew," she replied with a broad smile. Her presence lightened whatever weight I was carrying. I gestured toward the back of the room.

"Is it just me, or does Gabriela feel like the early arrival to our party?" I said to Cecilia, chuckling.

Gabriela glanced around, her smile softening. She noticed Cecilia cutting out name cards at the kidney table near the playground door. That area, our only tiled space, would double as a second art center. Jorge told us to use the first art center, in the front of the room, as a garage or shed.

"¿Necesitas ayuda?" she asked Cecilia.

"No, gracias, Gabriela. Ya casi termino."

Gabriela turned to me. "¿Qué va a hacer Mr. Andrew con tanto espacio?"

"We were wondering the same thing. It's a lot of space," Cecilia said, smiling. "I'm sure he'll figure it out."

Gabriela tilted her head and switched to English. "Is that right, Mr. Andrew? Do you have big plans?"

I walked over and answered in Spanish. "Estoy seguro . . . um . . . no . . . tienes? Tendré? Ningún problema. Sorry, you know what I mean." I grinned. "I'm sure it won't be a problem."

She laughed. "Qué bueno." Then with a light sigh, she squared her shoulders. "All right, Mr. Andrew. What do I need to do before Ernesto can start in your classroom?"

"Help me practice my Spanish," I joked. Then I added more seriously, "Actually, we'd like to go over some classroom details. Cecilia, Lillie, and I decided I should lead the conversations with families who speak Spanish. You're our test subject."

Gabriela's tone shifted. "Entonces, cuéntame. What do I need to know before the school year starts?"

We sat down at the kidney table across from Cecilia. "Let's start by learning more about Ernesto and your family," I said.

After a while, we switched to English. I explained the new curriculum and how it would shape family involvement. Parent participation would be limited to take-home activities, with no in-class volunteering and likely no home visits, as we did the previous school year. Despite the undesirable changes, I tried to maintain a positive disposition. "Please send a photo of your family with Ernesto next Monday. It'll be part of our first unit." I reviewed arrival and departure routines, now simpler with our direct playground door, and went over a two-page safety document. Gabriela listened closely. I closed with a few friendly phrases in Spanish.

"If you agree to everything, just sign on the line and you're free," I said with a confident smile.

She signed with a flourish. "Bueno, Mr. Andrew," she said, her smile reaching her eyes. "It makes me very happy to have Ernesto in your classroom. I know he's going to learn a lot."

We took pictures of Gabriela and Ernesto to use in the classroom. The curriculum didn't require it, but it was one of the ways we made our room a place where children felt safe. That had always mattered most.

***

The overhead lights were off, leaving the room bathed in soft natural light from the single window and the back entrance. It was lunchtime, and the place felt peaceful, almost as if it was holding its breath before the rush of next week. I was alone at the kidney table, tying up loose ends on the mandatory paperwork. As always, Cecilia and Lillie had left the room for their break. We were in our final hours of planning before the weekend.

The last family of the day, the Torreses, were new to the Vista neighborhood. We had met them during a home visit on Monday, but Beatriz Torres wanted to bring her son Jimmy to the classroom when she came to register him. She had heard about our class from a neighbor and was excited for her son to join a space as diverse as room 122.

Beatriz came through the back door with a toddler on her back in a carrier and Jimmy, a young boy with shaggy oak-brown hair, shyly glued to her side. His eyes moved quickly across the room. He looked alert but unsure. I saved my document and closed my laptop, standing to greet them.

"Mr. Goff! It's so nice to see you again. Thank you for welcoming us," Beatriz said warmly, resting a hand on Jimmy's head. "You know Jimmy, and this is Ellie. She was napping when you came over."

I followed her gaze. "It's a pleasure to meet you, Ellie. And Beatriz, Jimmy, wonderful to see you again," I said, lowering to my knees. I scanned the room, trying to guess which center might entice Jimmy. "Please, come in."

I tried to catch Jimmy's eye. "What would you like to play with?" During our home visit, he showed us his puzzle collection. He had said he liked to draw, though we'd left before he could show us anything.

Beatriz knelt beside him. "Jimmy, can you tell Mr. Goff what you like? Look, there are blocks, puzzles . . . and over there, paper and markers." She gently guided him toward the literacy center, which doubled as the home office. Ellie, ready to roam, started to squirm.

"Is it all right if Ellie explores the classroom?"

"Absolutely."

Beatriz unstrapped her daughter. "Oh, and before I forget, here is a family picture for your first unit." Ellie took off without hesitation. Beatriz led Jimmy to the literacy center. I stayed a step behind, watching their quiet rhythm. Beatriz angled herself to give me a clear view as Jimmy investigated the shelf. He picked up a piece of paper and a basket of crayons and sat down. He still looked unsure, but he was starting to settle.

I crouched beside him. "Jimmy, do you want to draw?"

He nodded.

"What do you like to draw?"

Beatriz encouraged him. "Tell Mr. Goff what you like to draw."

Jimmy gave a small nod. After a moment, he picked up a red crayon and began scribbling.

"What are you drawing?" I asked, observing the paper.

"A car," he murmured.

"A car! Do you have a favorite kind of car?"

He shook his head, still quiet, but I saw a small spark of interest in his eyes. Wanting to give him space, I fetched an adult chair and set it beside him.

"Beatriz, please have a seat," I offered.

"Thank you, Mr. Goff," she said, easing into the chair. I saw her shoulders drop as she relaxed.

"You're welcome to call me Andrew," I added. "Most families do. But whatever feels right."

As I flipped on the overhead lights, I added, "It's nice to have a little more light in here." I returned to the table. "So, you told me about your weekend outings in the mountains. Is there anything else you'd like to share about your family?"

Beatriz smiled. "Well, that's Ellie over there." We looked toward the puzzle shelf, where Ellie was inspecting each puzzle like she was solving a mystery. Beatriz went on to describe their favorite spots around the region and mentioned that Jimmy had very little experience being around children his own age. She added that she was especially eager for him to be exposed to Spanish. "I was thrilled to hear this classroom has both English- and Spanish-speaking children. And children with disabilities," she added with warmth.

"Yes, Lillie and Cecilia are both fluent in Spanish. I do my best, mostly in small groups or one-on-one," I replied. "We also have six children in the afternoon class with disabilities. There's a richness to the diversity that strengthens our whole learning community."

Beatriz's face brightened. "That's wonderful. And I don't recall, do you have a special education teacher or specialists working with the kids?"

I paused. "We have Mr. Tom, a speech-language pathologist who visits weekly to support children during natural classroom routines, along with a few other therapists. I have a master's degree in early childhood special education as well as early childhood education, so I serve as both. I've always believed any adaptation we make for children with disabilities or those learning English benefits everyone. I'm hoping to keep that approach this year, but we'll see how it works with the new curriculum. It's a bit of"—I looked toward Ellie, still surveying her options—"a puzzle."

Beatriz and I both laughed. Her eyes shone with appreciation. "I'm so happy Jimmy's in your class," she said sincerely.

We continued our conversation for over half an hour, covering routines, classroom expectations, and dozens of questions she had about child development. I gave her a tour and explained the curriculum. By the time Cecilia and Lillie returned, Beatriz was getting ready to leave. Lillie and Cecilia introduced themselves, then, with Beatriz's permission, invited Jimmy to the block area. They wanted to build a connection with him, too, and I encouraged it.

As the Torres family left and the door closed behind them, the warmth of the visit remained. Taking time to connect with each family wasn't always easy, but it was essential. It was how community began. Cecilia handled most of the conversations with families whose primary language was Spanish, and both she and Lillie started building their own meaningful relationships. Their roles in the classroom community were as important as mine.

That week, we had welcomed twenty of the twenty-three families who would begin the year with us. The curriculum still felt uncertain, but we ended the week feeling comforted by something more important. We had begun to build new relationships and strengthen established ones. We would figure out the rest day by day and piece by piece. What I did not yet understand was how often I would turn to those relationships to talk through what I could not handle on my own.

CHAPTER 4

P.R.I.D.E.

———

The first day of school had finally arrived. The room buzzed with early morning excitement as families entered through the back door. Parents guided their children through the morning routine of handwashing and answering the question of the day: "What is your favorite thing to do with your family? /¿Cuál es tu actividad favorita con tu familia?" The curriculum included this practice to build routine and connection. For me, these questions reflected inclusion in its truest sense, offering a window into each child's interests, experiences, and family culture while laying the foundation for trust and belonging.

Lillie and Cecilia retrieved the three children who had arrived by bus. Each had an Individual Education Program and lived outside the neighborhood. Our Foundations classroom was their closest program to their home. Lillie and Cecilia followed the other families, each holding the hand of a bus rider who needed help navigating the unfamiliar crowd.

Ten adults and eleven children filled the room. Most of the conversations were in Spanish. We had partitioned the classroom with folding tumbling mats turned on their side, one fold opened to allow adults to move between the front and back halves of the room. Some children sat at tables for breakfast while others chose books to read or toys to play with. They filled the back half with a mix of curiosity and caution.

I moved between groups, checking in and asking about the question of the day, using either Spanish or English. I wanted every child and family to understand that their voice belonged in the room, regardless of the language they used. As 8:10 approached, I gently encouraged families to say goodbye. In past years, this had always been optional. Now, the Every Early Learner Succeeds curriculum required that all families leave before activities began, a shift I already disliked.

By Wednesday, most of the children had adjusted to the routine. When the last parent left, Lillie opened the partition. I settled onto the carpet in our "community center," which was framed by two low shelves of blocks on one side and two low shelves with complementary toys on the other side. Most children joined with a verbal cue in Spanish, though a few needed a physical prompt. David Alvarez—often referred to as David A.—and another child who had been in our class the previous year responded only when they heard our circle-time music. Lillie guided them gently to the group.

Circle time was now designated for introducing curriculum topics. After just three days, it was already clear that this structure clashed with how we built community. In past years, we used circle time for play, storytelling, and songs. Now we were expected to use it for scripted content and materials.

I began in English. For more complex directions, I turned to Cecilia. During my summer course from the English Language Development Department, we were told not to repeat instructions in both languages. "Children won't listen to English if they expect Spanish," the instructor warned. So, I used visuals and gestures, reserving my Spanish for play and small groups.

"In my family, I am the dad," I said slowly, holding up a picture of my family. "My wife, Natalie, is the mom. We have two daughters." I repeated the sentence, watching the children. "Who is in your family?"

Ernesto raised his hand. "I have a mom and a dad," he said in Spanish.

"Yes, you do," I replied, holding up his family photo. "He has a mom, dad, and a dog." Ernesto grinned proudly.

"Who else has a family like Ernesto and me?" I asked. Nearly every child, even David A., looked my way. "Ms. Cecilia, do you have a family?"

She held up her photo. "Yes, Mr. Andrew. I have a husband, two daughters, and a son."

I turned to Brandon and held up his picture. "Brandon, do you have a family?"

"¡Sí!" he exclaimed.

"¿Y quién está en tu familia, Brandon?" I asked, then caught myself. I needed to use English.

"Tengo mi mamá y papá. Y mis abuelos. Viven en California," he said proudly. "Nosotros vamos a Disneyland y yo manejo los roller coasters." He traced roller-coaster dips through the air.

"Wow, Brandon, that sounds fun!" I said. His joy was contagious, but other children had drifted. Nelia and Mateo, a charismatic, curious child, were talking about their dogs. Another child lay staring at the ceiling. David A. paced near the block shelf. I glanced at the clock. Four minutes. Not bad.

"Okay, todos, levántense," I said, raising my arms. Circle time was done. I used Spanish to transition. Most children stood. I turned on a high-energy song, hoping music would draw them in. Cecilia and Lillie joined, helping guide the group. I chose a song familiar to David A. and the other child who was with us the previous year.

The next few minutes were a dance, not just to the music but in response to what each child needed. By the end, all but one of the children who had disengaged had rejoined us. I gestured to Cecilia, asking, "Should we do the curriculum learning time?"

She shrugged as if to say, "Your call."

I nodded and began the transition to the curriculum learning time. We had planned to act out family roles, but I adjusted. "Lillie, can you head to the grocery store?" I asked, pointing to table toys. "Skip the family props. Just let them play. Foster trust and relationships." She guided David A. there. "Cecilia, literacy center?" She nodded. I stayed in blocks.

I lifted the butcher paper draped over the shelf and held up a cardboard tube. "Who wants to help me build?" I asked in Spanish. Several children rushed over. During the fifteen minutes designated for the curriculum learning time, we played and built together. It wasn't what the lesson intended, but it was real cooperation and real connection—the foundation for a community.

The afternoon class went similarly, with a more even mix of Spanish and English speakers. Language didn't seem to matter for community building. After dismissal, Cecilia, Lillie, and I debriefed.

"Three-year-olds are three-year-olds," I said, half to myself. "We're doing pretty well after three days."

"If you say so, Andrew," Lillie replied skeptically. "It would've been better if we could do things the way we did last year."

"It takes time. The first week's always an adjustment," I said. "The children will settle in, just like last year." I paused. "Maybe we could try two groups for the curriculum, one in Spanish and one in English, like we do for story time."

They didn't hesitate. Separating children in any form wasn't exactly inclusive, but we believed that approach honored both the curriculum's intention and our students' abilities. Honoring abilities had always been central to our classroom culture.

***

Lillie and Cecilia were already on their way home. I was crouched by the Promethean board at the front of the community center, sorting through a pile of learning materials, when I heard the steady clap of wing-tipped shoes approaching. Jorge stepped in with an air of purpose. I rose slowly to receive his words.

Jorge scanned the room. "You're making progress, Andrew," he said, nodding at the learning centers. "I know it's not easy but keep at it. It'll come together."

I forced a smile. "Thanks. Honestly, some of my students with disabilities are struggling with the most basic curriculum learning activity concepts. We're just encouraging them to explore the materials, even if it's not scripted."

Jorge's smile tightened. "Take notes. You can discuss your concerns with your early childhood education team. We need high expectations for every child. You can make minor adaptations but don't let them stray away from the curriculum goals. It sets a bad example."

I felt a twinge of discomfort. "Yeah. I agree, but—" I stopped short. I believed in high expectations; however, those expectations had to reflect each child's developmental abilities, shaped by their interests, experiences, and family culture. Understanding those took time, observation, and a meaningful connection with each child.

He leaned in before I could continue. "Trust me. It works. The goal is self-regulation and literacy development. If they don't understand everything, that's okay for now. Just stay open and follow the process."

"I will," I replied, trying to sound professional, though a quiet resistance stirred within me. I reminded myself that change was hard. I was grateful he was listening at all.

Jorge's tone shifted. "I need to address something else. I was notified earlier today that your classroom is designated as an English Language Development–Spanish class. Do you have that credential?"

I blinked. "No . . . and I didn't know that." I thought of Ana's and Esmeralda's Explorer classrooms. "How can that be?"

"It's complicated," he said. "But we have to follow the Binding Compliance Order. Classrooms designated English Language Development–Spanish must have teachers qualified to teach in Spanish. Can you connect me with your special education director? Or . . . would you consider taking the Spanish Language Proficiency test?"

He must not have remembered my response to the question during our first conversation back in May.

I inhaled deeply and exhaled slowly. "My Spanish is good enough for preschoolers. Beyond that, no promises."

Jorge remained serious. "How many of your students are native Spanish speakers?"

I tallied them in my head quickly. "Seven of eleven in the morning. Eight of twelve in the afternoon. But three of the four English speakers in the morning are nonverbal and have Individual Education Programs. The four in the afternoon are meeting developmental milestones."

"That's what I was afraid of," he muttered. "If parents choose your classroom expecting Spanish instruction, we're legally required to provide it."

A cold pang shot through me. "So . . . have parents raised concerns? Are you saying they might be transferred?"

"No complaints yet," he said, "but it's a legal issue. Your assignment may have been made in error."

My stomach dropped. This had never come up in my previous two years. "I wasn't supposed to be hired?" My voice quivered as I spoke.

He sighed. "I'll see if there's a waiver for your role. But yes, if Spanish was expected, there could be serious repercussions. Not just for your class, but for the school and district."

"The families met us before the year started," I countered. "If Spanish was a priority, wouldn't they have said something or withdrawn?"

"You'd think. But many parents don't understand the distinction between English Language Development–English and English Language Development–Spanish. It's confusing."

"Yeah. I'll reach out to Diana Carter. She's the new early childhood special education director. She might know more." I felt sick thinking about compliance and oversight, especially from someone at the district level.

Jorge nodded. "Good. I'll follow up with you soon." He peeked at his watch, then rattled off interim guidelines for Lillie, Cecilia, and me. His final instruction struck hard: no Spanish should be spoken to the children.

My throat tightened. *After all the Spanish I have learned. After two years of building relationships with Spanish-speaking families, how can I not speak it?*

"But Cecilia and Lillie . . . they were hired to speak Spanish with the children."

Jorge softened slightly. "I don't want to lose you, Andrew. But my main concern is avoiding a lawsuit."

I nodded numbly. *Lawsuit.*

His footsteps faded down the hallway.

As I stepped into the corridor, a familiar chill of insecurity swept over me. The legal revelation unsettled me. *How can I form meaningful relationships or establish expectations if Lillie, Cecilia, and I cannot speak a child's native language, if we cannot create a community where everyone feels they belong?*

Just before the stairs, my eyes landed on a glossy poster I'd barely noticed in the past: five bold letters: P.R.I.D.E., which stood for Perseverance. Respect. Integrity. Diversity. Excellence.

Those values had once been Vista's foundation under the previous principal, Kris. Her leadership had brought them to life. Now, under Jorge, I wasn't so sure. At our first meeting, he had emphasized different words: collaboration, innovation, and equity.

Were the original values still alive or just relics on the wall, waiting to be torn down?

An ache of uncertainty rattled in my chest as I passed the sign. *Am I being cynical? Too quick to judge?* I tried to quiet my thoughts. Maybe it was too soon to grasp the significance of the Binding Compliance Order on room 122 or Jorge's leadership.

The unease pulsed as I walked the long corridor to the front of the school. During the drive home, the image of those five bold letters, P.R.I.D.E., and the implications of Jorge's words refused to fade. I wanted to believe the five words would hold their meaning, even as I began to sense how easily words could be outpaced by the structures meant to support them.

CHAPTER 5

VOICES

———

At the time Jorge told me we could no longer speak Spanish in the classroom, David R. and David A. had already spent nearly a year with us.

David Ramirez—or David R. as we called him—joined our classroom community midway through my second year at Vista. From the beginning, he struck us as a deeply curious child, like a scientist in the middle of an experiment. His eyes scanned the room with purpose, darting from one object to the next as if searching for just the right variable to observe. When something caught his attention, he approached it slowly, his head tilted, studying it with quiet intensity as though through an invisible magnifying glass. Some textures, especially anything squishy like slime, overwhelmed him and led to distress. We came to see those responses as windows, not barriers. His reactions revealed what felt safe, what invited exploration, and what could be adapted. What some might view as peculiar, we recognized as communication. David R. was helping us learn how to include him, not only in the classroom but also in the co-creation of the curriculum.

One Wednesday morning in the spring semester of his first year with us, David R. went to the art sink after his mother left, as he often did, and let the water flow over his hands in a calming, meditative rhythm. Meanwhile, we began clearing breakfast and preparing for morning group time. Cecilia approached him with a visual cue to show him that the class had gathered in the community center for circle time.

"It's time to go to circle time, David," she said gently in Spanish, attempting to guide him to dry his hands.

Disliking the sensation of dripping water, he screamed, shook his hands, and ran off to the casita, our dramatic play area. We let him go; circle time was optional. He typically opted out unless we were dancing, and he wasn't alone. He didn't dance, but he would stand in our presence.

As I led the class in our morning songs and started reading a story from our unit on buildings, two children noticed David R. moving around the casita, studying objects. One stood up, then the other. In my early years, I would have asked them to sit down, reassuring them that Ms. Cecilia would help David. But now I decided to let them go.

In the periphery of my vision, I observed them join David R. One child took dishes from the shelf, and the other sat at the table and made a playful request. David, eyeing the teapot with a squint, approached cautiously. I continued reading, allowing the children to navigate their interactions.

Lillie confronted me after the morning class left. "Why did you let the children leave in the middle of circle time?" Her blunt questions about the mechanics of the classroom were common. I met them with the openness of a teacher, and her inquiries often forced me to reflect more deeply on my professional practices.

"I'm not sure. It just seemed like the right thing for our community. It's February. Most of the children understand the classroom expectations and routines. They know circle time is about coming together to learn with one another. I trust that learning happens in different ways. Our expectations of each child have to reflect their developmental abilities, shaped by their interests, experiences, and family culture. Whether they're sitting with us or exploring nearby, they're still part of our community. Does that make sense?"

Lillie nodded. "But things could have gotten out of control. I know most of the kids get the expectations, but I noticed a few still got distracted. They stopped paying attention to you. How's that good for the community?"

"I agree. That's why I started adding hand and body gestures to the story. Did you notice that once I got the children physically involved, all of them followed? It comes down to what motivates them and how I can adapt on the spot to balance what has motivated the community all year with the outcomes I want to achieve in the lesson."

"Wow. I didn't pick up on any of that."

"I'm sure this is not the last time I will have to pivot. Keep watching me with the lens of community building, especially when the events include David R."

Cecilia, as usual, did tasks on the periphery while Lillie and I spoke about the children's behaviors and my teaching approaches. She had told me months earlier that she liked to listen and didn't have those types of questions. "I just follow your lead, Andrew," she had said.

By mid-March, Cecilia, Lillie, and I had created a classroom community where routines flowed naturally, supported by the children, families, and teachers. Each of us contributed to the harmony that allowed moments like the one back in February with David R. to unfold without tension between the children and adults.

David A. joined our afternoon classroom when Cecilia and I were just starting to teach together. Each afternoon, David A.'s mother arrived with her sister-in-law, whose son Leonardo was also in our class. During our first home visit, we learned both families, monolingual Spanish speakers from El Salvador, had immigrated to the US about seven years earlier. They shared a two-bedroom bungalow near the school. While the close quarters presented challenges, the two families found joy in their shared home.

As I got to know them, I saw how much they valued education, even though it was unfamiliar territory. Neither of David A.'s parents, nor his aunt and uncle, had consistent access to formal schooling as children, but they wanted their children to have the chance they never had. When David was diagnosed with autism at two, his mother described the family as "desgarrado," or torn apart. They accepted home visits from interventionists yet remained wary of outsiders. Though she was unsure of what support was available for her son, David A.'s mother was determined to give him every opportunity within her reach.

The start wasn't easy. Cecilia, Lillie, and I were still working out our classroom rhythm, and conventional interventions for a child with autism didn't resonate with David A. His mother stayed behind periodically to help us. With Cecilia's support, we encouraged her to focus on the other children in the classroom rather than David and his cousin. It was a challenge at first, but after Cecilia modeled how to support groups of children during play, his mother caught on quickly.

David A. loved arranging toy cars in precise patterns. His mother provided insight regarding this behavior through Cecilia, which helped us consider additions and modifications to the class. In November, during our unit on balls, I brought in a set of white gutters, hoping to see children create magical experiences in the classroom I could never have come up with on my own. It was a common event. While I envisioned rolling balls, David took it to the next level. David A. saw the gutters as elevated car tracks he could prop up on chairs. He figured out how to create inclines that provided enough energy to move the vehicle or ball to the end. His creativity captivated the other children more than my planned activity. Instead of following the lesson I prepared at the start of the unit, I let the children take the lead and revised my lesson plans.

For the rest of the year, the children collaborated on complex tracks, changing them with each unit in the curriculum.

The sparks of connection and wonder extended far beyond the white gutters. The collaborative spirit and creativity the children developed reportedly carried over into the pre-kindergarten year in the Explorer classroom.

As the end of the year approached, we decided to keep David A. and David R. in our class for an additional year. We believed staying with us would help them strengthen their skills for kindergarten rather than moving them to Ana's Explorer class or Esmeralda's. I knew from experience that once children were placed or kept in a more restrictive setting, they were rarely included in general education a majority of their school day, so the decision was not made lightly. I wanted to have all the evidence possible to recommend they transition into general kindergarten classrooms in a year and a half, and the Individual Education Program team decided that transition would be more likely if the boys stayed in our classroom.

Earlier that Thursday morning, after Jorge told me we couldn't speak Spanish in the classroom, I realized we might have miscalculated. Without the language support that David A. and David R. depended on, and with a new curriculum that didn't align with my instructional instincts, it would be difficult to sustain the progress and trust we'd built with the Davids and several other children.

***

When our first day not speaking Spanish ended, I sat at my desk after everyone in the early childhood education wing had gone home. My thoughts circled around the families and children in our classroom, not just those of David A. and David R. *How are we supposed to support the development of a community if we can't speak Spanish?* It wasn't just about the children currently enrolled. It was every child who might come through our door, with or without an Individual Education Program, and their families. We still had space for seven more kids.

I opened a new email draft; my mind crammed with questions. *How could our classroom be classified as English Language Development–Spanish?* We'd been part of Vista for two years, and this had never once come up. My teaching assistants spoke Spanish. I'd thought that was the requirement. There was no mention of English Language Development–English or Spanish designations. Our focus had always been on supporting children with developmental delays, disabilities, and diverse linguistic backgrounds without conditions.

Every piece of feedback I'd received from administrators and instructors in the three English Language Development Department courses affirmed that my novice ability to speak Spanish exceeded the expectations and was appreciated.

I minimized the draft and scrolled through two years of messages from the Early Childhood Special Education Department. It triggered a flood of negative memories. Still, I needed to find anything that could help make sense of this sudden shift.

I leaned back in my chair. *What matters most for our classroom: a teacher experienced in early childhood special education who could teach children with developmental delays or a teacher fluent in Spanish but less equipped to meet the complex needs of twelve children requiring significant support?* There was no clear answer. There wasn't a scale for measuring all the soft skills and experience a teacher brings, but I imagined these were the kinds of considerations Kris and the hiring team had weighed before opening the position two years ago. I recalled Kris mentioning the need for at least one Spanish-speaking para before we hired Cecilia. Since then, language hadn't been an issue.

Now with the awareness of an English Language Development–Spanish designation, it felt like everything might change. I maximized the email draft and typed in the name of the new director of early childhood special education, Diana Carter. My cursor hovered over the subject line. I still wasn't sure how to phrase the message.

Finally, I began typing:

Dear Diana,

I hope the school year hasn't been too hectic. I have a quick question.

I was just informed that our Foundations classroom is designated English Language Development–Spanish. Are the requirements for a Foundations classroom designated English Language Development–Spanish the same as the requirements for Explorer English Language Development–Spanish?

Sincerely,

Andrew

The subject line was direct, no ambiguity or emotion: *Question About Foundations Classrooms.*

I looked over at the class roster, watching the names blur as more questions raced through my mind. Eight of our students, morning and afternoon combined, would be considered English Language Development–English. Most of the morning children had Individual Education Programs. The afternoon children did not. What did this mean for them? For those eight children and families? Would students who would be considered English Language Development–English be moved into other programs? I couldn't make sense of it.

David A. and David R. had been with us for more than a year. Would they be uprooted simply because I wasn't fluent in Spanish? *How will we possibly explain this to families?*

My pocket vibrated. I glanced at my phone. A message from Natalie lit the screen:

4:45! Are you on your way home?

With a sigh, I hit send on the email to Diana, then logged off. As I packed up and made my way down the long hallway separating early childhood education from the rest of the school,

I couldn't shake the restlessness pressing on me. Each beat of my heart felt like a reminder of the many unanswered questions, of the uncertain future facing not only the students and families, but also all of us working to support them.

As I approached the stairs, the laminated poster came into view.

Perseverance. Respect. Integrity. Diversity. Excellence.

I paused, letting the words settle over me like a soft instruction: *Breathe.*

***

The dinner routine was winding down. I cleared the kitchen table and counters while Natalie cleaned up the girls and sent them to the living room. I followed behind, settling on the carpeted floor to watch Citlali and Itzel play. With my university classes titled Leadership for Organizational Performance and Teaching in the Modern Classroom starting, I was fully in dad mode, committed to the agreement Natalie and I had made about balancing time with the family.

Citlali leapt onto the couch and then sprang off with a shriek of joy. Itzel crawled after her, giggling as her sister jumped. My eyes drifted to the laptop on the end table. My mind slipped back to the email I'd sent earlier. I pulled out my phone, pretending to check the time. It was 5:45 p.m. In truth, I was anxious for a reply from Diana.

I had no idea how this would unfold. I didn't know Diana or how she'd navigate the politics swirling through Metro Denver Unified and the teams she oversaw. I slid the laptop to the floor and opened it. The girls didn't notice.

A reply had arrived.

Her response was brief. She said she wasn't sure and wanted to know who was asking. I explained that the principal was inquiring about special education policy for dual-language learners. It was terminology I had recently been taught that more accurately described children who are non-native English speakers learning English than the term English language learners. "Every young child is learning English," one of my peers at the university told me. In the email response to Diana, I added a question, trying to gather more information before returning to the commitment that mattered most.

Before I could close the laptop, another message appeared. She'd listed a few contacts in other departments and asked how things were going overall. I stared at the screen, confused. *More departments? More layers?*

"Daddy! Watch!"

Citlali's voice snapped me back. She stood on the edge of the couch, arms outstretched.

I shut the laptop and slid it under the couch. Citlali's eyes sparkled as she readied herself. Itzel grinned, a single tooth gleaming. I scooted closer, hoping to intercept Citlali before she landed on her sister.

Too late.

"Kaboom!"

She missed Itzel by inches. The toddler burst into giggles.

"How about I lift you over Itzel instead of you jumping on her?" I offered.

"Yeeeaaah!" Citlali squealed, running toward me with arms out like a tiny zombie. I hoisted her up as Itzel patted my leg and plopped down. I helped Citlali fly over her sister safely.

"Kaboom," I roared as she landed. She echoed it, beaming with laughter. The girls took turns until I called, "One more time, then it's bath."

Later, after they were tucked into bed, I told Natalie I needed to catch up on emails. I stepped into my closet-office and opened the laptop, rereading Diana's message. I felt the weight of everything I wanted to say. How personal it was. How deeply it cut. How much the families trusted us. How this wasn't just a policy change, that it felt like a betrayal.

Did I need to say all that to Diana? This was an email to the director of early childhood special education. I needed to focus on professional concerns.

I typed carefully, apologizing for the frequency of my messages. I explained my concern for the children and families. I noted that two-thirds of my class spoke Spanish and that I'd been told my teaching assistants and I could no longer speak Spanish with them due to me lacking the credential. I described how hard it would be to sit across from families and explain we could no longer offer what they had trusted us to provide.

The original subject line felt too clinical. I changed it: *Supporting Children and Families.* That was what this was really about. I reread the message, thought through the power dynamics, and hit send.

I stepped into the bedroom. Natalie was reading. The girls were asleep beside her. I grabbed my water bottle and returned to the closet-office.

Another reply had arrived.

Diana's words were swift and clear. She was stunned. She saw the problem too. The tension in my shoulders loosened. I wasn't overreacting. This wasn't just personal; it was professional, and someone with influence understood.

I drafted another email, this time to Jorge. I asked if he'd be willing to meet with the parents of the monolingual Spanish-speaking children. I told him how painful it felt to face these conversations alone, that it felt as if we'd misled families for years. I admitted I was struggling to carry this alone. The weight of it was personal, but Jorge was the principal. Since the day I met him, he reiterated I go to him with professional concerns that felt personal.

After sending the message, I stepped outside. The cool night air greeted me like a quiet embrace. I inhaled deeply, trying to slow my heart and collect my thoughts.

When I came back in, Natalie was in the kitchen getting water.

"What are you doing?"

"Just some emails," I said softly. "Nothing important."

I returned to the closet-office and reread my message to Jorge. Moments later, his reply came. It was one sentence. He told me he'd talk to parents at the next "Pastries with the Principal" event.

My thoughts wandered. *Good. At least a path forward is beginning to emerge.*

I returned to Diana's thread and sent one final update. I was diplomatic. I knew that, as director, Diana's role was first and foremost about ensuring compliance. The well-being of children and families wasn't her primary focus. Still, I ended the email asking whether she'd be open to a phone call the next day.

When I finally shut the laptop, I checked the time: 8:55 p.m. My body was restless, my mind still racing. I grabbed my journal and curled up on the love seat in our living room. The pen moved quickly.

My final sentence: *Time to sleep.*

I closed the journal and let the silence settle around me.

***

The moment I returned to work Friday morning, the emails began. Two exchanges came in before lunch and four more after Cecilia and Lillie had left with the children. After a few missed calls, Diana and I scheduled a phone conversation for the following Tuesday. Until then, my focus remained on room 122. *Perseverance, respect, integrity, diversity, and excellence,* I reminded myself.

I also had to respond to Mr. Tom's email from earlier that morning. He was going to be in the Vista neighborhood and preferred to stop by in person rather than prepare for his first day with us through email. We both knew how easy it was for collaboration or friendship to get lost in translation when filtered through technical discussions about district business.

"We moved to room 122. It'll blow your mind," I'd written in my reply.

It was the first time I had seen Tom since late May, back when I still had hopes he might contribute to the classroom curriculum. He arrived midway through the morning class, stepping through the threshold of room 122 like no time had passed. Charismatic as ever, he appeared at my side. His neatly groomed gray hair, round brown glasses, and button-down shirt paired with brown khakis made him instantly recognizable.

I crouched beside one of the four-seat rectangular tables set up in what was labeled the literacy and home office center. At that moment, it was neither. It was where the four native-English-speaking children in the morning class sat. Two of the children did not have verbal language. One could say a few unintelligible words. The fourth did not have an Individual Education Program, but was not yet socially interacting with children or adults. The four children practiced drawing "people" on white dry-erase boards. We had intended to complete the activity during circle time, but with the distractions and limited attention spans, we shifted to smaller groups instead. I worked with the children who were native English speakers because I could provide special education support. Although we were prohibited from speaking Spanish, Cecilia and Lillie divided the seven native Spanish-speaking children between two other tables for the same activity.

"Mr. Andrew, how have you been?"

"Mr. Tom!" I said, looking up. "It's great to see you, my friend. Bienvenidos a la sala 122."

"Gracias, amigo." That was the extent of his Spanish.

"This is quite the room," he said, pushing up his glasses. I stood so we were eye to eye.

"It's great. We've got a closet, a bathroom, a door to the playground, a ramp, and actual space. It's a little overwhelming, but in a good way."

Tom's default expression was a smile. "That's great. And what's this I hear about a new curriculum?"

I gave him a general overview of Every Early Learner Succeeds and shared how the first week had gone. Then, more quietly, I added, "Oh, and we're not allowed to speak Spanish."

I left it at that. I didn't want to drag Tom into drama, especially when so many questions were still unresolved. "But we're adjusting. I took my third course with the English Language Development Department this summer, and it helped me apply strategies that can support dual-language learners. Still, it's been difficult to build relationships or implement interventions without Spanish."

"That's tough," he said with genuine empathy. He never asked questions that might place others in procedural conflict. Then he added, "As always, I'll follow your lead."

"I asked our new principal, Jorge Sanchez, if you could take on more activities this year, like we discussed last spring. But that doesn't seem likely anytime soon."

"You do the heavy lifting five days a week. I'll hang back and observe, get to know the kids, and we'll do our thing."

Tom's "thing" had always been showing up for our classroom with a commitment to providing special education services as part of the natural routine in the classroom. Although his training in speech-language pathology spanned birth through adulthood, his gift for connecting with three- and four-year-olds with developmental delays or disabilities was unmistakable.

We chatted briefly about his caseload. He shared kind words and a few laughs with Lillie and Cecilia before leaving. His visit reminded me of the joy that still existed here, despite the politics swirling around us.

After the morning children left, Lillie and Cecilia approached my desk. Their postures made it evident something pressing was on their minds. They hovered for a moment before Lillie said, "We were talking about this Spanish thing." Her arms were crossed and her tone was firm. "You can't just let this slide, Andrew."

Cecilia nodded, eyes lowered.

Lillie continued. "Seriously! Jorge has no idea what we've built. He just got here. And now he thinks he can tell us not to speak Spanish? That's BS." She glanced at Cecilia, then back at me. "Total BS. What if families say something?"

"It's not that simple," I replied, looking down. "I get it. I do. But I've dealt with district policies before, especially in special education. There's a chain of command. Burn one bridge, and you risk burning them all. Parents can speak up, but if they don't have a legal understanding of what they're up against, it won't go anywhere."

Lillie rolled her eyes but let me finish.

"The only way we make change is with support from upper administration. In the past, I had Kris's backing. Jorge might listen, but we need people with more authority. The new director of early childhood special education, Diana Carter, and I have exchanged a few emails. She might be able to help. Whoever we talk to, we need to be strategic, objective, rooted in policy, and focused on the ethical conflicts of the policy. If we come across as defensive or emotional, it will hurt our case. It won't be easy, but we need to try not to make this sound personal."

Cecilia finally spoke. "I just . . . I don't want to lose my job. We can adapt. It's hard, but we always find a way."

Lillie's expression tightened. After a pause, she sighed. "Okay. I hear you. I just don't want to sit here and watch this fall apart. What we've built . . . it matters."

"It does. And you're right. We can't stay silent. But we have to be strategic."

Lillie nodded slowly. "Then work with the early childhood special education lady. Don't let this die quietly. Fight for the families and us."

"Maybe she'll listen. Maybe she'll help, but I doubt it. They're always in it for themselves. They don't care about us, the kids, or the families," Cecilia added.

I didn't respond right away. My instinct told me Cecilia was right. Diana might not do much. But I also knew I had no other choice.

"I'll keep pushing," I said. The words sounded steadier than I felt.

Cecilia and Lillie packed up for their lunch break. None of us felt good about the situation, and I had a growing sense that this was only the beginning.

****

Parents, grandparents, older siblings, and the occasional toddler hovered outside our classroom's back door, waiting for dismissal. It was 2:45, and the twelve children in our afternoon class sat around the perimeter of the carpet in the community center. Their wiggles intensified as I sang the final lines of our goodbye song. Cecilia propped the door open, letting in the muffled clamor from the ramp that sloped toward the playground. One by one, families began trickling in.

To keep the children from racing toward the door, we had set up tumbling mats as a divider between the front and back halves of room 122, just like we did during breakfast and snack time. The barrier couldn't contain the children's excitement. The chatter from the back door rose steadily. Several children craned their necks for a glimpse of the back half of the room.

I used my usual strategy, singing a fingerplay to quietly cue the children with the least patience to grab their backpacks when I spotted a family member. For the three bus riders, all of whom were Spanish speakers, I gave a subtle prompt, but they stared at me blankly. My heart urged me to speak their language, to connect with them in the way that felt most natural. My head, full of rules, kept me silent. Lillie, ever intuitive, stepped in. She gently tapped each child on the shoulder and told them in Spanish it was time to go. They responded instantly, two of them taking her hands. Ricky, a boy whose laughter carried easily across the room, volunteered to help the third.

Once the last child was safely with their family or on the bus, I straightened a few things in the community center and made my way toward the remaining adults. Beatriz, Jimmy's mom, and Kelly, Ricky's mom, lingered near the door. Their posture was easy and familiar, like lifelong friends sharing a moment. Beatriz leaned lightly against the frame, arms crossed, dividing her attention. One eye followed Ellie, her toddler, who had once again wandered to the puzzle shelf. The other kept watch over Jimmy and Ricky. The boys were dissolving into giggles at some joke only a three-year-old could understand. Kelly stood slightly behind her. Tall and slender, her hands rested lightly on Ricky's backpack straps. A smile as warm as a hug lit her face as she glanced between Beatriz and the boys.

"Mr. Andrew!" Beatriz called out, her voice bright. "It's so fun to watch Jimmy. How was your first week?"

I hesitated, weighing how much to share. "It was great. Jimmy, Ricky, and another child, Eric, are quick learners and natural leaders. I can't tell you how excited I am to have them in our community."

Her expression softened, joy flickering in her eyes as she turned back to Jimmy. The boys had already formed a friendship with a native Spanish-speaking child, and I knew from experience that those connections would likely grow in English before long.

Despite everything that had unfolded this week, watching those friendships develop gave me hope for the classroom we were building.

"That's good to hear," Kelly added, her tone gentle.

"Jimmy loves coming to school. He talks about Ricky, Eric, you, Lillie, and Cecilia all the time," Beatriz said. "I'm curious. Do you think he'll learn Spanish?"

"Well, maybe from the other kids," I said, pausing, "but we're not allowed to speak Spanish to them in the classroom."

Their smiles faded, curiosity giving way to confusion.

"You've been speaking Spanish with them all week, haven't you?" Beatriz asked.

"Not yesterday or today," I admitted. I decided to share what I could, sticking to the facts. "There's a court order in Metro Denver Unified that says students must be taught core instruction in their native language while developing English. Some classrooms are designated English Language Development–Spanish, others are English Language Development–English. These designations depend on the students' language needs. On Wednesday, I learned that our classroom is designated English Language Development–Spanish. But because our program is unique for Vista, there's still a lot of confusion about what that actually means. That's why Jimmy and Ricky won't be learning Spanish from us."

Both women looked puzzled. Kelly responded first, her voice soft. "That's too bad."

Beatriz frowned. "That doesn't seem right. If you all speak Spanish, you should speak Spanish. Wouldn't that help Jimmy connect more with the children who don't speak English?"

My beliefs about professionalism halted me. "I don't know," I said carefully. "We're still trying to sort things out. There's not much else I can say right now."

Kelly sighed and called Ricky over. "I'm sorry to hear that. Ricky, come on. We have to go. Maybe we can get together with Jimmy this weekend to play."

Beatriz corralled Ellie into the baby carrier and reached for Jimmy's hand.

I watched them leave, the boys laughing all the way to the sidewalk. As the door closed, I could hear the muffled sounds of Lillie, Cecilia, and Maya's conversation about English Language Development–English and English Language Development–Spanish drifting in from Ana's room. It was a debate I didn't have the energy to join.

The week had been long and draining. A stack of graduate school homework still waited for me, but I resolved to spend as much of the weekend as I could with Natalie and the girls because being with them reminded me of what truly mattered.

CHAPTER 6

DEPARTMENTS

Natalie and I agreed that my weekends would begin at 6 a.m., taking the train downtown to the university library. Since telling her about the circumstances at Vista, we agreed that boundaries between work, home, and college were even more important than previously considered.

The private study room I reserved was rectangular and modern, with one wall of frosted glass that softened the hallway's light and three walls of smooth, taupe paint. An oblong table, four feet wide and ten feet long, stretched across the center of the room. At the far end, a whiteboard ran almost wall to wall, leaving only a narrow two-inch border on either side. I set down my coffee, opened my laptop, and spread eight articles across the table, their corners overlapping like layers of thought. Looking down at the documents, I could see theory on top of lived experience. So far, the concepts from class had not felt abstract. They showed up in room 122 every day.

By late morning, I was ready to pack up. There was one last assignment. A reflection paper.

What are the three patterns fundamental to Cashman's Theory of Results-Based Leadership inside your organization, school, or classroom?

The prompt was simple: integrate personal experience with the readings.

I began drafting:

While addressing the concept of leadership within a classroom, school, or organization, Cashman (2008) describes authenticity, influence, and value creation as the core elements that shape effective leadership. He emphasizes that meaningful leadership grows from a willingness to assume both personal and social responsibility. In the inclusive early childhood classroom, I enact these fundamentals by approaching my work with authenticity, building responsive relationships with children and families, and ensuring that each child's developmental abilities, interests, experiences, and family culture . . .

I stopped writing. I had never considered those actions to be leadership until my summer courses, where the line between teacher and leader began to dissolve. My mind began to wander. That was me in years past. Who was I now, in room 122, as a leader?

Maybe it was too early to know. I had begun forming relationships with a few parents, but nothing felt steady. Alone in the study room, I could not shake the feeling that my actions— my leadership—no longer aligned with the way I was being asked to teach. Was it appropriate to draw on past success when the present felt more urgent to analyze?

Still, I kept going.

In practice, I apply authenticity by reflecting daily on each child's engagement and communication style. I consider conversations with families during home visits, classroom family events, volunteering, and at drop-off and pickup. These reflections influence my decisions as I work toward Individual Education Program goals and developmental benchmarks . . .

Again, I hesitated. Was that truly how I was leading this year? Without home visits, classroom family events, and volunteering, I knew I would not be able to engage with families in ways that built authentic trust or encouraged them to share meaningful information. Even if those conversations took place, the curriculum and Jorge's expectations would prevent me from using what those families shared to implement effective interventions.

The tension was not just intellectual. It lived in my chest. What I believed about teaching—about leadership in the classroom—no longer matched the conditions I was working in. I had once taught with confidence and openness. Now I was being asked to follow scripts that silenced children's stories and distanced me from their families.

I thought about my upcoming conversation with Diana on Tuesday. *Will she help? Can she? Can anyone?*

I closed my laptop and took three deep breaths. Natalie had said years ago, when I was struggling to find purpose in a childcare center in Minneapolis, and repeated numerous times since, "You can only control what you can control. Letting go isn't giving up. It's survival."

Still, as I packed my bag, a deeper question rose in me. *What does leadership look like when systems are misaligned with our values?*

***

On Tuesday afternoon, September 2, after Lillie, Cecilia, and Mr. Tom had already gone home, I sat alone, staring at the white mug on my desk: "Best Teacher Ever." The words mocked me. I knew I could do better. I had an obligation to do better. My stomach churned as I prepared for the phone call with Diana. The line between compliance and connection had grown thicker than I'd ever experienced.

"Hi, Diana," I said, forcing my voice to sound steady.

"Andrew! Wow, I can't imagine how you're feeling right now. Let's get this figured out. Where do things stand at the moment?"

I exhaled. Her warmth made the conversation feel less daunting. "We can't speak Spanish to the children. I feel lost. How am I supposed to build relationships when we're not allowed to speak their language? My teaching assistants, Cecilia and Lillie, aren't even allowed to use Spanish."

"That's ridiculous," she said, her voice sharp with frustration. "I'm trying to get in touch with Rick Jackson and Janet Thompson in the Early Childhood Education Department. We need answers on what the Binding Compliance Order actually requires in Foundations classrooms. I can't even find enough qualified teachers with early childhood special education credentials, let alone those who are bilingual. There's only one bilingual early childhood special education teacher in the entire district, and she's tied up interpreting for meetings. Can you send me a breakdown of the children's home languages and Individual Education Program status?"

"Absolutely. Thank you so much, Diana. This whole situation is overwhelming."

"I can tell. But hey, I hear you're getting your doctorate. You're carrying a lot right now."

I laughed. "Who told you that?"

"Nothing stays a secret around here," she said playfully.

"Classes just started. The assignments actually help me process what's happening at school. As long as I keep a routine, I should be okay."

"Well, you're doing an amazing job managing the challenges at Vista."

Her kindness caught me off guard. "The English Language Development–Spanish designation is just one piece of it. Still, I try to treat it as a learning opportunity."

"That's a good mindset." She paused. "Hey, we have an open position on my team. We're looking for an itinerant teacher to support Explorer Early Childhood classrooms in the southeastern region. You'd be incredible in that role. Interested?"

The offer startled me. "I really appreciate that. I actually applied for an itinerant teaching position when we first moved here from Tucson, but right now, I'm committed to staying for the kids and families. Lillie, Cecilia, and I need each other."

"I understand. Just think about it," she said warmly.

Even amid the policy fog, I felt heard. Diana's understanding steadied me, at least for the moment.

After we hung up, I turned to a copy of the class roster on the wall next to my desk and began tallying the data she requested. Every number represented a child. Every language reflected a home, a culture, a story we were being told to ignore. I opened a new message and began typing.

Hi Diana,

Thank you for taking the time to talk to me. Here are the numbers you requested.

Morning:

11 children, 5 with Individual Education Programs

English: 3 (2 are nonverbal, 1 uses words in isolation)

Spanish: 2

Peer Models:

English: 1

Spanish: 5

Afternoon:

12 children, 4 with Individual Education Programs

English: 0

Spanish: 4

Peer Models:

English: 4

Spanish: 4

Thanks again,

Andrew

As I hit send, the tension in my forehead, jaw, and shoulders remained. We were being asked to follow a policy that contradicted everything I knew about inclusion, everything I had taught others to practice. Compliance was not neutral. It was protection. Not for children or families, but for administrators and the district. I was no longer sure where compliance ended and ethical responsibility began.

***

We were only a week and a half into the school year, but it felt much longer. We were tiptoeing around the new mandates in the classroom, intentionally or not. David A., David R., and several others hadn't connected with the new curriculum in any meaningful way. We were struggling to build a sense of community in the morning class, and my patience with the bureaucratic hoops was running thin.

As usual, I arrived at the classroom long before Lillie and Cecilia. The whisper of a computer fan in the empty room wrapped around me. I sat at my desk and waited for my email account to open. When my inbox appeared, one message immediately caught my attention. It was a reply to the message I had sent Diana the day before.

Her message was brief, but it carried a quiet promise. She thanked me for the information and said she would be in training over the next two days but wanted to meet soon. Out of respect for my space, she suggested we schedule something next week.

A small spark of hope flickered in my stomach, but I knew I could not wait for Diana. We needed to provide special education services. I needed to speak with Jorge directly. Still, I decided to wait until the school day was over. Whatever the outcome of that conversation, I could not allow it to pull me away from the children in front of me.

After the classroom emptied, I made my way to speak with Jorge when Gabriela, Ernesto's mom, caught my attention. She was leaving the office with a stack of flyers tucked in her right arm. As the Vista community liaison, she was a model of how to connect with families, and I knew nothing was more important than doing the same.

"Hey, Gabriela," I greeted her, slowing my pace.

"Mr. Andrew," she said, shifting the papers in her left arm and reaching out to me for a side hug. "I was hoping I'd see you. How's Ernesto doing in class?"

I smiled, the tension in my shoulders loosening slightly. "He's doing great. He's so observant . . . and those songs? He leads half of them now!"

She laughed, her eyes twinkling. "Oh, I know. He sings them at home, all the time. But if any of us try to join in, he shuts us down. 'Only Mr. Andrew can sing the classroom songs!' he says. We're not allowed."

I laughed with her, imagining his scowling face. "That sounds about right."

She came closer and lowered her voice. "He also talks a lot about Mateo and Nelia. It's sweet hearing him talk about friends so naturally."

"That's great to hear," I said. "He's definitely forming bonds."

Her tone shifted, quiet and serious. "Hey . . . I heard you, Lillie, and Cecilia aren't allowed to speak Spanish in the classroom anymore. Is that true?"

"You heard correctly," I said reluctantly.

She shook her head. "I'm not happy about it. And I've heard other families grumbling too. I just wanted you to know. You all have been incredible for our community. Truly. I don't want that to change. But"—she glanced toward the hallway, her voice softening further—"I also don't want to lose my job. So please, let's keep this between us."

"I understand," I said sincerely. "And I appreciate you saying that. Really."

Just then, Jorge emerged from his office, walking briskly with a clipboard in hand. I gave Gabriela a quick nod. "I should catch him before he disappears."

She returned the nod, her expression knowing. "Good luck."

"Jorge, sorry to bother you. I was wondering if you had a minute?"

He turned to me and glanced at his watch. His measured expression met mine. "I'm on my way to a meeting. Is this quick?"

"I'll try." I thought about Lillie's demand. *Don't let this die quietly. Fight for the families and us.* The words tumbled out of me, rushed but anchored by facts. "I need to meet the Individual Education Program requirements. Some of the children need up to four hours of special education services each week. I cannot be as effective with intervention strategies if I'm not able to communicate basic concepts with children in their native language. These are children who don't understand complex language, so there needs to be simple directions in the language they are familiar with, along with pictures." I wanted to say more, but I refrained.

Jorge's expression softened, but his voice remained careful, wrapped in layers of administrative distance. "I know you're doing great, Andrew. The curriculum is designed to help address the Individual Education Program goals. But we also need to follow the Binding Compliance Order. And you know, of course, we have to be mindful of potential legal concerns with special education."

The words landed heavily. *Legal concerns.* Not the children sitting in front of me each day. Not the families who trusted us. *Compliance. Avoiding lawsuits. Protecting the institution.* Those were his priorities.

Jorge shifted his eyes. "I'm sorry, Andrew. I really have to run. Let's set up a meeting next week and talk it through. I'll also connect with the head of early childhood special education. What's her name again? Diana?"

"Yes, Diana Carter. Would you like me to connect you with her?"

He nodded and turned, the heels of his shoes clicking swiftly against the tile as he disappeared down the hallway. I stood for a moment, listening to the sound of his footsteps fade, then I returned to room 122.

I opened my laptop and typed quickly.

Hi Diana,

Jorge Sanchez, the Vista principal, would like to speak with you directly about our Foundations classroom. He's focused on staying within legal guidelines for the Individual Education Programs. I think he's willing to listen. Thanks again for your support.

Best,

Andrew

Minutes later, her reply arrived. She welcomed the invitation. My fingers did a quick dance over the computer keys.

Wonderful! Thank you!

Andrew

I turned my attention to classroom responsibilities. Within moments, the class phone rang.

"Andrew," Diana's voice came through, steady and energized. "I just spoke with Jorge. We're setting up a meeting with the folks from the Early Childhood Education Department. A few others may join too. I'll keep you updated."

I was still processing how quickly she was able to contact Jorge and how fast the pieces were moving. "That's wonderful!" I replied reflexively.

We exchanged words of caution and compassion, then her tone lightened, and she said, "And by the way, I get the sense you might be reconsidering the itinerant teacher position."

I leaned back in my chair and chuckled softly. The offer was flattering, but the answer remained the same.

"I appreciate you asking. But no. I'm not reconsidering. The work with the kids and families, the relationships, being present with them in the day-to-day . . . that's where I need to be. That's what makes this meaningful."

"I understand," she said. I could hear the quiet smile in her voice. "But I figured it couldn't hurt to ask."

As the call ended, I sat still for a moment, letting the weight of it all settle around me. The road ahead was uncertain. Layers of administrators, departments, and policies still stood between us and a solution. But for the first time in more than a week, I felt something shift. I was no longer entirely alone in the fight. And for now, that was enough.

***

When I got home, Natalie and the girls were playing on the living room floor. My words tumbled out quickly. They carried a mix of exhaustion and cautious optimism. I told Natalie what Diana had said and ended with the opportunity Diana had dangled in front of me, which I had rejected without much consideration.

Natalie looked up from watching Itzel and Citlali. Her expression softened as she listened, but her response came without hesitation, as if she'd been thinking about it for a while.

"The itinerant teacher position sounds like something better for you," she said evenly. "It would get you away from the stress of the classroom. Maybe you'd pay more attention to us."

Her words stung: not because they were harsh, but because I was already mindful of how I spent time with the family. A familiar tug of defensiveness rose in my chest.

"I pay attention to you," I said, careful to keep my tone steady. "I'm here by five every day. I don't even touch work until the girls are asleep. And I've been home after noon on weekends too."

She sighed, clearly not interested in arguing. Her voice was calm but firm, the way she spoke when she wanted to be truly heard.

"Okay, but can you keep it up? I can already see the classroom wearing you down. That stress affects you at home. Your class isn't going to be like last year. You either need to accept that or move on. I think you should consider Diana's offer."

I was reluctant but resolved. "I hear you, but no. I'll be present. I need to stay in the classroom. I promise I'll keep it up."

"Okay," she said. "But you need to take care of yourself and be present with us before you can be present for others."

Her words meandered through my thoughts long after the conversation ended. By the time I climbed into bed, they had taken root. Lying in the dark, staring at the ceiling, I replayed my conversations with Diana, Jorge, and Natalie, turning over every detail. *Should I consider the itinerant position?* The darkness above me gradually shifted from emptiness to a canvas. One where I could project new possibilities, both as a classroom teacher and as something else. But with every brush stroke of possibility came the fear of what change might mean, not just for my role, but for the children, families, and colleagues I might leave behind. I didn't want to let anyone down. Eventually, the thoughts became too heavy to carry in my head. I raced to the living room, grabbed my journal, lay on the love seat, and wrote.

The next morning, the classroom moved with the usual energy of children arriving for the day. Our routines were still forming, as were my thoughts. During a quiet moment, I brought up the dilemma with Cecilia, speaking softly at the kidney table. I didn't want to alarm Lillie.

Cecilia wasn't as surprised as I'd expected. Like Natalie, she encouraged me to do what was best for my family.

Later that night, after class at the university, clarity settled in on the drive home. When I arrived, I greeted Natalie in our bedroom and brought up the itinerant position again.

"I already told you how I feel," she said, steady but kind. "Worry about you. The children and families will be fine."

Her words were both a reassurance and a nudge. By Friday, September 5, at lunchtime, I was ready to take the next step.

Hi Diana,

You mentioned in a previous phone conversation that if I were ever interested in jumping ship, you have an itinerant teacher position open. I'd like to set up a phone conversation with you in the very near future to discuss the position.

Thanks,

Andrew

Later that afternoon, Diana replied. Her message was brief but enthusiastic. She said she was heading into another meeting and suggested we find time to talk on Monday.

I stared at her response, feeling a strange mix of anticipation and hesitation. The wheels were in motion. I didn't know exactly where this would lead, but I had taken the first step toward something new.

***

"Andrew, did you hear what happened last Friday?" Ana asked on Monday afternoon. She stepped across the threshold of my classroom with an energy that felt both urgent and personal.

I turned from the kidney table where I'd been sorting papers in preparation for an Individual Education Program meeting scheduled for the following morning. Her tone snapped me to attention. "No, what happened?"

"Maya was down in the office," she began, lowering her voice as she walked closer to me. "She joined a large group of parents there. She said there must have been at least twenty-five.

They were talking about your program, and they're concerned about you, Lillie, and Cecilia. What's going on?"

My stomach tightened. My mind raced, trying to decipher what could have sparked this gathering. "Oh my," I said, shaking my head. "I need to catch you up."

We spoke quietly for a few minutes, piecing together what Maya had seen and what the families were being told in the office. After a moment of silence, Ana's face lit up. "Guess what!?"

"What?" I was caught off guard by her sudden emotional shift.

"I'm pregnant!" she exclaimed. Her voice matched her radiant facial expression. Her excitement projected through every gesture.

I sprang up from my chair. "Oh my gosh, Ana, that's amazing! Congratulations!" I couldn't help but race a few feet toward her and pull her into a loving embrace. Her happiness was contagious. It was a bright light breaking through the concern of twenty-five families. "When is the baby due?"

"The middle of April," she said, her smile faltering just a little. There was a flicker of nervousness in her voice, as if the reality of what lay ahead was beginning to sink in.

"So, you just found out," I said gently. "Have you told anyone else yet?"

"No, just Maya," she admitted, the glow in her expression returning as she placed her hands over her stomach protectively. "Andrew, I can't tell you how excited I am."

"I know you are," I said, matching her smile. "Congratulations. I'm so happy for you and Sergio. I need to go tell Natalie!"

As she turned to leave, still beaming, I watched her, grateful for the unexpected brightness she'd brought to my day.

I drifted toward my desk, pulling out my phone to text Natalie the news. For a moment, I forgot about the day's concerns and the rest of the week. Ana's joy reminded me of life's capacity for surprise—both challenging and beautiful.

Then, the earlier segment of Ana's and my conversation returned: twenty-five families. They had shown up without fanfare, without demands, simply because they cared. That kind of presence didn't need to be loud to be powerful. It said more than any letter of support ever could.

I sat down at my desk, opened my email, and started a new message to Diana.

Hi Diana,

So . . . apparently, twenty-five parents (mainly of my students from last year and this year) showed up in the front office today demanding to talk with Mr. Sanchez about the news that I was no longer able to work with the children in Spanish. Mr. Sanchez redirected the families to join him at the "Pastries with the Principal" event scheduled for next week.

Knowing how district policies work, I doubt this will do anything to persuade him, but maybe it will make him pause long enough to reconsider who he should be advocating for. If he changes direction, I'll need to retract my interest in the itinerant position.

Andrew

Once the message was sent, I tried to focus on preparing for Tuesday morning's Individual Education Program meeting. Rather than dwell on the email I had just written, my thoughts settled on Ana, on the way she glowed and how her news had shifted the energy in the room.

Just as I was about to close my computer and head home for the day, I heard the chime of a new message. A notification hovered at the bottom corner of my screen. It was from Jorge, addressed to Diana, and copied to four district administrators. My name was tacked on at the end, like an afterthought.

I clicked it open. My stomach tightened as I read.

The message outlined concerns about the program's designation and raised questions about my qualifications to work in a Spanish-designated classroom. Jorge described the makeup of the class, emphasized that most students were Spanish-speaking, and questioned how the current staffing aligned with program requirements. The message was framed like a postmortem rather than a conversation between colleagues.

I stared at the screen for what felt like hours. The sentences, especially those highlighting my "lack of qualifications," dissolved into one another like ink smudged by water.

That evening, I couldn't stop replaying Jorge's words in my mind. *What is he implying? Is he planting the seeds to remove me? Has he already spoken with the families who had gathered in the office? Am I in the wrong?*

I knew I needed to talk to him face-to-face—not just to advocate for myself, but to understand his true intentions. I also knew something more painful: advocating for children and families might no longer be enough.

***

On Tuesday afternoon, I walked down to Jorge's office. After a long day, I needed clarity. We had to make a collective sense of what was and wasn't unfolding.

Jorge's door was closed. I heard Ana's voice inside, muffled but clearly distressed. Gabriela stood at Grace's desk, flipping through papers. I turned my attention to her, not wanting it to seem like I was listening in on Jorge and Ana's conversation.

"Hi, Gabriela," I said.

"Hi, Andrew." Her eyes flicked up. Her mind was somewhere else.

"Which desk is yours?" I asked.

"Every desk is mine!" she replied with a chuckle. "I use whatever's open."

"You don't have your own?"

"No. I move around so much between the school and the Vista community that I don't need one."

She paused, then added, "Did you hear about the families who came in last week to fight for your classroom?"

"I heard a little."

"Andrew, it was incredible. Parents I've never even met came in. They were passionate."

Before I could ask more, Jorge's door opened. Gabriela fell silent.

Ana stepped out, her expression subdued. "Hi, Andrew." Her voice was flat, her eyes glossy.

"Everything okay?"

"Yeah. I'll tell you later," she said softly.

I looked back at Gabriela. Her grin was unreadable. The rapid clack of Jorge's keyboard echoed in the background. I knocked gently.

"Jorge, do you have a few minutes?"

He looked up and smiled. "Sure, come in. How's the curriculum?"

"It's fine. Just adjusting as we go and trying to focus on building the classroom community."

"As it should be at the beginning of the year. Just maintain high expectations."

I nodded and sat down. *High expectations,* I repeated to myself, thinking back to a similar comment he made before telling me Spanish was prohibited in room 122. Determining those expectations was nearly impossible when two-thirds of the children spoke a language Lillie, Cecilia, and I weren't allowed to use. Without that connection, high expectations felt less like ideals and more like pressure.

"I wanted to follow up on your email from yesterday," I said carefully. "I'm confused. It felt like you were saying I'm not capable of teaching the children in my classroom."

"That's not what I meant at all. I'm just trying to understand the bigger picture. If what we've learned is accurate, we'll need to make changes for next year."

"What about this year?"

"This year is set. The children are in your class. Families are comfortable. The curriculum is underway."

"Does that mean we can speak Spanish with the children?"

"No. The legal situation hasn't changed. We'll keep doing what we've been doing. I'll talk to Diana about bringing in a Spanish-speaking special education teacher a few times a week. You just do what you can using your training."

I paused. A thought I'd never considered materialized. *Has anyone even reviewed why I was hired in the first place? Does Jorge know what the Binding Compliance Order requires for Foundations classrooms?*

"Got it," I said, aimlessly.

"When the year ends, you'll be released in good standing. You can apply for other positions, and I'm confident you'll be hired."

"What if a job opens before then?" I surprised myself with the question.

He hesitated. "Well, you're always free to apply. If that's what you want."

"Can I apply for a position in the district?"

"We'd need to find a replacement. Why? Is something open?"

"Diana mentioned an itinerant opening. I don't want to leave. I love the children and families. Lillie and Cecilia are like family. But given everything . . ."

"If we find a Spanish-speaking teacher, it might be less disruptive."

It was a reminder of his priority: not me, not continuity, just compliance. My heart pounded. I didn't need to leave the classroom if we were allowed to use Spanish.

"I'm trying to make it work. It's just hard to build a community and support the children with Individual Education Programs when my teaching assistants and I can't speak their language."

"I understand. We're legally responsible for providing a quality education in the child's native language."

My frustration grew. My tone was firm. "I'm here. I'm committed. No families have asked for a different teacher. A quality education is still happening."

Jorge's delivery remained steady. "They're doing well. The curriculum is strong. Your training will help carry you through. It's just that a fluent Spanish speaker could do more."

That landed hard. I heard what he wasn't saying. I stood up.

"Thank you, Jorge. I appreciate your time."

"My door is always open. I want what's best for you, Andrew."

I walked quickly back to room 122. I felt charged, unsettled, yet strangely relieved for having spoken up. I thought about my graduate course on power and privilege. *Would Natalie, or anyone who wasn't a White man, feel safe challenging leadership like this? Am I overreacting?* I didn't think so. Still, I needed clarity.

I texted Natalie:

I'll be here a little late. I'll try to get home by 6.

Then I sat down at my desk and searched for the Binding Compliance Order. Within minutes, I found the federal directive stating that in English Language Development–Spanish classrooms where specialized instruction was required, such as special education, a Spanish-speaking paraprofessional must be assigned if the teacher lacks the Spanish credential.

There was nothing about banning Spanish in a classroom like ours. Nothing barring Lillie or Cecilia from using it. Quite the opposite.

Jorge's claims were unfounded.

I opened an email to Kris.

Dear Kris,

    I hope your transition to your new position has gone smoothly . . .

I paused. If I contacted her, would it look like I was going over Jorge's head? Would I put her in a difficult position?

Before I could decide, an email from Jorge arrived.

He confirmed I would stay through the end of the year, then be released in good standing. Parents would be informed that the classroom was officially designated English Language Development–Spanish and that placements would change next year. He thanked me for my patience.

I sat back in my chair. I couldn't contact Kris. Not yet. I needed someone else. Someone I could speak with in confidence. Someone who could see what was happening and call it what it was. Someone who could help me understand how to navigate circumstances that were being framed as procedural but that felt deeply personal.

CHAPTER 7

SHIFTS

———

The library study room was quiet, save for the B-flat hum coming from the fluorescent lights. It was Saturday, and I was surrounded by articles about theoretical perspectives on learning. As I read, my thoughts kept drifting back to the previous week in room 122. The support from twenty-five families during their office visit to Jorge reminded me that what we had built mattered. Leaving the classroom would not just mean changing jobs. It would mean leaving a community.

By midmorning, the questions swirling in my head needed an outlet. Few people understood my passion for this work as well as Virginia. Every conversation with her, in and beyond Rocky Mountain Community College, reminded me that she saw me more clearly than I could see myself. She recognized me not only as a teacher but also as someone with potential beyond the classroom. Her steady voice and strategic mind had once helped me see the links between pedagogy and advocacy. I trusted her.

I minimized the document I was working on and opened my personal email account.

Good morning, Virginia,

How has everything been over at the community college? I imagine you are busy with the start of the semester. I started my third and fourth course: Leadership for Organizational Performance, and Teaching in the Modern Classroom. Every week, I become more and more aware of how little I know.

As you're aware, we have a new principal at Vista. I was notified that my position will be eliminated after this year due to apparent mix-ups in my hire, and the reasoning has frustrated the life out of my teaching assistants and me. The barriers this year have been overwhelming.

The rigid Every Early Learner Succeeds curriculum limits my ability to follow the children's leads, which eliminates the most meaningful opportunities for interventions. A district policy, being misinterpreted, prohibits my teaching assistants and me from speaking Spanish in the classroom. That restriction has fractured our sense of community and made it nearly impossible to facilitate any special education interventions with two-thirds of the children.

On top of that, I can no longer involve families as I once did. You know from the ECE 260 class I taught this summer that research consistently shows inclusion depends on honoring each child's developmental abilities, interests, experiences, and family culture through responsive relationships with both children and families. Yet now, every structure in place seems to contradict that research.

Between the inspiration from my coursework and the recognition that I will be released after this school year, I am thinking seriously about pursuing another job opportunity. I want to stay in the classroom, but circumstances are making me reconsider. Do you have any guidance for me? Do I stay in the classroom, or should I start looking elsewhere?

Thank you for your support,

Andrew

That evening, after dinner and the girls' bedtime, I opened my email. Virginia's reply was waiting.

Hi Andrew,

We're doing great here. The semester is well underway, and things are beginning to calm down. You're considering leaving the classroom?! Wow, things must be really difficult. You know I always feel you shouldn't pass up opportunities. It might help if I knew more details.

I would enjoy catching up with you soon. Perhaps lunch? I'm available around 11 a.m. on Wednesdays. If you're interested, we should get together. Let me know.

Regards,

Virginia

I had found the person I could speak with in confidence. It would not change the circumstances, but it was bound to help in one way or another.

***

"Diana, so you saw the emails?"

It was the morning of Monday, September 15. With everything on my mind, I needed to talk with Diana. She understood the dynamics of Metro Denver Unified in ways Virginia couldn't.

"This makes no sense," I said after a brief greeting. "Jorge is pushing me out next year, but he's doing nothing to help this year. The Binding Compliance Order clearly supports the setup in my classroom. We have not one, but two paras who speak Spanish."

"Can you send me the Binding Compliance Order," Diana asked, "and highlight the specific lines that explain your situation? Show me exactly where it says you're qualified to teach as long as you have Spanish-speaking paras."

"Of course. Anything else?"

"No. Let me talk to my people and figure something out. If you're determined to stay in the classroom, I'll work on making things more manageable. We won't place any more children with you. If you decide it's time to move on, you already know my offer stands."

"I almost applied for a lead faculty role at Rocky Mountain Community College last summer. But I stayed. I couldn't imagine not working directly with children and families. Still, the itinerant position might be a good alternative. It's early enough in the year that a transition wouldn't be too disruptive. My only hesitation is finding someone with the qualifications Jorge is requiring, Spanish-speaking and certified in special education."

"Don't stress over that," she said. "If the Binding Compliance Order backs you up, we just need someone qualified for early childhood special education. If you want to talk about the itinerant position, text me on my personal phone. I don't want to risk any missteps. We'll need to keep this under wraps until everything with Vista is sorted out."

She gave me her number, and we ended the call. Having her direct contact was reassuring, as it meant I had her support. Still, something about the secrecy unsettled me. *Isn't she the one who said nothing stays secret here after mentioning my doctoral work during our first conversation?* If this was how she wanted to handle it, I would follow her lead.

Later that afternoon, I updated Lillie and Cecilia as we cleaned up after class. I was about to tell Lillie I was pursuing the itinerant position, but Lillie spoke first.

"I've heard a lot of parents want to help," Lillie said, sweeping sand from beneath the sensory table. "I told them they'd have to take it up with district administrators instead of Jorge, since it's a district policy."

I paused while stacking chairs for custodial cleaning. "Lillie, I know you want to help. I really do. But please don't encourage parents to go to the district right now. They could say we told them to speak up, and that could cause more trouble than good."

She sighed. "I just thought . . ."

"I know," I said gently, "but we have to be careful. There's a lot happening behind the scenes. I'm working with Diana. She's helping us find a resolution."

I thought about sharing what I had discovered in the Binding Compliance Order, that a Spanish-speaking paraprofessional was all that was required in a Foundations classroom. However, I held back. It would only fuel Lillie's desire to act on her own, which could backfire.

I also didn't mention Diana's personal number. I wasn't sure if it was unethical, but it didn't sit right with me.

After Lillie left, Cecilia stayed behind. She walked over to my desk, lingering for a moment before speaking.

"I appreciate Lillie's passion," she said quietly, "but I can't do what she does. I need job security in the district."

I nodded, understanding what she was saying and what she wasn't.

"She has the world in front of her," Cecilia continued. "That's not a privilege I have."

Her honesty touched my heart. "I understand," I said. "You're not alone in this."

"Have you heard anything about the other teaching position?" she asked.

"Nothing definitive."

Cecilia was somber. "Do you think it's time to tell Lillie?"

"Not yet. I'll say something if the job is offered."

When she left, I remained in room 122 as the shadows stretched across the floor. I stared out the window, thinking about what to do next.

I had confidence, perhaps because of my privilege as a White, educated man, but Diana had authority. I needed to trust her and follow her lead. Still, I could not ignore the deeper discomfort I felt. *What does it mean to comply with a system misaligned with my values? What does it mean to lead when silence sometimes protects others and other times protects only the institution? Is resistance, under these circumstances, leadership or unprofessional?*

***

It was a typical afternoon in room 122. Five children were gathered around the rectangular table in the writing center with me. The Every Early Learner Succeeds curriculum guided our activities, and today's task was to write the plan for the activities they would do in the kitchen. I'd demonstrated how to draw a picture and write about who they wanted to be and what they planned to do during the curriculum learning activity.

"Let's think about what you'll do in the kitchen," I encouraged, holding up my own example. I showed them the picture of the dad. Then I drew it myself.

David R. was peering down at the palms of his hands. As I finished drawing the dad, he glided out of his chair and wandered across the room to the community center. He peeled up the paper that covered the block shelf and picked up a wooden block. I took a breath, determined to stay focused on the children at the table. Ricky's eyes followed him. "Why does David get to play with the blocks?" Ricky asked, standing up from his chair. His learning plan was blank. His tone was both curious and accusing.

"It's not play time right now," I said gently. I walked around the table and crouched down to Ricky's level. My finger pointed to the schedule hanging on the wall. "Right now, we're making our learning plans for the kitchen. After that, we'll do our learning activity. Then, you'll have play time and can choose to play in the block area."

Ricky frowned. "I don't want to play in the kitchen. I want to play with the blocks like David."

Before I could respond, two girls working at the table slipped past me on their way across the room to the puzzle shelf. Jimmy remained at the table, drawing something completely unrelated to the kitchen scene I'd tried to demonstrate.

"David," I called, approaching him. "Come back to the table, mijo. Por favor. We're working on our learning plans right now." I knew from experience that he wasn't going to respond, but I wanted Ricky to see that I was trying. Then it struck me that my words might be sending another message—that David was being defiant or that Ricky could also avoid the task by walking away. I could hear Jorge's voice in my head: *Have high expectations.* My own voice answered quietly, reminding me that expectations needed to be differentiated for each child. In an inclusive classroom, the children needed to have meaningful connections with one another and feel a sense of belonging—the very things Ricky and David could build if I simply let them play with the blocks together.

I glanced over at the two girls. They had already taken out a box of puzzles. I quickly grabbed a visual prompt from the table that guided the creation of learning plans. I couldn't find one that reflected what the expectations meant in practice: an invitation to participate, not just to comply. I walked toward them and squatted down. I asked, "¿Vamos a sentarnos a hacer nuestros planes, sí?"

They hesitated. I internally chastised myself for breaking the English Language Development Department guidelines by attempting Spanish. I recalled feedback from office visits with Jorge. I switched back to English and pointed to the table and visual prompts. Repeating instructions in two languages was another breach of the English Language Development Department guidelines. This time, they sighed but followed me back to the table. Their reluctance was written all over their faces, but at least they were back.

As I returned to the table with the girls, I noticed Ricky had joined David R. in the block area. They were playing side by side, both laughing softly as they stacked the blocks. David R. never played cooperatively with other children. It was a breakthrough I couldn't celebrate. Jimmy, still seated, watched them wistfully while continuing to draw.

The noise in the room felt louder than it probably was. I stared at the table, where the two girls sat dispassionately holding pencils, their movements slow and disconnected. Jimmy was the only child staying within the parameters of the task, but even then, his body was tense with visible restraint.

The scene around me gnawed at my insides. This wasn't building on the children's interests or prioritizing relationships like I had envisioned when Jorge described the Every Early Learner Succeeds curriculum back in May. It wasn't the vibrant classroom where children felt empowered to explore and co-create. This felt stifling, almost mechanical.

I knew the gap between what the research described, what my eleven years of experience had taught me, and what I was managing to implement was widening. David's and Ricky's behavior, though disruptive to the day's agenda, was a clear signal that David needed embedded interventions. He didn't need me to speak Spanish if his peers were facilitating those supports through play. That was exactly what Ricky was trying to do. I also didn't want the other children to see David A. as separate from our community. Inclusion depended on that shared sense of connection and belonging, where every child's abilities, interests, experiences, and family culture were honored through their relationships with one another.

What does inclusion mean in this moment? Is it forcing them back to the table, or is it meeting them at the block area to find a way to connect their interests to our learning centers? My thoughts ricocheted between articles and experiences, full of theory but short on immediate answers.

I turned my focus back to the table, giving Jimmy a smile. "That's an amazing picture," I said, hoping to encourage him. But even as I spoke, my mind was still on David and Ricky, wondering how to bridge the gap between them and the rest of the group without further alienating anyone or anything.

The afternoon carried on, but the unease stayed with me. I felt the absence of the embedded interventions I once relied on to support children with Individual Education Programs in natural, relational ways. Without them, inclusion began to feel conditional, shaped by compliance rather than connection.

I wasn't sure I knew how to hold that tension anymore.

***

The next morning, an email from Diana appeared in my inbox. She had responded to Jorge, copying two of her supervisors. In her message, she clarified that Foundations classrooms fell under the jurisdiction of the Student Services Department and reiterated the licensing requirements for teachers in those positions. She acknowledged my commitment and expertise in inclusive early childhood classrooms and offered to review student needs or speak with concerned parents if needed.

There it was. Jorge could not use the Binding Compliance Order to remove me from the classroom at the end of the year. Nor could he prohibit the use of Spanish instruction. Yes, the class should be reclassified as English Language Development–English, but under Student Services, my practices aligned with district expectations. I knew this wasn't the outcome Jorge wanted. He wanted a shift. He had already replaced the curriculum. He got room 122 assigned to me. He would get a Spanish-speaking teacher in the classroom. Jorge would get what he wanted.

After the morning class left, I walked through the passageway into Ana's room. She sat at her desk, likely documenting children's progress. "Hola amiga."

"Hola Andrés David."

We chatted briefly in Spanish. There was no policy banning me from speaking to colleagues in Spanish—at least not yet, we joked.

"You looked upset when you left Jorge's office last week," I said, switching to English. "I've been meaning to ask about it."

She nodded, her eyes dropping. "I told him I'm pregnant. Sergio and I are trying to take care of everything, and I asked Jorge if I could take time for appointments and go on maternity leave in April." Her voice dropped. "He said I could use my personal days. When those are gone, I can't take more time off. He said it kindly, but it didn't feel real. It felt like he was reading a book."

I exhaled slowly. "I'm so sorry. That's not right."

Ana looked like she might cry.

"Hey. I was thinking . . . how do you feel about eating lunch together in your room from now on? You've got a microwave, which means I can upgrade from peanut butter and jelly. We can talk about anything other than work."

She smiled faintly. "I'd like that."

I stepped back. "Are you ready for the team meeting this afternoon?"

Her face clouded again. "I thought we were avoiding work talk."

We both knew what was coming. Two years of personality clashes, power struggles, and philosophical differences had only deepened under the new curriculum. The relationships across the early childhood team had frayed. The focus was less about child development and child progress monitoring and more about distrust and tension. Could I apply what I was learning in my university classes, like Cashman's Results-Based Leadership to our team? I wasn't expecting a breakthrough, but maybe we could be more supportive and responsive to one another.

***

Our early childhood education team meeting that afternoon focused on setting shared literacy and math goals for our classrooms. The plan was to align specific routine activities from the Every Early Learner Succeeds curriculum with the Colorado state standards, determine how we would track the children's progress, and develop methods for reflecting on what worked and what didn't throughout the year. Jorge joined us that day to help guide the discussion at Sharon's request. Up until then, he had sent a veteran teacher, Stephanie Peters, to act as an "instructional coach" and mediator.

Stephanie had been a teacher at Vista for ten years and aspired to move into an administrative role. I didn't know the details, but Ana and I connected the dots. Stephanie's role as an instructional coach appeared to be Jorge's way of giving her an opportunity to mediate the ongoing conflict within our team, a conflict he preferred not to address. She was well respected by everyone on the early childhood education team and had a clear understanding of the transition from Kris's leadership to Jorge's principalship. She recognized that our team's challenges were deeply rooted, and her steady respect helped keep things on track. Still, Ana and I both knew that stability was fragile, ready to give way at the slightest strain. For that reason, our meetings began with new team norms, grounded in an activity Stephanie had led three weeks earlier to help us identify our shared values.

Seven adults sat around a table in the early childhood education atrium: Jorge, Stephanie, and the five early childhood education teachers. A large piece of chart paper with the words "Early Childhood Education Team Norms" written in bold blue marker hung on the wall that faced three of the classrooms. We all looked at it.

Stephanie initiated the meeting. "All right, team. Let's get started by reviewing the norms you all created and agreed to," she said, making the formalities clear to Jorge. This was a thoughtless ritual for us, but we understood the stakes. "Andrew, would you like to start by reading the first one?"

I nodded. "Sure. 'We honor the time and contributions of each team member.'" I paused and looked around for the next volunteer.

Sharon spoke. "I think this one is really important. We have meetings where we go off topic, or some voices get ignored. This is a good reminder that everyone's input matters."

Ana added, "I think it's about more than just the agenda. It's about showing respect. If someone worked hard on something, we need to acknowledge that."

"But does that mean I can't respectfully provide my thoughts if I have an idea that will benefit our team?" Sharon countered.

Stephanie threw a wrench in the rusty wheels that were starting to derail. "Good discussion. Let's move to the second norm. Cindy, would you read it?"

"'Assume positive intent and address concerns directly.'"

Sharon spoke again. "This one feels important with all the changes this year. If we're frustrated or unsure about something, we need to talk about it without jumping to conclusions or being judgmental."

Everyone stayed silent. Sharon was always one to speak when words were not necessary, but this was going further than usual. It was a performance.

"Easier said than done. I know I can come off as blunt, but it's just my way. I'm not trying to be mean. I want us to work as a team," Ana stated.

"Good points, Sharon and Ana. Let's keep moving. All right, Esmeralda, would you read the third one?"

"Okay. 'Collaborate with openness and flexibility.'"

"I think this one is really important too. We're not just working in our own classrooms. Like Ana wisely stated, we're a team. If one of us needs help or has an idea, we need to be open to trying new things," Sharon interjected.

The mood began to feel familiar—passively hostile. Everyone stared at the norms as if imagining how to get through them without Sharon breaking them. Jorge watched us.

"Absolutely. And now the last one." Stephanie replied, attempting to exercise her mediation skills. "Ana, would you read the last norm?"

"'Celebrate successes and learn from challenges as a team.'" Silence filled the atrium for a few seconds.

Stephanie concluded her portion of the meeting. "It sounds like you all have a solid foundation with these norms. Let's talk about the literacy and math goals for your team."

The team nodded in agreement.

Sharon slid into the silence. "Sorry. I just want to say I appreciate Stephanie's support . . ."

Jorge took the reins. "Thank you everyone for welcoming me into this meeting. It looks like Stephanie has done a great job pulling this team together." He looked at Stephanie. "Thank you, Stephanie." He paused. "I want to point out that your norms align nicely with our school values: collaboration, innovation, and equity. In the spirit of your norms and Vista's values, I think it's time for your team to manage yourselves."

Did he not just see how difficult it was to get through the norms? I thought to myself. Our team had been through a lot with mediation. The previous year, the specialist for the district whose job was mediation and team building struggled to work with us. Our team was steady for a few weeks, and then things went haywire. Since then, there were always six adults at our table.

Jorge told us we needed to select a team lead to maintain group norms and keep the weekly hour-long meetings on track, just like every other grade level. "Who is interested in being the team lead?"

The question sparked disagreement. Some felt it would give too much power to one person, potentially leading to more tension. "The reason we're in the atrium for our meetings is because some of us felt it was unsafe to be in another teacher's classroom for our meeting. It's going to cause more conflict," Ana pointed out.

I stayed quiet, observing the discussion until Jorge interrupted.

"All right, that's enough. This is very unprofessional," he said, his tone calm but firm. Everyone was silent. He went on to speak about what professionalism meant to the success of our team, clearly not expecting pushback or unaware of our past two years together. He finished with a statement that shocked everyone but me. "If anyone doesn't want to be part of this team, fine. You can step away from the team and your job at Vista. But this has to be resolved."

I sensed his words were for dramatic effect.

"Does anyone want to leave?" Jorge asked firmly.

The group was silent. I contemplated whether this was the place and time to make Diana's offer public. Finally, I spoke up. "Yes. I do. I want to leave this team, and I want to leave Vista." It sounded more abrasive out loud than I had intended.

All eyes turned to me, including Ana's. She looked particularly surprised.

"If that's how you feel, Andrew, then I'll honor it," Jorge said, keeping his composure. "Go ahead and return to your classroom. I'll join you in a few minutes."

Back in room 122, I paused to take everything in. The bickering of the early childhood education team had already faded, leaving a heavy silence. It felt like the close of a long saga. I wondered how I would explain this decision to the families. My connections with the children had been thin this year, even with David A. and David R. Without the ability to speak Spanish, it seemed impossible to rebuild the bond we once shared. Yet the families had defended me in Jorge's office and offered nothing but support. The thought of letting them down was painful.

I sat at my desk and looked at the mug. "Best Teacher Ever." Regrets accumulated, then Jorge's wing-tipped shoes brought me back to the present. He walked into room 122, moving authoritatively to the back half of the room.

"I have to admit, Andrew, I wasn't expecting that," he said, his tone matching the wing tips. I doubted him. "It took courage, and I'm glad you were honest. I think it surprised the team too. It seems to have made them more open to having a team lead, so in that sense, it was helpful." He paused, glancing around the classroom. "You've done a great job implementing the curriculum here. It's unfortunate that after all the work and time you've put in, you've decided to leave."

Jorge's words were both condescending and contradictory, leaving me unsure of how to respond. I opted to share something I knew would move the conversation forward.

"I've talked with Diana about the itinerant position." My voice was confident, steadied by the knowledge that I had Diana's support and personal phone number. "I want to apply, but I need you to release me officially. Are you willing to do that?"

"I will," he replied. His intensity softened, and empathy emerged. "But first, we need to find a replacement. Once we have someone in place, I'll release you."

"How long do you think that will take?" I asked.

"I'll have to check with the human resources department," he said. "There are a few procedural steps we need to follow. I'll get started on that right away, and hopefully, we can post the job in the coming weeks." His voice was now comforting. "Andrew, I want you to be happy in your work. You're a talented teacher, and I know you'll thrive wherever you go. If you change your mind about leaving, we'll find a way to make things work here. Don't worry about the early childhood education team, focus on your growth for today."

I nodded. *What kind of growth is he suggesting?* I wondered. Not trusting myself to respond constructively, I stayed silent. We were on common ground, and I didn't want that to be jeopardized.

"While the team finalizes the literacy and math goals, you can work on yours independently," he added. "It should work out fine. We'll move forward with your reassignment as soon as possible."

"Sounds good." I tried to sound responsive, but Jorge's request didn't make sense. *Why am I creating goals if I'm leaving?* "Have a good afternoon," I said, trying to conclude the conversation.

He looked at me with an ambiguous stare. "You too."

Jorge left. I sat in silence, processing what had just happened. It was a lot to take in, but at least one thing was clear: I was finally moving forward, and it wasn't a secret.

***

My pulse settled after a few minutes of staring blankly at my laptop screen. I reached for my phone, opened Diana's contact, and started typing a message. I read it over, made a few changes, and sent it. I didn't want to assume the itinerant position was mine, despite her earlier offer.

Hi Diana, crap hit the fan during our early childhood education meeting this afternoon. Things feel increasingly tense, and I think it might be time for a shift. I'm even more interested in the itinerant role we discussed. Also, Jorge mentioned he'd need to find a replacement before releasing me. I'm grateful for any insight you can share.

The dots under the text started bouncing almost immediately. She expressed dismay with the early childhood education team meeting, encouraging me to fill out the application for the early childhood special education itinerant position immediately.

I was relieved to hear from her.

Yes! I'll complete it as soon as I get home, I texted.

I stared at my computer, its inbox overflowing with unread emails. My mind was scrambled, too jumbled to focus. The clock said I had fifteen more minutes before I could leave, not that I'd ever really stuck to that timeline. I wanted to talk to Ana, but she was still in the early childhood education meeting. I needed to tell Lillie and Cecilia. Lillie was not even aware I was considering the itinerant position. No, I don't want to say anything prematurely. I can't say anything until everything is final, I thought. Going home and submitting the job application was my priority.

Ana walked into my classroom through the front entrance.

"Andrew. What happened?" she asked, her voice soft with concern. "You can't leave me here. Where are you going to go?"

"I've been meaning to tell you," I said, bracing myself. "You know Diana. She's the director of early childhood special education. Well, she told me about an itinerant position. I'm going to apply. Jorge said he'll release me as soon as I find a replacement."

"What's an itinerant position?"

"It's the special education teacher who comes into your classroom once a week to work with the children who have Individual Education Programs."

She looked like she was experiencing deep pain. "You can't leave me! It seems like a good job for you, but you can't leave me here alone."

Guilt sank into my stomach. "I'm sorry."

Compassion washed over Ana's face. "I understand. It's hard. This will be good. I'm sad." She paused momentarily. "Do you have proof Jorge said he would release you?"

From guilt to gratitude and now a rush of anxiety. "I think so, but I should check my emails," I admitted. "If not, you all heard him."

"You should get it in writing before you apply," she urged. "He could say you applied without telling him. That could get you into trouble."

I nodded, considering her point. "I'll make sure to do that. I have a lot of emails and text messages, but you're right."

"I'll miss you." I felt like she was hugging me with her words.

"We'll still see each other. It'll just take a little more effort."

She turned and walked out slowly, leaving me alone with my thoughts. I checked the clock again and pulled out my phone to text Natalie.

Big news!

She replied immediately. *Okay. Will you be home soon?*

I have class tonight.

Oh, I forgot.

I could feel her disappointment. Likely not because she wanted to hear my news.

I'll be home around 9:15. Will you be awake?

I'll try. Love you.

Love you too.

***

That night, I lay in bed next to Natalie. The room was dim, illuminated only by the faint glow of the moonlight filtering through the curtains. Natalie had her head nestled into her pillow. She was seconds from falling asleep, her breath steady and slow, the kind of rhythm that made me wish I could relax as easily.

I still had my shoes on, dangling one foot off the bed as if keeping myself tethered to the chaos of the day. "Are you awake?" I mumbled. "I'm feeling good about things now. I think it's going to happen. I'm going to apply for the itinerant position." My voice was low, careful not to jolt her out of her half-dream state. "I'm actually excited."

She turned her head slightly, her eyes barely opening. "That's good," she murmured. "Just stay focused on what matters right now. Worst case, you stay in the classroom for the rest of the school year, learn, and you find something new for next year."

I nodded, her practical tone grounding me. "You're right," I said with a jolt of motivation. "I'll go apply . . . and keep my expectations in check."

She rolled her head back to the center of the pillow. "Don't stay up too late," she whispered. "I love you."

"I love you too," I replied, watching as she settled back into the sheets.

I sat up, swung both of my feet to the floor, and let the moonlight lead me to the closet-office. The desk was big enough for my laptop and a book, not the emotional baggage I held.

The laptop screen glowed as the Metro Denver Unified School District jobsite loaded. I completed each section of the application carefully, with the awareness that more people than Diana would be reviewing it. Before clicking submit, it seemed necessary to check in with her to ensure everything reflected what her team would want to know. Near 10:30 p.m., the phone was in hand and a message half-typed when Ana's advice surfaced: *Get formal documentation of permission to apply.* I deleted the text and began again.

Hi Diana. I've heard that principals are notified when a teacher applies for another job within the Metro Denver Unified School District. I'd like to touch base with you first, and maybe we can loop Jorge into a discussion about logistics before I apply. He knows I am going to resign and apply for the itinerant position, but I want to be sure everything is clear. I'll submit the application once I receive official confirmation in writing. Hope that makes sense! :)

The dots on the screen bounced for a moment. Diana was empathetic and encouraging. She told me she would talk with her team first thing in the morning and then communicate with Jorge.

I took a deep breath and shut my laptop. After failing to sort through the stories in my head, I decided I needed to journal.

Almost there. I'm grateful for this opportunity. My gratitude was restless as I closed the notebook for the first time that night. I returned a few minutes later. *I will submit my application as soon as Jorge confirms I can apply for the job.*

***

The next afternoon, I heard Cecilia's and Lillie's cheerful goodbyes to the other early childhood education teaching assistants fading into the vacant early childhood education atrium. I sat at my desk, phone in hand, and focused on the text screen. Still no messages from Diana. I was getting used to her instant responses. The silence from her was unnerving, but I told myself to be patient. I hesitated, considering whether to follow up. My emotions wavered between excitement and a growing fear. Yesterday's early childhood education team meeting felt like a storm that had blown through, leaving no visible damage but unsettling the air. Ana and I had spoken three times since our conversation after the meeting, and she did not bring it up once. It was as though the meeting had never happened.

I couldn't stand the waiting. My fingers hovered over my phone screen before finally tapping a string of words.

Swing any deals?

With the message sent, I slid the phone onto my desk, inhaled a room's worth of oxygen, and exhaled. My chest was tight, and my mind was racing. I needed more air. Sitting there, ruminating, wouldn't help. I stood and made my way to the community center, organizing materials that didn't need much organizing. My hands moved through the tasks, but my thoughts stayed fixed on the text.

When I returned to my desk, I couldn't resist. I picked up my phone. The screen lit up with Diana's reply. She told me her team granted her approval to move forward and organize a meeting to discuss logistics with Jorge. After exchanging a few humorous, affirming messages, I set my phone down. Relief washed over me. It was moving forward. The weight of uncertainty had lifted. I could focus. I wrapped up a few loose ends in the classroom, packed my things, and checked the clock. My contracted hours were over. There was no need to stay around and perfect room 122 before Thursday's class. Jorge had made it clear that my time in this classroom was temporary.

When do you think I'll get to say goodbye to this mess? I texted Diana as I walked out of Vista's front doors.

On the drive home, doubt crept back in. Should I have been more serious in my text? Would Diana interpret my question the wrong way? By the time I pulled into the driveway, there was still no response. I left my phone in the car intentionally, a small but deliberate act to ensure my attention was on Natalie and the girls. They deserved all of me, without distractions. Tonight, I needed their laughter and hugs to ground me in what truly mattered. Or at least that's what I told myself.

After the girls were asleep, I slipped outside. The breeze of the emerging autumn season brushed against my skin. My phone was still in the car. I retrieved it quickly, heart pounding as I saw Diana's reply, time-stamped 6:17 p.m. It was already 7:45. Her text was tinged with playfulness, telling me things were moving quick and urging me to fill out the application immediately.

Don't worry about Jorge, she said at the end of her last text.

I knew she had things under control. There was no room for hesitation now. I logged onto my computer, navigated to the Metro Denver Unified School District job site, and hit "Submit" on the application I'd completed the day before. It was done.

Still, I felt compelled to let Diana know. I picked up my phone and hastily typed a message.

All right. I've submitted my application! Please make this work.

Her reply came almost instantly. I peered at the screen, her promising words echoing in my mind. Abruptly, I realized that if anyone asked about why I applied for a new position while serving in another, my private messages with Diana wouldn't save me. I still did not have evidence that Jorge approved my departure. *Ah well. I'll be out of Vista, and it will all be behind me,* I told myself with a feeling of liberation.

CHAPTER 8

STUCK

―――――

The waning days of September carried a fragile mix of hope, frustration, and trepidation. My transition to the early childhood special education itinerant role felt tantalizingly close, yet each update seemed to nudge the finish line just out of reach. I found myself in emotional limbo, trying to balance growing impatience with professionalism and commitment to the children and families.

On the morning of Thursday, September 18, I received an email from Diana's administrative assistant. A new student was being placed in my morning class.

Less than a half hour later, another email arrived. Another child. *Why would Diana approve two new children in my class if I'm leaving? Am I still leaving?*

I texted her:

Hi Diana. Do you have any updates?

In an effort to keep my focus where it needed to be, I had started keeping my phone in my bag while the children were present. It was a decision I should've made earlier, but part of me had been clinging to the idea that Diana might message at any moment, asking me to collect my things and meet her at her office to begin the new position. That now seemed less likely. Still, the possibility hovered over me all morning.

When I finally checked my phone, Diana had replied. She confirmed that a meeting with Jorge was in the works and ended her message with a smiling emoticon. Her optimism brought brief relief. I responded, trying to mask my anxiety:

I'm sitting on pins and needles. Can you put a hold on the placement of children with Individual Education Programs in my classroom? Two were just placed here, giving us six in the morning and five in the afternoon. That's going to make my departure much more difficult for me and for my caseload at Vista.

Thursday turned to Friday. The classroom buzzed as the children transitioned from handwashing to the community center carpet. I started the music and led them through movement, arms swaying and hands clapping. In the back of my mind, though, I was still waiting for Diana's response.

By late morning, I sat at my desk reviewing intake paperwork for the new students. My pocket buzzed. A text from Diana said the placement of the two children was being reconsidered. Relief washed over me, but only for a moment. The cycle would repeat in the days that followed—cautious hope, a spike of panic, fleeting reassurance, and then more waiting.

On Tuesday, September 23, the cost of it all began to surface: avoiding Spanish, shelving responsive interventions, and enforcing a curriculum that ignored the children's realities undermined my sense of purpose. The moment the classroom emptied, I messaged Diana again:

Any status updates?

She replied quickly:

I'm anticipating a phone conversation with Jorge this afternoon. :)

I clung to the smiling emoticon as if it were a lifeline, a sign she was still in my corner. As the midday break passed, uncertainty crept back in. The children were lined up outside the back door with Lillie and Cecilia. I stayed back for a minute to text Diana:

Thank you.

Minutes later, I added:

Jorge is expected at our early childhood education team meeting at 3 today and asked me to attend. If there's any chance you'll connect with him beforehand, I'd really appreciate it. I know you're juggling a lot, and I'm doing my best to stay patient. Just wondering what you'd like me to share with the parents of the two children placed in our class. One of them is hoping for an update soon.

My phone stayed still in my pocket. At 1:36 p.m., while pretending to be the mommy in the dress-up area, I felt the vibration. I shouldn't have checked it, but I did. Shame rose as I recognized I wasn't fully present.

Had a conversation with Jorge. I'm confident things will go our way. In the meantime, let's move forward with the two new children in your class.

The message confused me. If things were going our way, why enroll new students? I exhaled hard and replied:

Give me a call as soon as you have a minute. :)

The pattern became maddening—obsessive phone checks, Diana's updates, teasing progress, but never delivering closure.

By Friday, September 26, frayed beyond words, I finally received the text I was waiting for:

Your start date is set for Monday.

I stared at the screen, stunned, then typed back:

Wow! So quick. Sounds great!

Just as I was transitioning into the weekend, Diana followed up:

You won't officially start on Monday, but the hiring process will begin.

Her words were confident and filled with optimism. They centered me.

On Monday afternoon, however, nothing seemed to come together. The early childhood education team was in shambles. I broke my silence with blunt frustration:

Hi Diana. Please get me out of here. Any word on my transition?

She replied later that day, her response laced with humor. A few exchanges later, I began to relax. There was no reason to worry, or so she told me. However, my patience was failing me.

Each day at Vista tested my endurance. The interventions I couldn't deliver in Spanish, the mounting paperwork, and the overall lack of support was exhausting. And I knew an exit was just around the corner.

That evening, I texted Diana again, mixing hope and humor: *Teammates yet?*

The next morning, she replied that she'd be meeting with Jorge at Vista that afternoon to finalize the plan.

If you can, come to my room when you're done.

She agreed.

At 4:45 p.m., still no visit. I texted:

I have to head out. Send me a text or call me when you're done.

Her reply came quickly. She asked if I was still in my room. Then she reminded me to stop discussing anything until it was official, assuring me they were doing everything they could. I responded:

Yes, I'm in my room. Are you coming down to visit?

Forty-five more minutes passed. Natalie texted me to tell me to let go and get home. I left for the day without seeing Diana. Everything afterward was a blur.

Wednesday brought more of the same: a delicate dance between hope and resignation. That afternoon, Diana called.

"Hi Andrew, it's Diana," she said. As if her phone number wasn't the only one I'd answer before the first ring was complete.

"Hey, Diana! I'm happy to hear from you. What's the scoop?"

"I'm sitting here with Mel Jones, and . . . you do not officially have the job yet. We're working on it from a new angle. Once it happens, Mel will be your mentor. Mel is here with me."

I heard Mel chime in from the background. "Hi, Andrew! I'm excited to work with you."

"Hi, Mel. I look forward to getting started," I replied.

Then Diana added, "Andrew, it's really important right now that we keep this on the down-low. It's not official yet, and I don't want anything to jeopardize it."

I nodded silently as she spoke. My throat tightened at the words "not officially." I appreciated her honesty, but I couldn't shake the omnipresent fear that it might all fall apart.

Thursday was heavier than Wednesday. Jorge's refusal to support the early childhood education team, the growing distance from children and families, the missed opportunities for authentic teaching—all of it chipped away at my resolve. The uncertainty was intolerable.

I finally texted Diana again:

Considering we don't know if this will happen, do you have any suggestions for outside jobs or organizations that I may be interested in?

Her reply was measured but not comforting. She asked if I'd be okay leaving Vista without a replacement early childhood special education teacher and hinted she could pull some strings. I replied with conviction:

No question. But I would like to be prepared for something. I don't think I'm as optimistic as you are.

Diana's final message that evening promised she was making deals that would settle everything by the end of the following day—Friday, October 3.

The weekend arrived. Her words were all I had to hold on to. At the library, I kept turning pages, searching for answers. In the classroom, I kept waiting, holding my breath. Both left me restless, and neither offered release.

***

On Tuesday, October 7, the children in the afternoon class and the adults who were picking them up scrambled near the back door. The usual flurry of shoes, backpacks, and energetic chatter filled the space. Beatriz and Kelly waited by the back door as the room emptied. Jimmy and Ricky saw me approach and recognized the opportunity to break free from their mothers and play with puzzles. I greeted the two mothers, knowing they were interested in talking to me.

"We wanted to tell you that we had the boys over on Saturday," Beatriz said. "Kelly brought Ricky and Eric to my house. They were in our backyard for hours hunting for bugs."

Kelly nodded along. "Ricky told me on the ride home that it's what they do at school."

"They really love that, don't they?" I said, laughing. The mothers followed, adding more details about the backyard playdate at Jimmy's house. Listening, I began thinking about their play and the fact that none of the parents had been able to observe their children, let alone participate, this year. Then the activities from the curriculum came to mind. We sent information about them home in our newsletter. I figured Beatriz and Kelly were practicing them with their boys, but I wasn't sure. "Have they been doing the family activities in the September room 122 newsletter at home or with each other?"

Both women shook their heads.

"No, it was mostly just running, hiding, and looking for bugs. Lots of laughing. Jimmy insists on drawing pictures of his friends when he's alone," Beatriz said. "The boys had a whole game. Not much talking, really. They just play together. Whatever they were doing, they had a lot of fun!"

"That makes sense," I said, nodding. "They've been working on activities related to families during the family unit. They've done well, but they don't stick with them very long. There's a letter in their backpacks about the new unit we're starting: grocery stores. Perhaps we can try to think of activities they can transfer to their play at home."

As I said it aloud, the realization struck me harder than expected. These boys weren't mimicking the family role-play or following our scripted storylines. They were replaying the moments that had sparked real connection: digging in the dirt, chasing insects, creating roles with no script at all.

Beatriz must have caught the change in my expression. "I'd love that! Anything to help Jimmy learn more," she exclaimed. "Is it bad that he's not doing the curriculum activities?"

"No," I said quickly. "Not at all. It's actually . . . good. It's real. It shows he's remembering what matters to him. If he can write or dictate a story about what he's doing, that would be helpful."

As we parted ways, I felt a pang of guilt. The Every Early Learner Succeeds curriculum was full of carefully designed components, but it wasn't rooted in the children's lives. The bug hunts and unstructured play were the pieces children carried home, not the carefully curated activities.

I walked slowly back into the classroom, the tension between the theories I was learning about in my Teaching in the Modern Classroom class and practice pressed down on my shoulders. Jorge expected cohesion across early childhood classrooms. The early childhood education team was supposed to follow the same pacing, the same unit plans. *No unit can compete with the curiosity of a child in the dirt, hands cupped over a tiny beetle. And there's no certainty that would be an interest of children in the other classrooms*, I thought.

As the mothers walked out the door with their children, I returned to my desk and re-reviewed the paperwork of the two students who would soon be joining our classroom. Lillie and Cecilia came over to me.

"Hey," Lillie said, her voice quiet but deliberate. "We've been meaning to check in with you. Are you okay?"

Cecilia tilted her head. "You've been kind of . . . less present today and last week."

I exhaled, grateful for their honesty. "Yeah. I've been feeling stuck," I admitted. "I don't think this curriculum is clicking with the kids. I feel disconnected, especially in the morning class. It's like we're just a group of individuals moving through a schedule, not a community that supports each other. During my first two years at Vista, when children had more support needs, we built something stronger and more interdependent. Now I feel like I'm falling short of creating that."

"It's Spanish," Lillie said. "Our classrooms need it. It's like we're only giving them part of ourselves . . . and, like, we are only letting them give us a part of themselves." She took a deep breath and sighed. "The curriculum doesn't do us any favors."

Cecilia didn't say anything, but I noticed the way she looked down, the way her shoulders stiffened.

Lillie continued. "Maybe we just . . . speak Spanish when Jorge's not around? Keep it quiet."

I looked at her and shook my head. "We can't subvert authority. It's not just about ethics. It's about sustainability. Burning one bridge in this district can burn all of them."

Lillie nodded, her mouth tightening into a thin line.

"We'll figure something out," I said gently. "I know this isn't working. But defying Jorge won't work either. I'm trying to be as direct with him as I can. I'm taking a page out of your book, Lillie."

Lillie laughed, and Cecilia's posture loosened.

"I think I've hit a brick wall. Like I said, I feel stuck," I said, resigning to better descriptions.

Cecilia spoke gently. "Andrew, just let us know what we can do to help. I know it's not the same as last year, but no matter what happens, things will come together in the classroom . . . even if you're not the teacher."

Lillie's expression shifted. Her brow arched, and her voice came out quieter than usual. "Wait . . . not the teacher? Are you leaving?"

I hesitated. I felt horrible having withheld my intentions from Lillie. Then I gave both the simplest version of the truth, explaining the possibility of the itinerant role and the uncertainty around its timing. They both nodded slowly, absorbing it. Though their responses were kind, steady, even affirming, it was clear the news hit hard. It was the first time we'd spoken openly about the possibility of my departure, and the implications were painful for all of us.

I listened as they floated ideas, trying to ease the transition or soften the impact. Still, I felt strangely separated from the conversation. The truth was, I didn't know how to let them help. I couldn't tell if I was staying or leaving. Beneath it all, I felt like I was breaking something sacred: trust. It was something I had built not just as a teacher but as their teammate.

***

During lunchtime, Ana's classroom was a psychological refuge from the emails, special education paperwork, planning, and inner voice of doubt that wove it all together in room 122. The environment was serene with no artificial lighting and a "no screens at the table" policy. That was one of the stipulations. Ana welcomed me with nurturing words and a captive Friday smile. I collapsed into one of the small green plastic chairs, setting my lunch bag on the child-sized table. She looked up from her Tupperware of Spanish lentils. Her brow furrowed as she studied my face.

"You look like you're barely holding it together," she said, her tone a mix of concern and understanding.

I sighed, running a hand across my scalp. "Yeah. This is killing me."

"What's wrong?"

"Same story," I said, swallowing a bite of my sandwich. "The itinerant role is right there, but Diana keeps telling me to wait, to trust the process. Meanwhile, the curriculum feels like it's killing me. I mean, the children provide so many opportunities for me to jump in and guide them into a deeper exploration of topics, but I have to restrain myself. I just feel . . . stuck."

Ana nodded, setting her spoon down. "I get it."

"How are things for you?" I asked, gesturing to her stomach.

"I'm tired," she admitted. "Between the nausea and trying to meet these expectations, it's hard. I feel like I'm failing."

"You're not failing," I said empathetically. "Your room looks amazing. Your kids are doing incredible things." I looked around the room pointedly. "The things you share during the early childhood education team meeting are fantastic. You're juggling more than most people could handle, and you're still doing really well."

She gave me a small, grateful smile. "Thanks. But it's hard. And the new unit in the curriculum? Grocery store? It's a disaster."

"Oh, I know," I said, leaning back in my chair. "It felt like I spent half the morning today trying to explain how to stir pretend batter in a bowl . . . in English, to Spanish speakers. It seems so easy. More than half the kids were not interested. The few children listening looked at me like I'd lost my mind."

Ana laughed, shaking her head. "Yesterday, I tried to do activities with the cash register. It took twenty minutes just to set up, and then the kids spent five minutes doing it before they decided it was boring."

We both laughed. The shared frustrations eased some of the tension at the table. "That's what happens when we take control. I know you didn't see my classroom last year or the year before, but it's amazing to watch when the children guide the play, and we learn right alongside them."

I then realized it was probably exactly what she had been doing in her classroom for the past two years, too. "Sometimes I wonder who these lessons are really for," I said. "It's something I've been reflecting on in my Teaching in the Modern Classroom class at the university. The lessons feel out of touch with what the kids in my classroom actually need in the day-to-day interactions. Yes, they need the self-regulation skills, but at three years old . . . in a foreign language? It just doesn't land the way it's supposed to. And the hardest part?" I glanced down at the table. "I want my class to work like"—I paused to think of a metaphor that made sense—"the cardiovascular system."

Ana raised an eyebrow, curious.

"You know," I continued, "a system where everything's connected—every part doing its job, feeding and fueling the others. The heart keeps things moving, but it only works because the whole system is in sync. That's how it used to feel when kids brought all of themselves, when families were involved, when we, as teachers, responded to what was really happening in the room. It felt alive. Now?" I sighed. "Now it's like I'm the only one pumping, but the rest of the system isn't responding. We're not circulating. We're not connected."

"I think I understand," she said, closing her Tupperware. "We can't measure the heart with a checklist, right?"

I nodded. The metaphor was pulsing in my mind. "And without that connection between us, the kids, and the families, it's like the system's clogged. Everything slows down or starts shutting off. We're left doing CPR on something that's supposed to be alive."

Ana tilted her head, thoughtful. "I don't completely understand the heart . . . what's the word . . . the heart comparison," she admitted, "but I think I understand what you mean. The classroom doesn't work without those relationships."

"Yeah," I said, bobbing my head. "And right now it feels like we're both short on oxygen . . . okay, maybe this isn't a great comparison," I professed.

She looked at me across the table. "Andrew, we'll get the blood flowing. When you get the itinerant job, you'll have a whole new rhythm."

"Thanks," I said, and my shoulders softened. "And if you need someone to cover for you while you sneak a nap, you know where to find me. I hear sleeping is good for heart health."

She laughed, the sound warm and genuine. "Deal, but only if you bring snacks. No blood, just snacks."

***

The roar of water filling the bathtub echoed through the bathroom. I leaned against the doorframe watching Natalie gently assist the girls in the tub. She turned off the water and began scrubbing bubbles through Citlali's hair. Itzel, sitting with her legs out, splashed her hands in the water, giggling. Their laughter was infectious, briefly easing the discomfort I still carried from Vista.

I watched Natalie closely, the way she always seemed to know just how much soap was needed and how to keep the water at the perfect temperature for their sensitive skin. I admired her calm. Her attention to the girls meant the world.

"What's up?" she asked, not looking up.

I leaned my head against the wood molding and sighed. "Same old. I know you don't want to hear it, but I feel . . . stuck. The ideas around inclusion and leadership I'm writing about in my papers just don't transfer to room 122. And in our daily work, I can only get so much support from Lillie and Cecilia. Then there's Ana. She's not doing much better than me . . . for different reasons."

"How's her pregnancy?"

"It sounds like yours with Itzel. She's nauseous and exhausted. She's just trying to keep her head up and show up for the kids."

Natalie didn't respond; her focus remained on the girls.

I watched her for a moment. "Diana keeps telling me it's all in the works, that the itinerant position is almost there. I want to believe her, but I don't feel it. And I can't shake the sense that I'm losing touch with my passion to teach. Maybe it's because my university work is validating everything I did in the classroom before this year. Now I feel like I'm not ethically meeting my commitments to children and families . . . or maybe I'm just stubborn."

Natalie paused, setting the washcloth down in the tub and turning toward me. "I don't know. It's hard when everything feels like it's in limbo. Do you think the work at the university is affecting you negatively?"

"Maybe . . . but I think it's the opposite. It's giving me perspective; I can see things with curiosity rather than just judgment. I don't think I'd be able to notice the gaps in the curriculum or in school leadership if I didn't have the ideas I'm learning there. I'd just stew in my frustrations. It's actually what keeps me motivated. That said, it would be easier to analyze all this from the outside without the emotional guilt. I'm just trying to hang on," I said, rubbing my scalp. "I'm trying to stay patient. It's just hard when I know nothing will change in the classroom. I don't even feel like I'm making an impact . . . not the way I want to."

Citlali started splashing Itzel.

"Citlali, stop," Natalie said gently. She shifted Itzel into a safer position and leaned back against the edge of the tub, meeting my gaze. "I can see that. But you are making an impact. You're still teaching the children. The world isn't going to give you a certificate for that. Have the parents communicated any dissatisfaction?"

I shook my head. "No. They stood up for me to Jorge. They support me more than I could ever ask for, which makes this whole thing even harder. They don't even know what their children are missing out on."

"I think you take yourself too seriously," she said. "If you leave the classroom, there will be a replacement who can pick up where you left off, especially with Lillie and Cecilia's help."

I wanted to explain the idea of the classroom as a cardiovascular system. The longer I stayed in room 122, the more it became a system I couldn't step away from, even if it wasn't healthy. Still, none of that seemed to matter at the moment.

"Yeah, if we can get a new teacher soon." I looked at the mirror in front of me, wondering, *If someone else can speak Spanish, would that be a bigger benefit to room 122 than my skill set?* "All I can do is wait, wait for someone to actually follow through."

Natalie turned back to the girls, continuing to wash them as she spoke. "Yeah. You've always done what you need to do for the children and parents. Just do your best. Forget about Diana."

I watched her with the girls. I wanted to believe what she said, but the doubt still gnawed at me. She could never understand the spell Diana had cast over me or the dynamics of a classroom.

"I know," I said quietly. "I just have to keep pushing."

"Exactly. And in the meantime, focus on us when you're home. Go get me two towels."

Natalie turned the water on again. Citlali hovered her feet under the flowing stream and giggled. Itzel splashed in response. The two of them were lost in their little world of water and laughter.

For a moment, everything felt right. The noise of the world inside my head seemed to disappear, and I remembered why I had to keep going.

"All right," I said, pushing off from the doorframe, "I'll get some towels."

"Thanks, babe," Natalie said, giving me a soft smile. "I know it feels tough right now, but you'll get through it. You can only control what you can control. Letting go isn't giving up. It's survival."

It was hard, but hearing her say that centered me. As I turned to get the towels, I couldn't help but glance back at the bathroom and see my daughters carefree and radiant in their joy. That was a blessing I couldn't ignore.

Maybe I didn't need all the answers right now. Maybe I just needed to keep showing up and let go of what I couldn't control.

***

The early morning air on Saturday, October 11 was cool and crisp. I stepped onto the Denver light rail to go to the university library. The whoosh of the train cutting through the stillness of the city was peaceful. The seats were mostly vacant. Just a few commuters, with their faces turned toward the glass of their phones or leaning on the windows beside them. Like me, they were probably lost in their thoughts.

I couldn't stop thinking about Diana's texts. She had said everything would be settled by Friday afternoon last week, yet the silence that followed was all I could hear. I checked my phone every few minutes when I wasn't with the children in the classroom or my family. It felt obsessive. I kept hoping for a new message, something to push the frustration down and give me something to hold on to besides old texts. All I had was waiting. It felt like I had been caught in a strange enchantment, unable to break free. Diana's promises kept me waiting. Jorge's authority kept me stuck. Or maybe it was just me.

Then there was the conversation with Natalie in the bathroom as she gave the girls their bath. Her words: "You can only control what you can control. Letting go isn't giving up. It's survival." I wanted to believe her. I really did. But it was hard to shake the layers of everything, of the feeling that I was stuck in something I could not see beyond.

I knew Diana was trying to reassure me that everything would eventually fall into place, but from where I stood, the path was shrouded in fog. The harder I tried to find my way, the thicker it seemed to grow, like storm clouds folding in on themselves. Every thought and decision was tangled within the haze, impossible to separate or see clearly.

Then there was Ana. Her voice echoed in my mind. *"They want us to check boxes and hit benchmarks, but they're not in the classroom with us. They don't see what we see."* The Every Early Learner Succeeds curriculum was at the center of the early childhood education team's frustration. Despite the training and Jorge's coaching, it felt like it restricted everyone's love for teaching. Every day felt as if we were being asked to teach with a frayed power line at our feet. We were never sure when it might spark or fail. I had no idea what the next step was, and neither did Ana. Yet she had this quiet resilience that seemed to rise above the chaos. I could hear the exhaustion in her voice, the way she was holding it all together just enough to keep going. I wondered if I was doing the same. No one besides Lillie and Cecilia understood the true gravity of the conditions in room 122.

The city outside blurred as the train entered downtown. Just like the events inside the classroom, everything was moving too fast, but at the same time, everything was stuck in one place. The train slowed at the stop for the university. I was jolted out of my thoughts. I pressed my palms on top of the seat in front of me to get up.

Walking toward the library, I pulled my phone from my pocket and scrolled through the playful texts Diana sent nearly a month ago telling me I would be on her team within the week.

The familiar tone made me smile despite my anguish. Diana had a way of using humor to defuse the tension. She made the unbearable seem like just another bump in the road. But in the back of my mind, there was a nagging doubt. *How much longer will I be stuck? No Spanish, no child-centered teaching, no family engagement, and no high-quality interventions for children who did not understand English?*

For now, it was just me and the library. All I could do was wait, control the things I could control, and keep pushing forward, even as I began to wonder how much waiting could be asked of someone before it started to change what they believed was possible.

CHAPTER 9

RIPPLES

The mid-days of October felt different. My relationships with the children who spoke English were strong. The content I was learning in my Teaching in the Modern Classroom class continued to stir ideas about creating a more inclusive classroom, despite the barriers. At the same time, the need to leave the classroom felt more urgent. I no longer wanted to invest more emotional energy into a classroom that asked me to suppress what I knew about high-quality, meaningful inclusion. During circle time, I found myself barely present, just going through the motions. My smiles felt thinner. Every conversation and every email with Diana carried a tinge of something I could not quite name: a blend of hope and dread that pulsed beneath the surface.

On Monday, October 13, at 1:26 p.m., I received another text from Diana. They had found a teacher to replace me, and she would have more details on Tuesday.

I stared at the screen, heart thudding, reading the sentence again to be sure I hadn't imagined it. I leaned back in my chair and exhaled sharply, trying to keep it together. A knot of relief mixed with an uneasy excitement formed in my chest. *This could be it*, I thought. My fingers hovered over the screen before I typed back:

YAY!!!!! I will ask for no other information until tomorrow . . . unless you have any other details to share. I don't want to be tempted to spread rumors :).

I was giddy, waiting for something good, something real, to finally happen. Yet letting myself hope felt dangerous. I had celebrated before, only to be left waiting again.

That night, after returning home from class, I lay in bed for an hour before deciding to write in my journal. My mind replayed the dozens of text exchanges from the past month, still trying to piece together if this was really it. I imagined I was living inside M. C. Escher's *Relativity* sketch, the one that adorned the closet-office wall, a world where the rules of logic bent with every step. Like climbing stairs that led nowhere, I kept thinking I was moving forward, only to realize I was still on the same floor, still under someone else's ceiling. It was a chance to take on a role that would remove me from the daily grind and place me where I could make a difference for a larger population of children. I could already picture it, touching lives and breaking barriers.

Then the doubt crept in, as it always did. Maybe this would fall through too. Yet I could not ignore the possibility that it wouldn't. Wasn't that why I kept showing up?

***

We were in the third week of the Every Early Learner Succeeds grocery unit. The morning class was in full swing. Curriculum learning time was gradually transitioning into playtime. Allowing the two to bleed together was my way of reconciling the reality that I ethically could not ostracize children who were less engaged in the curriculum, as I had with Ricky and David. R. I was doing my best to balance my research and lived experience with Jorge's expectations.

Eleven children were exploring the world through their own eyes. The casita/kitchen had been transformed into a bustling Starbucks. David A. stepped in as the consumer, tentative but curious. Nelia eagerly claimed the barista's orange Home Depot apron, while Ernesto, quick to seize any chance to lead, became the cashier, standing at the register without knowing exactly how it worked. Sofia tended the bakery in the neighboring center with her baby doll, a quiet, steady presence. On the edge of the scene, Antonio, new to our classroom, spun slowly and flapped his hands in his familiar way.

Only Sofia and Ernesto had created learning plans. I'd coached all the children, but my expectation for Antonio was simply to stay in our presence. Abstract thinking and understanding social roles weren't yet in his developmental repertoire. David A. had scribbled on his paper but gave no indication he understood the connection between the plan and the play. Nelia had enthusiastically scribbled a picture of what she identified as a "muffin" but quickly set her paper aside.

Was it truly realistic, or even helpful, to expect these children to conform to a rigid framework like learning activity plans? The more I considered this and other parts of the curriculum, the more I wondered if teaching the value of socially constructed roles was doing more harm than good. Wouldn't it be better to let them be themselves, to play in ways that reflected how they saw the world? How much did they really know, or need to know, about coffee shops?

"¿Señor, qué le gustaría tomar?" Nelia asked David A., pointing to the funnels hanging from the shelf representing a soda machine and the coffeepot below it.

David glanced at her briefly before looking away. Nelia turned to Ernesto and said, "¿Necesito un plato?" Ernesto hurried from the cash register to the shelf and handed her a plate with a cup on top. It wasn't exactly the language or actions we were teaching them, but they weren't complaining.

In the bakery, Sofia looked up from her baby doll and noticed Antonio. "Antonio, ven siéntate junto a mi, mijo," she said, patting the chair next to her.

Antonio kept spinning. Sofia tilted her head, looking over at me for guidance. I stepped closer, crouching to her level.

"Show him what to do," I whispered, adding in Spanish without thinking.

Sofia nodded and turned back to Antonio. She gently touched his arm and repeated, "Antonio, ven conmigo. Siéntate aquí." This time, he stopped spinning and looked at her. Slowly, he allowed her to guide him to the chair.

"Gracias, Sofia," I said softly, catching myself slipping into Spanish again as I added, "Lo estás haciendo muy bien."

Ernesto glanced over from the Starbucks, noticing Antonio nearby. "Antonio, necesita comida!" he declared, laughing as he scribbled something on a sheet of paper.

David A., however, had already grown restless. He wandered out of the Starbucks and into the deli, his attention immediately caught by the blocks I had strategically placed there. He sat down on the carpet and began stacking them, completely engrossed.

Ernesto followed, setting his piece of paper aside. "¿Necesitas ayuda?" he asked David A., picking up a block to help.

David didn't respond verbally. Ernesto placed the block on top of his tower without hesitation.

Sofia looked at David in the deli, then at Antonio, slipping out of the chair next to her. "Antonio, vamos a jugar con los bloques," she said, motioning toward the blocks. She stood and held out her hand.

To my surprise, Antonio followed her without hesitation. They joined David and Ernesto at the blocks, where Sofia declared herself the mother of both boys. "I'm taking care of my children," she announced in Spanish, patting Antonio on the back as he began to spin a block in his hands.

As I watched the scene unfold, I felt a strange mix of emotions. On one hand, it was beautiful to see the children creating their own world, communicating in Spanish, and finding roles that included everyone. On the other hand, a pang of guilt clawed at me. I knew the restriction about the language used during instruction.

Brandon interrupted my thoughts, walking over from the art table across the room. "Play?" he asked in English, looking at the block area.

The question jolted me. I realized how natural it had felt to let Spanish flow. I hesitated, feeling a wave of guilt. Had I crossed a line? No, this was for the betterment of the community. We were still using the curriculum, right?

"Of course, Brandon," I said, leading him toward the blocks.

"Nelia, ven a la . . . deli," Ernesto called out, looking in her direction.

Nelia, who had been organizing the clay breakfast food in the Starbucks, straightened up. She looked toward Ernesto and joined him.

From my spot at the edge of the scene, I watched Brandon, Nelia, Sofia, Ernesto, Antonio, and David play with blocks. Ernesto helped David balance a one-foot-long rectangular block against a stack of two-inch-by-two-inch cubes. Sofia whispered something to Antonio, who was now tapping two blocks together rhythmically. Brandon and Nelia collected blocks for a castle.

Language wasn't a barrier here. Abilities weren't barriers. The children were creating a world that was theirs, one where everyone had a role and belonged. It reminded me of my previous eleven years of teaching, when play had no limits, only possibilities.

I thought back to the differences I noticed between the curriculum I used in my first two years at Vista and the Every Early Learner Succeeds curriculum. Embedding interventions into play was not just a strategy; it was an opportunity. Embedded interventions made inclusion feel seamless and natural.

Watching the children now, I realized this was one of those rare moments where everything clicked. I hadn't observed this often with the Every Early Learner Succeeds curriculum. But now, stepping back and letting the children make sense of the roles and take the lead in transitioning from the curriculum learning activity to playtime, I realized that making the curriculum work in a way that honored inclusion might be possible.

It was becoming more and more clear in the morning and afternoon classes that embedded interventions could work. They did not require me to speak a child's language; they required children to be able to communicate with one another, authentically and meaningfully, as they were.

***

It was Friday, October 17. The week had wound down, and I had not heard much from Diana about the teacher she said would replace me. I thought I could finally set her promises aside as something that would happen when it happened. I could only control what I could control: how I showed up in the classroom, my home, and my schoolwork. Still, I could not help sending a text message when I had a few minutes.

Hi Diana. :) Is the English Language Development–Spanish teacher on track?

Diana's response gave me a little hope, though I remained cautious. According to her, everything was still moving forward. She was working with Mel Jones, my future mentor, to identify the schools where I would be assigned.

Sounds good, I replied, trying to keep my nerves in check.

Then she let me know that she was sending an email to all the early childhood special education Foundations teachers for a training on October 31, but that I could ignore it because I would be on board with her team by then.

I sat there for a second, reading the words, knowing she was trying to keep me level. It had the opposite effect. I set my phone down and stared out the window at the golden leaves falling from the trees across the street. Everything outside seemed in transition, yet I felt caught in the past. The tension between the teacher I was the previous eleven years, the teacher I was at that moment, and the leader I wanted to become kept me straddled between Diana's spell and room 122.

The days that followed were still a roller coaster: emails, text messages, brief moments of hope followed by deep frustration. I stopped checking my texts during the day. On Tuesday, the twenty-first, I waited until my arrival at the university before classes to read a text Diana had sent earlier that afternoon.

Her message said she was sealing some deals and would be in touch shortly.

I replied while waiting in line for coffee, my thoughts drifting to Eric, Ricky, Jimmy, and the new student with autism as they searched for insects on the playground this morning during class. Their curiosity and laughter always rekindled my passion for teaching. I pictured the morning class building elaborate block structures, their focus and cooperation reminding me why this work mattered. As the line inched forward, I could almost see Sofia gently placing a cup into Antonio's hands or hear Ernesto's giggle as he scribbled a menu. The thought of leaving those moments behind tightened my chest. More than anything, I wanted the uncertainty to end. I knew now that the longer I waited, the harder the separation would become.

I'm guessing you didn't get the chance to talk with Jorge? I wrote.

Diana replied right away, letting me know that she was still waiting for a call from him.

I quickly dictated a voice-to-text reply.

I can't express how much I am soooooooooo ready for this to conclude.

Diana assured me the deal would be done and that we had to put faith in karma.

Karma? Interesting choice of words. Was spirituality the missing piece for completing this puzzle? I thought.

The following evening, after a rich conversation in my university class about the overlap between learning theories related to teachers and students, I felt the need to speak up about my growing concerns with the approach I was being asked to take in room 122. I began drafting an email to Jorge, sharing my perspective and asking him to connect with Diana for clarity on the future of my position.

Good evening, Jorge,

I'm writing with a heavy heart, but also hope. I know you understand how much this itinerant position means to me. It is more than just a step in my career. I see it as a way to bring the inclusive practices I've refined during my time at Vista to a larger scale. As I move through the doctorate program, I feel a growing urgency to support more children, families, and educators in making inclusion a reality.

For eleven years, I've worked tirelessly to create environments where every child feels they belong. I've seen the beauty of high-quality, meaningful inclusion in action, but I've also faced the barriers in the system-level gaps that hold us back. The itinerant role feels like the bridge between what I've accomplished in the classroom and what I can do for others on a broader scale.

I'm asking if you can reach out to Diana tomorrow. I need clarity so I can focus on my work here without the constant question of "what if" festering in the back of my mind.

Thank you for your support, always. It's something I deeply value in the midst of this uncertainty.

Take care,

Andrew

Jorge replied twenty-four hours later. I sat in my closet-office reading his message, feeling my jaw tighten as disappointment crept in.

In his response, Jorge let me know he had reached out to Diana and left a voicemail, expecting to hear back from her soon. Then the tone of the message shifted. He reminded me of the values at Vista: collaboration, innovation, and equity. He expressed concern about how I was structuring language in my classroom and emphasized that English should remain the sole language of instruction for both direct teaching and student interaction. He asserted that switching between languages was not best practice for second language acquisition and outlined specific expectations for my use of the curriculum, learning plans, and strategies to ensure students engaged in complete sentences with one another rather than relying on support staff for interaction. He concluded his email by saying he would be in touch once he heard back from Diana.

I stared at the screen for a moment. It struck me that Diana always spoke of children and families in terms of possibility. Jorge, even when well-meaning, seemed bound by systems that reduced inclusion to compliance. I didn't want to lead that way. Inclusion was no longer just about individual connection; it was about shaping systems that allowed connection and belonging to flourish. Jorge had cited best practices as if they were absolutes, but none of the research he referenced considered contexts like room 122.

I carefully composed my reply, trying to walk the line between what I saw as professionalism and resistance.

Good evening, Jorge,

Thank you for calling Diana. I think it would be valuable for both of us to have a conversation about room 122 as a whole and how it aligns with the Vista values of collaboration, innovation, and equity. Among the many things we have discussed, I don't think we've ever talked about me as a teacher. We've never really discussed why I do what I do in the classroom and how I've had to adapt my teaching based on what I observe of the children.

I really look forward to a conversation about the human side of my classroom, beyond standardized observations, published curricula, and legal requirements. I hope we can connect in person tomorrow.

Andrew

The next morning, I received a text from Diana. It shed light on a step in the process I didn't anticipate.

She informed me that she had sent an email, inviting me for an interview later that afternoon. Her words were simple, but the message was clear. The job now felt more real than ever.

My pulse quickened as I typed back.

I just saw that. What does that mean exactly? Did you talk with Jorge, and now we're moving forward with formalities?

A quiet wave of relief washed over me as I read Diana's reassurance and confirmation that conversations had taken place. It wasn't finished yet, but finally, I could see the end drawing near. Each day I had spent waiting for a resolution had quietly chipped away at my capacity to be fully present with the children. I was still showing up, but less whole each time. Now, at last, something concrete was taking shape.

***

Lillie, Cecilia, and I sat at the blue kidney table. Their faces showed a mix of exhaustion and quiet attentiveness. That Monday morning had been chaotic, but now, with the room calm, a necessary moment of peace settled over us. I was about to share something that had been building beneath the surface for weeks.

"I've got some news," I said, my voice cracking. I could already feel the tears welling in my eyes. "I had my interview for the itinerant position."

They looked up, their eyes searching mine.

"Diana said it was mostly a formality. I have the job." I tried to soften the words, not to make it sound dramatic, but this wasn't hypothetical anymore.

Lillie gave a faint smile. Cecilia's face shifted, her eyebrows dropping into that expression she wore when something ran deeper than words.

"I'm excited," I added, "but I also feel horrible about leaving . . . leaving you, the children, and the families. I care for you all dearly." The words slipped out before I could stop them.

Cecilia exhaled, her hands now busy with an artifact from the morning's play. "So, it's finally real," she said, her voice thick with something between sadness and resolve.

I nodded, brushing past the tightness rising in my chest. "I know you're both in a tough spot." I looked toward Lillie, who held my gaze with quiet strength.

She spoke softly. "We're on a good track. I feel better about the class now that you've stepped up to Jorge and helped us create something that works better for the children and for us."

I listened, unsure I deserved her affirmation.

Cecilia gave a tight smile. "The kids and families are going to miss you. No one can replace what you've brought here."

I swallowed the lump in my throat. "I'll miss you both too. Probably more than I even realize yet." I paused. "But I'll still be around. I won't just disappear. I may be assigned to schools nearby." I smiled gently. "I'm not abandoning you. I'll look for other opportunities for both of you."

Lillie's lips twitched into a small smile. "I'll take anything that lets me work with children and families in a way that's right for them and me." There was harnessed conviction in her voice that hadn't been there a few months ago. She understood choices have consequences. She was advocating for a just system.

I thought back to the start of the year, how unsure we'd all felt, how often I had carried the weight alone. Now, I saw something steadier. Their voices had grown more confident, their instincts more attuned. Leadership was knowing when to step back so others could rise.

Still, I wondered if I was leaving too soon. Antonio had just begun responding to Sofia's invitations. David A. was taking initiative during play. Would anyone else notice these subtle shifts? Would their strengths still be seen?

A shared silence followed, but it wasn't uncomfortable. We all knew change was coming, even if none of us wanted to face it.

I stood, trying to move into the rhythm between the morning and afternoon class. Cecilia and Lillie didn't move. I paused, then said, "We've got this, together, for the next few days, okay?" My voice was quieter now. They both nodded.

The future still felt uncertain. But their trust in one another and in our work with the children and families made me believe we could face it head-on.

As Lillie and Cecilia walked toward the door for lunch, Cecilia turned back and met my eyes. She smiled, and for a moment, it felt like maybe everything would be okay.

Perhaps this next step was exactly where I was meant to be. Yet I knew the hardest part wasn't over. Questions remained, and decisions were being made in rooms I wasn't part of yet. I didn't know what my first day as an itinerant teacher would actually look like.

***

The bell rang, signaling the end of the school day for the kindergarten through fifth grade children. Our students had been gone for forty-five minutes. I sat in my chair and swiveled from left to right, right to left, feeling a rare sense of relief. The classroom community was well established. After talking with Cecilia and Lillie, I was confident they'd be fine without me. I was excited for the new chapter about to unfold.

I pulled out my phone and found Virginia's name. She would be a good person to share this news with. She could understand the complexity of the situation, see the win for what it was.

Just got the news this morning. I'm about to get the job I've been waiting for, I texted.

Moments later, she responded. *Yea!! That's amazing! The itinerant position? What's the next step in the process?*

I smiled at her words, feeling her enthusiasm through the screen. She always had a way of making me feel like I was on the verge of something bigger than myself. It was both comforting and motivating, like someone shining a light up ahead while I was still trying to navigate the shadows.

The next step is just waiting for the official offer. I'm excited. But I'm also still feeling a little . . . torn. You know, about the kids and the families. They're doing well, but I can't help but feel like I'm letting them down.

I stared at the pulsing ellipses at the bottom of my screen.

I get it. You've been invested, and it's hard to think about leaving that. But what you're moving into is bigger than any one classroom. You're going to be able to make a bigger impact across the board. More kids, more families. You've been preparing for this.

I read her message twice, letting the words settle in. It was true. I had spent so much time focusing on the daily dilemmas in room 122 and just getting out that I had not allowed myself to think deeply about the itinerant position, its implications, and its possibilities. It was an opportunity to be a leader, to practice what I was learning in my university courses on a broader scale. Yet it was hard not to feel the tug of the kids with whom I was just starting to make progress. There were also the families, the ones who had stood up for me in Jorge's office earlier that fall.

Yeah. I'm trying to reconcile the two. I can't help but feel like I'm abandoning them in some way.

As the ellipses dangled for, what felt like more than a minute, I felt the all-too-familiar sense of insecurity begin to surface again.

It's okay to feel that way. It's a big change. What you've done already will have a ripple effect. Just think of the direct and indirect impact you'll have on kids and families in the itinerant role. ;)

Her words felt validating. She had a way of peeling back the emotion to reveal the meaning underneath like a mirror that showed not just who and where I was, but where I was going, and who I was becoming. I looked around the classroom, the familiar space that still felt new. The possibilities of this room, if I had been allowed to teach the way I had the previous two years, were endless. Maybe I needed to give it more time. But Virginia was right. The work wasn't finished, and I wasn't abandoning it. I was expanding it.

You're right. I need to stop focusing on what I'll be leaving behind.

A few minutes passed before Virginia's response appeared.

You're always going to do right by them, even from a different place. And it doesn't mean you won't still be there for them. You just won't be in the trenches every day. And you're going to give someone else the chance to step up and make their mark too.

I didn't completely agree with her last sentence. Virginia wasn't privy to the details of who might replace me or how that might affect the community we had built. I decided to keep things simple. Her messages were soothing, and she was right about one thing: This wasn't an ending. It was a new beginning. Even if the next person didn't do things the way I would, maybe that was the point. The work wasn't about replication; it was about transformation, creating something strong enough that others could build on it in their own way.

Thank you, Virginia. You always know how to put things into perspective. :)

You've got this, Andrew. I'm cheering for you!

I sat back, absorbing the text conversation. Outside the window, the light of the afternoon faded. I finally felt a sense of peace settle within me. Yes, this was going to be a hard transition, but it was the right one. It was time for me to step up and be a part of something bigger.

***

It was early Tuesday morning, October 28, just before the first bell rang. I stood by the front door of room 122, tying up loose ends before the children and families entered. The halls echoed with kids chattering, families corralling, and teachers scrambling. Ernesto's mom, Gabriela, entered the front door of the classroom with purpose, her usual warmth subdued.

"Good morning, Andrew," she said softly.

"Morning, Gabriela. How's everything?" I kept it light, but her tone made it clear she wasn't there for small talk.

She glanced around, then lowered her voice. "I heard you're leaving."

I felt a lump rise in my throat. I had rehearsed this conversation in my mind, but I wasn't expecting to have it so early in the day. "Yeah. You heard correctly."

Her expression softened. "We'll miss you, Mr. Andrew. You've been incredible. I'm sad to see you go."

Her words hit me hard. The thought of leaving these children and the families I'd come to know felt like an impossible choice.

"I know," I said, my voice thick. "I'm sad too. It's . . . a new opportunity."

She nodded, her smile thin. "Just know what you've done here matters. Not just this year."

I looked down. Gabriela understood more than most. "Thank you. You probably know more than I do about what's coming next."

She sidestepped any further comments. "Don't forget about us."

"I won't, Gabriela. I won't forget any of this."

She turned toward the front door and left without any additional consideration. I nearly called after her, but the words stayed inside. Her affirmation didn't ease the weight of leaving. It made it heavier. I wasn't ready to walk away from the children, the families, or the relationships we had nurtured. Still, I knew it was the right next step, even if it meant leaving something precious.

Later that morning, Lillie, Cecilia, and I were doing our thing. The hearts of fourteen children were beating strongly with play. I was near the front of room 122 when two unfamiliar faces walked in with clipboards and neutral expressions. One introduced herself as a representative of the Department of Justice's Civil Rights Division in Colorado, the other from the Congress of Hispanic Educators. They were there to evaluate adherence to the Binding Compliance Order, specifically how our dual-language learners were being supported.

They took seats along the wall. I was alarmed. At the last staff meeting, Jorge had mentioned observers might visit, but I hadn't expected them in the early childhood wing, let alone room 122. I didn't know how to alert Lillie or Cecilia without drawing attention.

That week marked the end of the grocery unit in the Every Early Learner Succeeds curriculum. I was in the science center, which also served as our pretend produce section, with Brandon and Nelia. Their engagement in the curriculum learning activity involving shelf-stocking had faded, and they were now immersed in the magnifying glasses and nature objects: rocks, leaves, and shells.

"Why aren't the leaves green anymore?" Nelia asked in Spanish, holding up a brown, dried leaf.

Normally, I would've said, "¿Qué piensas?" Not that morning. I scanned the room for ways to demonstrate my English language instruction. I pointed to the poster of leaf types. "Good question, Nelia. Do you think all leaves turn brown?" I gestured to pine needles, then to a maple leaf. She didn't respond.

I saw the observers scribbling. My face began to burn. Did it look as unnatural as it felt?

My thoughts didn't stall. Brandon pointed to a stone. "What's inside the rock?" he asked in English. I knew it wasn't because of my modeling, but I was grateful.

"Let's see if we can figure that out," I said, keeping my voice light despite the churn in my stomach.

Across the room, I could hear Cecilia speaking in Spanish with children painting clay food in the art center. Their animated voices carried joy. At the sensory table, Lillie supported Antonio. Spanish, paired with visuals, was the only way he engaged.

The language that built bridges was the very thing that broke protocol.

I looked at the clock. Usually, we'd be heading outside. I hesitated. I didn't trust myself to manage transitions without using Spanish. I kept us inside. As I moved around the room, I discreetly notified Lillie and Cecilia of the observers.

Lillie, no longer holding Antonio's attention, guided Sofia to join them in the deli area. Antonio spun in circles near the shelves. Lillie handed Sofia a unit block and whispered a prompt. She tapped his arm gently. "Come play," Sofia said in Spanish.

I spotted the observers whispering to each other. The questions they might be asking swirled through my thoughts. *Am I using English as the primary language for instruction?*

Ana's words echoed in my head. "*They want us to check boxes and hit benchmarks, but they're not in the classroom with us. They don't see what we see.*"

After about twenty minutes, the observers approached. One observer asked, "Can you explain how you address the needs of your English language learner students during this unit?"

I gestured toward the classroom. "We're in the grocery unit. We integrate language development into all activities. During play, I speak English. I encourage children to speak English, but I don't prohibit them from speaking Spanish so they can fully engage. I use visuals to guide structured learning."

The second one asked, "How do you support children like the one . . . I think his name is David . . . those who struggle with both language and social interactions?"

I explained our embedded interventions. "We place familiar materials in multiple centers to help him transition. We pair him with verbal peers like Ernesto, Nelia, Mateo, Brandon, and Sofia to support interaction."

They nodded, walked around the room a bit longer, then thanked me and left.

We had ten minutes to go outside. The children needed it. We transitioned with the help of some Spanish. As they lined up, I saw Jorge near the door. His face was unreadable. I knew a debrief was coming. Perhaps we would talk about the concepts I had shared with the observers. Several were parallel to what I had requested to talk about in the email I recently sent him. I wanted to explain my philosophy of teaching in an inclusive classroom, not only through embedded interventions, but through a learning environment where systems, relationships, and expectations worked together to support each child's growth. Many of those ideas came from my course Teaching in the Modern Classroom, where I was beginning to frame inclusion not as a method, but as a way of leading.

***

That afternoon, Jorge called, asking me to come to his office to discuss the report from the observers. I braced myself as I stepped inside, the memory of the morning's visit still fresh in my mind. He greeted me with his usual professionalism, but there was a tightness in his tone as he began.

"Andrew," he said, his tone more abrasive than usual. "I wanted to talk about the feedback from the observers this morning. They had a lot to say about your classroom."

I nodded, sensing this was not going to be a conversation about authentic, meaningful connections, embedded interventions, or any concepts from my courses at the university. Regardless, this conversation was procedural. I was leaving for the itinerant position.

"They were impressed with how engaged the children were," he said. "It's clear you've created a classroom where the kids feel comfortable exploring and expressing themselves."

I felt a flicker of relief but knew better than to relax.

"They also noted some concerns, specifically around language use and curriculum fidelity."

I nodded again, working to keep my expression neutral. *Is that their concern or his?*

"For instance," Jorge said, consulting his notes, "they mentioned your interaction with a boy and girl in the science center. They noticed that you spoke to them in Spanish before switching to English. Their concern is that the primary language of instruction needs to be English, especially in those moments of direct interaction."

I didn't recall speaking Spanish, but if I did, it was instinctual, meant to honor the children's questions, not to undermine instruction. I wanted to explain how using Spanish built trust and curiosity, but I could tell this wasn't the time for nuance.

"They also observed Cecilia and Lillie using Spanish," he added. "While I understand the intent behind it, we need to ensure that English is the language of instruction across all routines. That's what the district expects, and it's what we've been asked to uphold."

This wasn't feedback. It was a warning. The message was clear: fidelity to policy over responsiveness to children.

"The observers felt that the teaching in the centers did not meet the expectations of Every Early Learner Succeeds. While it's great to see the children engaged, we need to ensure that they're following the structure of the curriculum and that their activities align with the learning objectives."

I resisted the urge to respond. I could have cited research about learning theory—play, engagement, developmentally appropriate practices, and more. But this wasn't an invitation to dialogue. This was about compliance.

During a recent early childhood education team meeting, Jorge confirmed that children were expected to participate in curriculum activities only as long as they could stay focused. By the time the observers arrived, most had moved on. How would stricter adherence to a grocery store theme help children, like Antonio or David A., who needed social and emotional support, sensory exploration, and a sense of authentic, meaningful connections?

Jorge must have sensed my internal resistance because his tone softened.

"Andrew, I know you're doing your best. And I know how much you care about these kids. That's obvious to anyone who spends time in your classroom. You embody most of our values at Vista."

"Thank you," I said, unsure whether his praise was aligned with Diana's encouragement or meant to keep me in line.

"I want to remind you what those values are," he continued. "Collaboration. Innovation. Equity. That's what we center our work on here. And I want to help you think about how you can lean into those more, especially collaboration. You have a strong team. I think you'd benefit from partnering more with the early childhood education teachers so you're not carrying this alone."

That caught me off guard. Ana, Esmeralda, Linda, and Sharon had all voiced frustrations with the curriculum, and they weren't the ones being asked to support children with complex support needs in a language they weren't allowed to speak.

Jorge continued. "I also want to encourage you to view the Binding Compliance Order through an equity lens. These children need exposure to fluent speakers, people who can model academic language so they can have access to better educational opportunities in English or Spanish in the future. When they hear nonfluent speakers like yourself, it can actually be detrimental."

His words landed like a slap. I clenched my jaw, nodding outwardly while my thoughts burned beneath the surface. Was he implying I was harming the children? That my bilingualism, still in progress, was more than a liability? Was it dangerous? I flashed back to the email he sent in September, insinuating to four district officials that I was not fit to teach in room 122.

What about Lillie and Cecilia, who spoke Spanish fluently? They weren't being empowered to use it. They were being silenced. How was that equity? And what about the curriculum itself? The Every Early Learner Succeeds grocery unit featured roles that didn't reflect most of our students' lives. It wasn't rigorous; it was irrelevant. *If children can't see themselves in the material, they won't engage. That's not inclusion. That's exclusion dressed up in academic language, I thought to myself.*

Jorge looked at me with what I assumed was meant to be encouragement.

"Let's work on this together. I can talk with the early childhood team more about building consistent collaboration. And you just keep reflecting on how you bring the Vista values into your classroom. I can help you with that, too."

I nodded slowly, my head swimming with contradiction. "I understand," I said finally.

As I left his office, the weight of the conversation sank deep in my chest. This wasn't just about observer notes or curriculum fidelity. It was about whose vision of education was legitimate. I wasn't sure how much longer I could pretend that mine still fit within his, but that didn't matter. I wouldn't be there much longer. My vision would fit where I was going.

***

The house was quiet when I walked in. It felt like a pause in the chaos. Natalie had taken the girls to a family friend's house, whom she'd met through her mom's group. I was alone but not at ease.

I hung my bag on a hook near the door and stood still for a moment, letting the hum of the refrigerator fill the quiet. My mind was tangled in the conversation with Jorge, replaying it like a loop I couldn't escape. His words, "see it through an equity lens" and "nonfluent speakers like yourself can be detrimental," stayed under my skin. It wasn't only what he said; it was the assumption behind it, that I didn't understand equity, that I was the barrier.

It wasn't just my fluency he questioned. He questioned my place in the classroom and, by extension, Cecilia and Lillie's ability to fulfill their professional obligations.

I took a slow breath and tried to convince myself it was only an ego bruise, a passing sting. Yet even as I reasoned through it, I couldn't shake the feeling that something deeper had been exposed.

I grabbed my phone and pulled up Diana's number.

'Sup Diana! Just checking in. Everything still on track for the itinerant position? I had a weird conversation with Jorge today. His comments suggested I would be at Vista for the rest of the year. I just want to be sure.

I hit send and walked into the kitchen. I pulled salmon out of the fridge, set it on the counter, and started prepping dinner.

I knew Natalie and the girls would be home soon. I wanted everything to be ready before they burst through the door, hangry and tired.

My phone buzzed.

Absolutely. Everything's still on track. It looks like you'll start in two weeks. Not sure why Jorge would speak to you like you were staying at Vista. I'll text you next week with the details. Let's plan on meeting up with Mel, your mentor, soon.

I exhaled. Not relief exactly, but a kind of loosening.

Thanks. That's all helpful. I've got to get dinner started before Natalie and the girls get home.

Her reply came quickly.

I totally understand. I'm excited to start working with you and getting to know your family better. My team values family deeply.

I stared at her message a little longer than necessary, letting it settle. "My team values family." Those words felt like medicine. Jorge had made it clear through his treatment of Ana that family wasn't something you brought into your professional identity. It was something you hid, something you worked around, not something to be honored.

I seasoned the salmon and set the oven to preheat, smiling softly as I moved around the kitchen. I was stepping into a role where I didn't have to perform. I didn't have to prove myself by silencing parts of who I was. I could bring my whole self—my family, my questions, and my convictions—and be seen not as a problem but as a person.

This wasn't abandonment. It was a transplant, lifting what had grown in room 122 and finding new soil for it to take root.

The oven beeped just as I heard the key in the front door. I smiled. I was ready.

CHAPTER 10

HOPE

The parent-teacher conferences at the end of October were a bright spot within Vista's policies and procedures during an otherwise overwhelming school year. Sitting with Cecilia, Lillie, and occasionally Tom, I had the rare opportunity to pause and see each child through the eyes of their families. These conversations offered a glimpse into who the children were at home, beyond the structure of the classroom, and reminded me of what we were missing by not engaging families more regularly in our daily work as we had the previous year.

Gabriela, Ernesto's mom, radiated joy as she described how her son loved organizing games with his cousins. His father chimed in, sharing how Ernesto took charge at family gatherings, inventing elaborate stories and assigning roles for everyone to play. I nodded, thinking of his imaginative play in the bakery center.

"He's a natural leader," I said, recalling how Ernesto had encouraged David A. to join in by helping him build a tower with blocks in the waiting room center. "He notices what everyone needs and finds a way to include them."

His parents exchanged a proud glance.

"That's exactly who he is," Gabriela said. "He's always looking out for others."

The conversation with Sofia's grandma was equally heartwarming.

"Sofia's so gentle," her grandma said in Spanish, her voice soft and welcoming. "She's always talking about Antonio at home."

I thought of Sofia inviting Antonio to sit with her in Starbucks, patiently repeating her invitation until he followed her.

"She has this quiet way of making people feel safe," Cecilia replied. "The way she helps Antonio join in. It's like she knows exactly how to reach him."

Beatriz, Jimmy's mom, laughed when I mentioned his conviction for following his imagination.

"Jimmy's funny like that," she said, shaking her head affectionately.

I told her about his learning plans, how he'd drawn the same scene every day for a week, staying focused and determined.

"It's patience and creativity rolled into one," I said. "He has this ability to stay on task, no matter what's happening around him."

Then there was Nelia's mom, her eyes lighting up as I recounted Nelia's time in the bakery, deli, and Starbucks.

"She's a superhero there," I said. "She takes care of everyone, handing out food and making sure no one is hungry."

Her mom laughed, sharing how Nelia often pretended to work at a bakery at home. "She likes cooking desserts."

Each family's story reminded me of the vibrant world we could nurture together if only the policies and curriculum allowed more room to breathe. No matter what the conditions, children and their families were never truly separate. I had learned years earlier that I could not fully include a child without also including their family. These conversations brought that truth back into focus and reaffirmed why I loved this work. I carried a bittersweet pride as I listened, knowing how much these relationships mattered, how fragile they were, and the ache I'd hold once I left.

As we wrapped up the conferences on Friday, October 31, I packed up my notes. The emotions from the week settled heavily over me. A question that had simmered since early in the semester kept echoing in my mind: *What does leadership look like when systems are misaligned with our values?*

I had wrestled with that question again in a recent paper for my organizational leadership course, where I concluded that true leadership does not compromise inclusion to satisfy subjective interpretations of policy. Instead, leadership holds firm to authentic relationships, cultivates a culture of belonging, and engages family voices as central to curriculum and decision-making. When policies misaligned with this view of inclusion, I relied on professional ethical guidelines to resist thoughtfully and with care. The parent-teacher conferences reminded me how far we were from a classroom fully capable of inclusion, how much policy and structure continued to limit it, yet how survival was still possible when I focused on what I could control and let go of everything else.

Writing about inclusion in theory and living it in practice were not the same. On paper, the pieces fit together; in reality, they felt disjointed and fragile. Still, I began to recognize that this tension was teaching me something I would not need to solve inside a single classroom. The itinerant role offered the possibility of stepping outside daily curricular constraints and using what I was learning about families, relationships, and ethical leadership to support multiple classrooms without having to reconcile those lessons in real time with rigid instructional demands. For now, my responsibility remained with the children and families in front of me. I stayed present, held what I was learning, and waited, knowing that this knowledge would matter when the conditions finally allowed me to use it fully.

***

David A.'s Individual Education Program meeting began promptly at 10:45 a.m. on Tuesday, November 4. Tom, Lillie, Cecilia, Esmeralda, the occupational therapist, David's mom, and an interpreter gathered around the blue kidney table in room 122. Each carried pieces of David A.'s story. No one sat in the center. I had scheduled the meeting last week to ensure it would be held before I transitioned into the itinerant role.

David's mother greeted everyone quietly in Spanish. Her hands rested in her lap, and her expression was composed but fragile. The interpreter leaned toward her, slightly apart from the rest of us, poised to translate the conversation without interfering.

It had been more than a year since David's mom had first confided her fears to us. "I thought he would never have friends, never speak, never be happy like other children." That day remained vivid in my memory. But since then, I had seen the light return to her eyes as David began to grow, first in his language, then in his confidence, and now in his relationships.

As she looked around the room today, her gratitude was palpable.

"Muchas gracias por todo lo que han hecho por David," she said. Her voice was thick with emotion.

The interpreter translated: "Thank you very much for everything you have done for David."

"It's been a privilege to witness his growth," I replied. "He's such a bright, curious child. We're all so proud of him."

She nodded, her eyes glistening. "Yo tenía miedo de que nunca pudiera hacer amigos o aprender cómo otros niños, pero aquí lo ha hecho."

"I was afraid he would never make friends or learn like other children," the interpreter echoed, "but here, he has."

Tom added, "He's even starting to use verbal language to initiate play during centers. That's a huge step."

David's mom smiled. "At home, he reads books and plays with his cousin. He's even helping me with small chores."

The occupational therapist described his progress with fine motor skills. "He can now complete puzzles and use writing tools with confidence. His frustration tolerance has improved so much."

Moments like these affirmed the purpose of inclusive education, not just as a legal or theoretical ideal, but as practices centered on authentic relationships.

We turned to the question of placement. The team had been preparing for this for weeks.

"Given how well David is doing, we believe he's ready for a classroom where he can learn alongside children his age," I said. "We're recommending he transition into your class, Esmeralda, where he can continue building the skills needed for kindergarten."

Well-planned transitions mattered. They could either open a path to high-quality, meaningful inclusion or quietly reroute children toward isolation. I knew the stakes, but I wasn't sure Esmeralda saw it the same way.

I looked at David's mom, then at Esmeralda. "David has most likely made more progress in our classroom over the past year than he would have in a separate setting for children with autism. Being with same-age peers who share his language and cultural background gives him models for both language and social development."

The interpreter translated as I continued. "When Ernesto or Nelia invites him in Spanish to play, he responds instantly. That kind of connection is what fuels learning. And you've seen the track-building. He's taught every child in this class how to build ramps using gutters."

Tom nodded. "Peers his age will stretch that even further. It's the right next step."

Esmeralda listened carefully. "That makes sense. I think being with children who speak Spanish and are his age will help prepare him."

David's mom added quietly, "Gracias, maestra."

Then Esmeralda asked the question I was beginning to anticipate. "Will there be a Spanish-speaking special education teacher to help him in my class?"

I hesitated. "To my knowledge, no. The itinerant teacher assigned to support you may not speak Spanish. You'll likely be the primary person implementing his supports."

Her face tightened, and David's mom looked down.

My thoughts turned inward. *If Diana is asking me to join her team, maybe it's because the current education system doesn't serve kids like David as well as it should. Maybe that's the point. She sees that we cannot just support one child, but that we need to make sure the education system itself begins to shift.*

"I'll need help," Esmeralda said.

"You'll have it," I promised. "Reach out anytime. Tom, Lillie, and Cecilia—we all know David and can help you problem-solve. You also have my personal phone number."

Cecilia smiled. "He'll do great in your room."

David's mom nodded slowly, hope flickering behind her eyes.

I looked at Esmeralda and then at David's mom. "Every step forward, no matter how small, is worth celebrating. Please continue to share his celebrations with us."

As we wrapped up, I felt both pride and unease. David was ready. Esmeralda was willing. Yet the education system beyond my classroom that he was entering was not yet built to recognize his brilliance. That reality stirred something deeper: maybe my next role wasn't just a shift, maybe it was a responsibility. If I could influence placement decisions, coach teachers, and protect inclusive practices from falling through bureaucratic cracks, then perhaps leaving room 122 could serve a purpose greater than my grief.

***

I stared at my phone, the voicemail notification glowing like a warning light on a car dashboard. It had been there since midmorning, waiting for me to find the courage to listen. After finishing the paperwork from David's Individual Education Program meeting the day before, I took a slow breath and pressed play.

"Hi, Andrew, this is Diana. I just wanted to follow up on our conversation from last week. Mel Jones and I have been talking, and we think we know what area of Metro Denver Unified we'll have you working. It will be a perfect fit for you. Let's set up a time to meet. Give me a call when you get the chance. Talk soon!"

The message was exhilarating. I texted back, proposing a few meeting times. She replied that she and Mel couldn't coordinate during the day and wanted to meet as soon as possible. They suggested getting together for happy hour at a pub. I couldn't help but wonder, *Why a pub?* I was concerned, but I trusted that she was doing what needed to be done.

The plan was set: Riverside Pub, 5:30 p.m., the next day, Thursday, November 6. Mel and Diana were enthusiastic. I felt a small lift of anticipation.

The next evening, I arrived early with my laptop in tow. I chose a quiet corner table. My insecurities crept in as I pulled out the journal articles assigned for class that week and opened my computer. The place wasn't busy yet, but I still felt like every patron was silently questioning why someone would bring a laptop to a pub. I ordered some water and tried to blend in.

Mel arrived first, breezing in with an air of energy and confidence. "Hi, Andrew," she said with a glowing smile.

I quickly closed my computer.

"You're not hiding anything, I hope."

I gave an awkward laugh. "Only from my own overthinking."

She grinned, taking a seat. "No trouble in that. Feel free to share your overthinking with me. I'm happy to help you process."

We made small talk about work, our families, the changing seasons, and the pub's drink menu until Diana arrived, a few minutes late. She slid into the chair adjacent to me and immediately got to the point.

"Andrew," Diana began, "we've been talking, and your résumé speaks for itself. Your experience in early childhood special education is phenomenal, and your work with dual-language learners is exactly what we're looking for. Your focus on leadership in this position is what we need. We know the itinerant position is a perfect fit for you."

Mel's enthusiasm was contagious. "Seriously, Andrew, it's rare to find someone with your blend of classroom expertise, leadership potential, passion for inclusion, and emphasis on partnerships with families. We've been brainstorming how we can make this transition seamless for you and your classroom. We're also tossing around ideas on how to give you opportunities to be a leader for our program in the district."

As they talked, my mind flickered back to the children and families in room 122. The thought of leaving them, especially close to midyear, still made my shoulders tighten. At the same time, Mel's and Diana's words were validating. I had spent so much of the past two and a half months feeling scrutinized and inadequate under Jorge's leadership, my integrity constantly challenged. Here were two professionals not only acknowledging my skills and values, but also actively advocating for me. Maybe that's why we met at a pub. There was no interest in politics. It was about relationships.

"We know leaving midyear will be tough," Diana said, as if reading my mind. "But the position could be a game changer. It's a chance to expand your impact beyond a single classroom and bring your values to our team."

I nodded, mulling over her words. "It's . . . a lot to think about," I admitted, giving way to unbeckoned skepticism. "I've been at Vista for almost two and a half years now, and I know the challenges the kids face there. At the same time, I've been questioning how much longer I can keep doing this."

"Diana has filled me in on your situation," Mel responded. "It sounds toxic. I'm surprised you haven't found something else, considering your credentials."

It was jarring to hear it said aloud. Under Jorge, my work had been dissected and doubted. Here, it was being valued. Not in a performative way, but with action. Offers. Plans. Care. It felt like the aspects of leadership I talked about in my papers, not control.

The conversation shifted to logistics. They outlined how the transition could work: finding a replacement teacher, setting up interim plans for room 122, and ensuring the children and families were supported. I could feel their excitement, but my thoughts kept drifting back to what leaving would mean for me, my students, their families, Lillie and Cecilia, and even Ana.

Mel leaned in, her voice earnest. "Andrew, we're excited to have you on our team. You bring something really special, and we don't want to lose that opportunity."

I left the pub that night with mixed emotions. Their belief in me was undeniable. Diana had expressed that for more than two months. Still, the idea of leaving my classroom midyear was feeling more like a betrayal than the relief I should have felt. The pressure hung over me as I walked to my car, the November air cold against my skin.

At home, I replayed the conversation in my mind, trying to untangle my doubts from my hopes. *How will the children make sense of it? Will the parents feel abandoned? Will Lillie and Cecilia have adequate support if there isn't a substitute? What will it mean for our program's role in the Vista community if I walk away now? How long can I keep absorbing the tension without breaking?*

Maybe this was the only way to create real change, by stepping into a role where I could influence the system and protect children like David A., not only in room 122 but across the district. One thing was certain: whatever path I chose, something would be left behind. The next step would bring its own questions, pressures, and trade-toffs.

***

By the first weeks of November, the oscillation between staying in the classroom and leaving for the itinerant position was suffocating. My impatience with the delays sharpened. My inbox had become both a tool and a battleground. Every email felt like a new skirmish in the ongoing tension between what I believed in as an educator and what was being demanded of me. The emails included numerous threads from every Metro Denver Unified School District entity that influenced room 122: the Early Childhood Education Department, Early Childhood Special Education Department, English Language Development Department, Every Early Learner Succeeds, Vista initiatives, and the implications of the Teaching Observation Protocol. Sifting through messages about my transition to the itinerant position, I couldn't help but reflect on everything that had led up to this point.

I thought back to my conversation at Riverside Pub with Diana and Mel and the validation they offered. My mind jumped to past conversations with Ana, who had reminded me that observations rarely captured the full picture. *"They're not in the classroom with us,"* she'd said. *"They don't see what we see."*

I clicked on an email thread that started Wednesday, November 12. Diana had updated me. She expressed hope that the transition could happen before Thanksgiving. I grew unsettled hearing the word hope. Diana and I had been in regular contact since early September, and she'd been nothing but supportive. Now, everything hinged on Jorge's cooperation.

Jorge was impossible to pin down. I had reached out to him on November 13, asking for a meeting. He said he was booked. I followed up the next Monday, suggesting a quick ten-minute conversation. His reply came late that night: "The only opening I have this week is Friday at 11:00. Fifteen minutes max." He offered the option of emailing my concerns in advance. It was the kind of dismissive accommodation that let me know exactly where I stood.

Meanwhile, Diana was transparent: I wouldn't be officially hired until HR finalized it. She told me the real holdup was finding someone to take my place. I tried to help, reaching out to universities, suggesting teachers from other schools or districts who were interested in working in a Foundations classroom, sharing contact lists, and even passing along Virginia's suggestion to contact the Colorado Department of Education about newly licensed teachers. Diana seemed appreciative but wary, reminding me that Jorge needed to approve any candidate.

Still, I kept showing up for all the meetings, for room 122, and for my integrity. Even though the values Jorge claimed for Vista were collaboration, innovation, and equity, I hung onto Perseverance. Respect. Integrity. Diversity. Excellence. I stayed at work late, revising lesson plans and getting ahead of special education documentation for myself or a new teacher. I was trying to honor the mandated curriculum while still building on my students' interests. I continuously heard Lillie's words in my mind. *"Don't let this die quietly. Fight for the families and us."*

Each day demanded more emotional energy than the last. Holding space for my students while navigating this bureaucratic maze left little room to breathe. Yet I couldn't let that spill into the classroom.

On Friday morning, November 21, I met with Jorge during the narrow fifteen-minute window he had offered. I was composed but tired. I didn't bring up every concern, sharing only enough to signal that I was ready to move forward. He nodded a few times but didn't offer much in return.

That afternoon, I sent Diana more resources and a list of a few substitute teachers who might be interested in something more permanent. I knew I couldn't control the timeline, but I could control my P.R.I.D.E.

Each action, every conversation, and every carefully worded email no longer centered only on room 122. The concepts from my courses helped me to see each solution as part of a larger system, not just a response to isolated circumstances.

As I moved toward something new, I kept thinking of the families who had trusted me. I didn't want them to feel abandoned. I wanted them to know I had done everything I could.

As the sun set that evening, I closed my laptop and stared at the text box on my phone. The words to Diana read:

Let me know when I can start. I'm ready.

Despite the uncertainty, I chose to act with purpose rather than remain paralyzed. I was moving toward the work I believed in, work that stayed true to my integrity and expanded my impact beyond one classroom.

***

The smell of our small Thanksgiving dinner lingered in the air of the duplex. Citlali and Itzel were sprawled on the living room rug, their giggles spilling into every room as they played with blocks. Itzel, barely one, was learning how to stack the pieces, while Citlali proudly built towers and narrated grand adventures. As

Natalie and I cleaned the kitchen, we talked about the paper I was writing—the one that had kept us in Denver for the holiday instead of traveling to Wisconsin.

"Enough of your research. You're putting me to sleep," she said, half-joking. "I'm going to go into the bedroom and read something fun. Enjoy writing your paper."

I sat at the kitchen table. My closet-office desk didn't have the space to spread out everything I needed. The laptop rested in front of me, surrounded by printed journal articles and my working draft. I reread what I had written so far and tried to pull together my ideas. I was developing a conceptual framework for effective inclusion based on my experiences at Vista and the Division for Early Childhood of the Council for Exceptional Children and National Association for the Education of Young Children's joint position statement on inclusion (2009). The position statement identified three pillars: access, participation, and supports.

Still, a question echoed in my mind: *Inclusion, but how?*

Scenes from the classroom rushed back. Children in the dramatic play center. Children in the community center playing with blocks. Were they truly included if they participated only briefly before withdrawing again? And Antonio—he had started responding more when peers invited him to play, but had I given him the tools to move beyond fleeting moments of engagement?

I returned to the first pillar: access. Having materials available was only one layer. Another question emerged. How could access be meaningful if the curriculum itself imposed barriers? Every Early Learner Succeeds claimed to support students like David R. and Antonio, but without honoring their home languages or lived experiences, it felt misaligned. I thought of how Nelia came alive when she was allowed to lead or help, when we followed her strengths instead of a script. It wasn't just about access to materials. It was about access to meaningful learning opportunities and to authentic connections.

The second pillar, participation, felt even more complex. When children and adults spoke Spanish during previous school years, bonds between children formed seamlessly, but policies blurred those bonds in room 122. As a teacher labeled "English Language Development–English," I was left wondering how many children I unintentionally left out. Could I create better bridges across languages to cultivate stronger peer relationships leading to more participation?

Citlali ran over, holding up a LEGO tower. "Look, Daddy! It's taller than me!" she exclaimed proudly.

I smiled and nodded, my thoughts shifting to the third pillar: supports. My daughters thrived because of the web of relationships that surrounded them. In room 122, supports often felt more logistical than relational. Cecilia and Lillie worked tirelessly to create a sense of connection. Mr. Tom, on the days he was in room 122, offered embedded interventions that made a difference. The depth of our support was always tempered by systemic limits—too little time, too much policy, not enough freedom. What more could be done to foster collaboration that identifies the most effective supports?

After putting the girls to bed, I returned to the kitchen table. I typed late into the night, thoughts circling back to the children, the families, and the adults who made room 122 what it was. The framework I was drafting had to hold space for all of them, the children and the adults. Inclusion, if it meant anything, had to stretch beyond the community center and into the policies, the staffing decisions, the professional development, and the leadership structures that shaped our days. The paper was personal, but the vision had to be shared.

I wrote about barriers, some external and some of my own making. I wrote about the school's stated values and how they often clashed with its practices. I wrote about leadership and how it shaped, or stifled, our ability to build inclusive environments. I also wrote about myself, my intentions, my missteps, and my ongoing questions.

As I wrote, I realized this wasn't just a class assignment. It was my first attempt at building a new foundation, one that could reach beyond room 122 in the itinerant role. The more I named the gaps, the more I could begin to imagine structures that honored every child, every language, every adult. I wasn't just describing a framework. I was preparing to live it.

When I finally closed the laptop, the duplex was quiet, the mashed potato stains on my shirt had dried, and the doubts about the reality of the framework in my mind, while not gone, had softened.

***

The days leading up to winter break were a mix of chaos and longing. One reason after another forced me to see every glimmer of inclusion as a celebration. Room 122 was alive with holiday activities, giggling children, and the chatter of the three adults trying to keep everything on track. My mind, however, regularly revisited the events of the past few months, questioning how I could do better. The court observers, Jorge's critiques, and my own doubts about whether I was making a difference pushed me to rethink how I could teach more effectively. Something happened the week after Thanksgiving break that reminded me why I was struggling to let go of the classroom.

The children were gathered in the dramatic play area, which had been transformed into a winter market. This wasn't exactly part of the Every Early Learner Succeeds curriculum, but it was an extension no one opposed. We were in the restaurant unit, but the children wanted to return to the previous unit on grocery stores. In another setting, their idea might have been dismissed for not aligning with the week's lesson plan. In room 122, we let their curiosity lead.

That morning, the classroom buzzed. I circulated the room with a camera and notepad, documenting each child's progress toward expected developmental milestones. Brandon was playing the shopkeeper, and Ernesto was his assistant, confidently explaining in Spanish which items were on sale. Antonio spun circles near the cash register, twirling a red ribbon between his fingers. Sofia stood nearby, carefully arranging cloth fruits and vegetables, while Nelia ran around enthusiastically shopping for everything she could grab.

Antonio, as well as a few other children, did not make the connections between a learning plan and the activity. Sofia and several other children needed help staying engaged with the learning plan and activity process. Still, there they were, playing together, smiling and laughing, and no one was left out.

I set my camera and notepad on top of a nearby shelf and knelt down next to Antonio, who was still clutching the ribbon.

"What's that, Antonio?" I asked, my tone curious rather than directive.

He stood, unresponsive, his eyes darting to the cash register.

I switched to Spanish. "Ah, you're paying for your food?" I pointed to the cash register.

He nodded and handed the ribbon to Ernesto, who cheerfully said, "Gracias, Antonio!"

It was a small exchange, but it was significant. Antonio was engaging, however briefly, in the curriculum learning activity that had eluded him since he joined our community.

As I watched, I realized how far we'd come since August. The kids weren't following the curriculum perfectly, but they were still learning. They were collaborating, using language, and building relationships. They needed more than a curriculum. They needed connection, trust, and the freedom to explore who they were.

At that moment, it hit me. This wasn't just an opportunity for documenting progress toward curriculum student outcomes.

This tiny market scene, with its laughter and layered languages, was a reminder of what inclusion looked like when we trusted children more than the script. We hadn't rejected the curriculum entirely. We had reshaped it together, and the result was a space where inclusion grew in real time. That realization stayed with me. The most important component of the framework I was developing for my university class was strong: peer relationships. If I ever had the chance to lead beyond room 122, the other three components I had identified—leadership, collaboration, and training—would be my priority.

***

Winter break couldn't come soon enough. The children's chatter filled room 122 as Jorge walked in, clipboard in hand. His eyes scanned the room. It was the kind of day that could fool an untrained eye into thinking everything was running smoothly. Beneath the surface, though, I felt the tension.

We were ten minutes into our afternoon playtime. Children were scattered across the classroom, most in small groups. I was with three of them in the community center, playing with blocks. I watched as Jorge observed Lillie kneeling by the sensory table, her gentle encouragement keeping one of our new students engaged. Cecilia sat nearby in the literacy center, helping children create new menus for the restaurant inside the winter market. Their interest in the activity was unmistakable. I could sense Jorge's gaze shifting quickly from one center to the next, narrowing in on specific indicators from the Teaching Observation Protocol rubric and how I practiced those in relation to the curriculum and the English Language Development Binding Compliance Order.

My mind ran through the criteria in the Teaching Observation Protocol: classroom culture, instructional practices, and content delivery. The protocol emphasized observable, measurable interactions, how teachers responded to student cues, how seamlessly transitions flowed, and how deeply lessons connected to objectives.

I noticed Jorge pause and jot something on his clipboard. When he looked up, his expression was neutral but focused. He glanced at Lillie and Cecilia, eyes narrowing slightly. I sensed what was coming. I willed myself to focus on the learners.

Children shifted through centers with practiced ease. By the time they gathered for circle time, the room was calm. I stuck with activities from the curriculum I knew would keep them engaged rather than take risks. Lillie and Cecilia focused on David R. and a few others who struggled with circle time dynamics. It felt less inclusive than usual, more forced than natural. I thought I saw a flicker of a smile on Jorge's face before he exited. The observation passed in what felt like both an instant and an eternity.

Later that afternoon, I sat across from Jorge in his office, the clipboard resting between us like a silent referee. He flipped through his notes, lips pressed into a thin line.

"You're doing good work here," he said, his tone measured. "I can see your continued efforts to improve the classroom. The kids seem engaged, and your transitions are much smoother than they were earlier in the year."

I nodded, the knot in my stomach loosening slightly. "Thank you. I've been trying to really focus on the feedback from previous observations."

Jorge tapped his pen on the clipboard, his eyes meeting mine. "That's evident. But . . ."

Here it came.

"I noticed Lillie and Cecilia speaking Spanish with the children." His tone sharpened. "We've talked about this before, Andrew. It's critical that we maintain consistency in English instruction."

I hesitated before speaking. "I understand the policy, and I've reminded them of it. But some of our students"—I paused—"respond more readily in Spanish, especially during moments of frustration or transition."

His expression didn't break. "I get that, but the district has guidelines for a reason. Families expect us to follow them."

I nodded again, biting back my frustration. I wanted to lay the Binding Compliance Order on the table and show him exactly what it said. I wanted to quote Diana's praise and argue that we were building something inclusive. I wanted to beg him to choose one of the three educators I was told expressed an interest in my job. I wanted to say it all. Instead, I said nothing. I knew too much pushback could cost me more than credibility. It could close doors I hadn't even seen yet.

As I left his office, the exchange played on a loop in my mind. His comments were fair and even encouraging, but I couldn't shake the feeling of being held back. There was no space for nuance in the policy. No allowance for cultural context, for trust, for language as a bridge.

I thought about the strategies I had used in past years. The way I adapted lessons to reflect my students' lives. Back then, flexibility was seen as responsive, but now the scripted lesson plans and checklists ruled. The creativity, the relationships, the trust-building moments were being pushed aside.

I remembered Kris and how she welcomed different perspectives. She saw connection as the heart of educating. I hadn't learned to lead from a manual. I had learned from those who trusted me to know the children, work with my teaching assistants, and effectively implement a classroom curriculum.

***

I approached the study room at the university library. The motion lights flicked on as I stepped inside. The table seemed to invite the backpack full of literature I was about to unpack. Once I was set up, my final paper stared back at me. The words were sharp and definitive, as if daring me to challenge them.

The conceptual framework I had constructed was called the Four Core Elements for Effective Inclusion: leadership attuned to early childhood special education, a collaborative service delivery model, meaningful pre- and in-service education, and the use of peer models to foster authentic relationships. Each element had once felt transformative in my work as an early childhood professional, but now they seemed to exist in a world far removed from room 122.

I scrolled through my paper. In my section on leadership, I had written about the need for transparency, consistency, and uniting teachers, families, and service providers around a shared vision. In reality, leadership at Vista was anything but unified. Jorge's observation of our classroom revealed how fractured the system was, with district policies and agendas pulling in different directions. His critique of Lillie's and Cecilia's use of Spanish showed how those policies could undercut the very relationships that were essential to inclusion. The gaps in communication between him, Diana, the English Language Development Department, and the Early Childhood Education Department left me feeling stranded. I had studied models of distributed and responsive leadership, but what I saw each day felt disconnected from those ideals.

Collaboration, my second element, felt equally fragile. Specialists rotated in and out under the weight of the Binding Compliance Order, often arriving without context for our work with the new curriculum. Their recommendations came as isolated directives rather than as part of an ongoing, integrated plan. The transdisciplinary approach, in which specialists and classroom teachers shared responsibility for interventions, was not possible with Every Early Learner Succeeds. Even with Mr. Tom spending one day a week in our classroom, genuine collaboration never emerged. What we had instead was fragmented, inconsistent, and far from what children truly needed.

The third element, training, too, failed to match the needs of our classroom. My formal education offered theory, but the in-service sessions from the district were often irrelevant to the realities of our jobs: multiple languages, varying abilities, and a scripted curriculum that fit none of it. The professional development felt more like boxes to check rather than tools to strengthen our practice. The gap between what I was learning in my coursework at the university and what I was being given at work was wide and exhausting.

Even the peer models, the element that seemed most promising, was hindered by the system. I had seen small moments of connection, like those in the winter market, but these happened despite the structures around us, not because of them. Without stronger leadership, genuine collaboration, and training that prepared us for real classroom conditions, even peer relationships felt like they were balanced on unstable ground.

I scrolled to my paper's conclusion. The framework read like a roadmap: leadership, collaboration, training, and peer modeling. It was sound, and I believed in it. Yet I could not ignore the dissonance between what I had written and what I was living. Vista's systems were fragmented. Leadership was inconsistent. Collaboration felt fragile. Training was spotty. Peer models thrived only when the rest of the structure supported them.

I thought of Natalie's words: *"You need to take care of yourself and be present with us before you can be present for others."* The itinerant position had become more than a career move. It was my way forward in Metro Denver Unified—a chance to align my work with the vision I had laid out in this paper. I imagined visiting multiple classrooms and helping teachers and families apply these principles in the daily routine.

I closed my laptop and leaned back in the chair. This was not just an academic exercise. It was a reminder that inclusion was worth fighting for, even in a system that made it difficult to live any of it out each and every day. Still, as my mind kept naming contradictions, the concepts I was learning in school and the transfer of knowledge into my work with children and families were not going to come together until I was in the itinerant role.

CHAPTER 11

BEST TEACHER EVER

Three weeks away from the classroom for winter break had not brought the clarity I had hoped for. The weight of emails that greeted me on Monday morning reminded me of everything unresolved. Each day that followed felt like a continuation of last semester's uphill battle: unanswered questions, uncertain timelines, and the constant effort to balance my responsibilities in room 122 before stepping into the itinerant position.

The fluorescent lights overhead cast a sterile glow, dulling the late-afternoon sunset painting the playground outside. I sat at my desk that Thursday afternoon, glaring at my laptop screen. An email from Jorge announcing the long-term substitute posting had landed in my inbox earlier that day. The fact that they just determined the need for a job posting made me feel ill. Until reading that email, I had clung to the itinerant role as a step toward the vision I believed in: classrooms where access, participation, and support were a reality. Where I could witness the Four Core Elements for Effective Inclusion in action.

I glanced at the rows of neatly stacked chairs and organized learning centers. The order of the classroom could not compete with the cornucopia of negative emotions stirring my thoughts. I leaned back in my chair, staring at the ceiling. My memories circled, replaying the last few months of frantic text messages, conflicting directives, strained conversations with Jorge, and Diana's uplifting words punctuated by emoticons. Ana's words from her classroom echoed in my mind. I wanted to believe things would work out.

I began to close my laptop. Just before the lid clicked shut, a notification chimed through the speakers. A new email from human resources. I opened it.

Dear Andrew,

Great teaching is the single most important factor in driving improved student outcomes, which is why Metro Denver Unified School District is committed to ensuring that we have highly effective teachers to support the success of all our students.

The attainment of non-probationary status represents a meaningful milestone in a teacher's career and is the result of demonstrated effectiveness. We know that it takes time to develop the skills to be effective in the classroom and to demonstrate consistent levels of high performance.

School administrators will have the following options at the end of the school year, with respect to probationary teachers with at least three years of service:

- *Renewal with award of non-probationary status*
- *Renewal with continued probationary status*
- *Non-renewal*

Over the next several months, you will continue conversations with your principal. You should also be reviewing goals you have set, reflecting on your instructional practice, and analyzing student learning and achievement throughout this year.

If you have questions, please contact your principal.

Sincerely,

Helen O'Brien

Chief Human Resources Officer

Metro Denver Unified School District

I reread it. Once. Twice. My pulse quickened. On the surface, it seemed like a standard HR update, but the timing rattled me. The job posting. The itinerant position. The court-ordered observations. Jorge's Teaching Observation Protocol walkthroughs.

I shook my head. I had done everything I could to educate the children, support families, and collaborate with my classroom team. I was more than effective. Yet a shadow of doubt lingered. What if it was not?

I sat motionless, staring at the screen. Would any of it matter if I was not even at Vista next year? But that thought felt wrong too. Non-probationary status was not just a box to check. It was validation. Job security. A signal that my work mattered to the people I served and to the system I was still trying to believe in.

I closed my laptop. The silence in the room pressed in on me. Concerns and doubts that began when Diana and I had first started exchanging personal text messages screamed at me. I thought about the parents who had trusted me. I thought about Lillie and Cecilia, navigating responsibilities that challenged their ethics and kept them silent. Would my actions, or inaction, impact them? Would it impact the children next year?

The classroom phone rang. It was Jorge. He asked me to stop by his office before I left for the evening.

I slung my mailbag over my shoulder and walked down the quiet hallway. My steps were slow and heavy. Jorge was waiting at his desk, a few papers stacked neatly in front of him. The overhead lights cast a long reflection against the darkened windows. The custodian's cart squeaked faintly in the hallway, reminding me that we were among the last still inside the building.

"Andrew," Jorge greeted with a polite smile, gesturing to the chair across from him. "Come in, have a seat."

I sat. The chair creaked beneath me. My mind raced, but I let him speak first.

"I know it's been a long road, but I wanted to confirm you received my email stating Grace submitted the requisition for the long-term substitute today," he said, his tone steady and measured.

"Yeah. I received the email. The posting said the position needs to be filled by February 6. Is that correct?" I replied cautiously.

He nodded. "It's a tight deadline, but I'm optimistic. In the meantime, I want us to be clear on expectations. Whether this lasts a month or the rest of the year, I want to make sure you feel supported while we meet the needs of the school."

He walked me through a list of next steps: encouraging Cindy, the appointed early childhood education team lead, to structure early childhood meetings, providing Lillie and Cecilia with planning support, and addressing parent concerns more directly. Jorge's voice was steady. Thoughtful. Rehearsed.

They were all good ideas. Necessary, even. "Thank you," I said evenly. "I appreciate transparency."

He nodded. "I hope you can trust that I'm doing what I can."

As I stepped outside into the January night, cold air cut through the top of my coat. I replayed our conversation in my head. Jorge had said all the right things. Still, the gnawing doubt remained. Diana's unfulfilled promises. Virginia's encouragement. Natalie's gentle concern.

I no longer knew what action would look like. I only knew that waiting had worn me down more than any decision ever could. In room 122, I had already asked myself whether leadership was found in compliance that preserved the district, or in resistance that carried consequences I could not yet understand. Maybe this was the moment to stop waiting. Maybe this was the moment to resist. But how?

***

The scent of grease and fried potatoes greeted me as I pushed open the door to McDonald's. It was 11:00 a.m., and the restaurant was quieter than I had expected. The lull before the lunch rush left a calm stillness in the air. I spotted Virginia sitting by the window with her laptop closed and a steaming cup of coffee in front of her. She waved as I approached. Her warm smile cut through the frustration I had been carrying all week.

"Hey, stranger," she said, moving her purse off the table. "Happy New Year. How are you holding up?"

I took off my jacket and slid into the booth with a sigh. "Barely," I admitted. "I'm running on fumes, and it's only been two weeks."

Her eyes softened. "That bad already?"

I nodded, glancing at my phone before tucking it away. "The long-term sub situation is still a mess. I've accepted the uncertainty, but it's hard to focus on anything except what comes next . . . whether I'm still in room 122 or somewhere else entirely."

"What's going on?" she asked.

I told her about the back-and-forth between Jorge and the Early Childhood Education Department, Early Childhood Special Education Department, and Student Services Department on the various policies and contradictions. "Each new answer seemed to undo any sense of progress."

Virginia let out a low whistle. "Typical. Bureaucracy at its finest."

"Exactly. Every time we get close to a decision, another hurdle appears. Meanwhile, I'm trying to hold things together in room 122, knowing I might be gone before February 6. If they find someone, it would be irresponsible for me to stay. Oddly, I'm starting to see leaving as the more ethical choice."

She studied me. "How are Lillie and Cecilia handling it?"

"They're doing their best, but the uncertainty is wearing on everyone. Jorge has been helpful in some ways. He's encouraging

Cindy, the early childhood education team lead, to strengthen team meetings, and he'll help respond to parent concerns more directly, but the constant delays are exhausting."

"And how are you handling it?"

The question caught me off guard. "I don't know. I'm trying to keep it together for the kids and the team. Sometimes . . . I feel like it's pointless. My two classes this semester, Supports in the Inclusive Classroom and School Leadership, help me make sense of the circumstances. Still, hope feels like a stretch most days."

"It's not pointless, Andrew. You're doing the best you can inside a system full of paradoxes. That puts you in a rare position to bridge practice and theory, especially with your leadership work."

I told her about my vision for inclusion, the Four Core Elements, and my longing to create a classroom where both children and adults felt as if they belonged. She reminded me that change begins with people.

"You think I could still make room 122 into a truly inclusive classroom? One where every child has access, the necessary supports, and can participate? Where everyone feels a sense of belonging . . . if I stay?" I asked.

"I do. It may not look exactly how you pictured it, but start with the people and build from there."

Her words were blunt. What I studied for my classes made sense in the quiet of the library. In the rush of work, though, I was still reactive and barely keeping up. At that moment, I realized I had been so focused on leaving that I wasn't truly looking at the possibilities of personal growth in room 122. At what was still in front of me, most importantly of which were the people.

***

February 6 came and went. No one contacted me about the fate of the itinerant position. My energy, with the hope of refocusing on co-creating an inclusive classroom, was swallowed by daily fires. By the afternoon of Thursday, February 13, every frustration, disappointment, deception, and dismissal from the past six months had built into something I could no longer contain.

As I pulled out of the parking lot, the drone of the engine filled the silence. Exhaustion had settled into my body well before lunch that day. No amount of patience could smooth over the cracks anymore. At the root of it all was the absence of communication from Diana and Jorge. I needed closure.

I tapped the button on my steering wheel to call Diana, who answered on the second ring.

"Hey, Andrew," she said. Her voice was warm, but something heavy clung to it.

"Hi Diana," I replied. "How's it going?" I tried masking my intent.

She sighed. "Andrew, I'm so sorry. Things didn't go the way we had hoped."

There it was. The truth I had braced myself for.

"Yeah . . . I figured that when no one said anything after February 6. I kept telling myself maybe the deadline changed."

"I know. And I hate that you were left waiting like that," she said. "You deserve better."

"I appreciate that," I replied, keeping my voice steady. "At least I get to finish the year in 122. That matters. I've been rethinking my earlier approaches to inclusion and shifting my focus on possibilities." It wasn't a lie, but the gratitude sat beside deep disappointment. I could be grateful and still feel profoundly let down.

"I still believe in you," Diana said. "Everything I've told you about your value is true. You're exactly who we need. The good news is you can start the itinerant role next year. There's no need to reapply."

Her reassurance felt distant. I turned onto Diamond Avenue, unsure whether to believe in another promise.

"Can I ask something, Diana? Why did this fall apart?" My frustration cracked through.

"The system. Bureaucracy," she said. "I fought for this. I promise you that. But it's behind us now. There's a place for you next year. You have my word."

As I approached the on-ramp of Highway 144, the weight of the past six months pressed harder.

"Diana . . . how can I trust . . . you?"

There was a pause. "Because I won't let it happen again," she said. Then her voice dropped. "The truth is, Jorge never saw what you were doing as valuable. He never understood your leadership. Andrew, do you want the truth?"

I didn't, but I couldn't speak.

"He feels threatened by you. He wants to push you out of the district. If you left Vista, he'd no longer have control."

Her words slammed into me.

Jorge, the one who had smiled, nodded, offered support, assured me he was doing his best, and wanted me to do my best, had been undermining me all along. The curriculum, the compliance mandates, the silence, the undercutting . . . it wasn't just an oversight. It was intentional.

My jaw locked. My grip on the wheel shook.

The fury was too much, but I couldn't let Diana hear it.

"Diana, I just got home. I need to let you go."

"Oh, of course."

"Thanks again," I said, voice cracking. The call ended, and I pulled onto the shoulder of the highway.

Three lanes of traffic blurred past. I tried to breathe deeply, but my body refused. My chest collapsed. My throat closed. Tears erupted. My neck gave way. I fell forward, initially suppressing the urge to scream, but my will betrayed me.

Within a few minutes, I was able to catch my breath. The storm inside me slowed. I steadied my hands, stretched my face, and considered the ten minutes left in my commute.

Jorge was out of my control, but silence would not serve me. I needed to speak with him. Avoidance was not an option. Our past conversations had grounded me. He had offered support, however performative. I didn't know what to say that hadn't already been said, but I would not disappear. Not now.

I merged back into traffic and drove the rest of the way home.

***

Natalie and the girls had gone to bed hours earlier. I sat in the closet-office. The house was quiet except for the low hum of the space heater. The blinking cursor on my screen hovered over a draft of an email to Jorge. I leaned back and pressed my hands against my face. The words I had written felt raw and exposed. Like the drive home hours earlier, tears crowded the corners of my eyes.

I reread the draft. My frustrations spilled into sentences that felt both cathartic and terrifying.

Good evening, Jorge,

On my way home this afternoon, I broke down in tears. The breakdown was a product of ongoing job stress, and I want to share more clearly what has been weighing on me.

For the first time in my career, I am using an early childhood curriculum that requires an intense focus on general early childhood education. This would be manageable if it weren't combined with significant responsibilities for children with disabilities, while my teaching assistants and I are also restricted from speaking the primary language of most of the children in our classroom.

Working with children who have disabilities has always been demanding and deeply meaningful. In the past, flexible curricula allowed my team and me to balance diverse support needs effectively. This year, however, that flexibility is gone, and the result has been overwhelming.

I want to be both an effective early childhood education teacher and an effective early childhood special education teacher. Yet when I cannot provide the necessary, responsive support for the children, I struggle to sustain the quality of teaching I hold myself to.

You've often asked what you can do to help. I've hesitated to respond before, but now I believe I must. I need your help in finding a sustainable way to manage both roles without reaching the point of exhaustion.

One possible solution would be to request a substitute on days when my responsibilities as an early childhood special education teacher are especially heavy, such as during upcoming Individual Education Program transition meetings. On those days, I could remain on-site, completing paperwork, attending meetings, and ensuring compliance and quality. I'm also open to other ideas if you have alternative recommendations.

Considering that the deadline for hiring a long-term substitute has passed, I hope we can identify an immediate way to make this workload more manageable for the remainder of the year.

Happy Valentine's Day, and thank you for your ongoing support.

Andrew

I didn't want to send the email without a second opinion. Virginia's wisdom had steadied me before, and I hoped she could help me make sense of what I was trying to say. Without overthinking it, I copied the draft into a new message and typed a quick note:

Virginia, I need your thoughts. Am I being too honest here?

I hit send. The laptop's glow faded as I closed the lid. I crawled into bed next to Natalie, the words of the email looping through my mind.

The next morning passed in a haze. I left the duplex before anyone else woke up and drove to Vista in silence. Throughout the morning, I thought obsessively about the email, waiting for Virginia's response. It finally arrived just before the afternoon class.

Andrew,

This email is all you. It's raw, honest, and reflective. I wouldn't change a thing because it needs to come from your heart. Be true to yourself and don't overthink it. The words are there. Let them speak for you.

Virginia

Her encouragement steadied me, though it didn't erase the fear of laying myself bare in front of Jorge. Still, I knew I had to send it.

That afternoon, as the children played outside, Lillie and Cecilia offered to take the lead. I stayed behind, grateful for the solitude. The classroom was quiet except for the distant sounds of laughter and the occasional shout from the playground. I sat at my desk, laptop open, rereading the email one last time. The mouse arrow hovered over the send icon.

The words captured everything: the impossible task of balancing a scripted curriculum when two-thirds of the children have Individual Education Programs or speak a language the teachers aren't allowed to speak, special education responsibilities, and the daily emotional toll of everything in between. They carried the weight of the past few months and the reality that I would be finishing the year in room 122, no longer protected by the illusion of a pending transition.

With a deep breath, I clicked send.

It was Friday, February 14, 1:53 p.m.

Happy Valentine's Day, I thought cynically.

***

The weekend stretched on endlessly. I checked my email countless times at the library, waiting for a response from Jorge. Every notification made my heart race, only to be followed by disappointment when it wasn't him. I tried not to let it interfere with family time, focusing on playing with Citlali and Itzel, though anticipation hung over me like an ominous gray cloud.

His reply finally came at 9:15 p.m. on Sunday night.

When I saw it, I hesitated. Part of me didn't want to open it. What if it dismissed everything I had shared? What if it confirmed the creeping feeling I had that I was on my own?

Still, I clicked.

Jorge opened by recognizing that I was going through a difficult time. He hoped the experience would lead to professional growth and offer me insight into my values and what motivated me.

His tone was professional, even empathetic on the surface, but the subtext stung. The reference to "insight into my values" felt like a veiled critique, as though my struggles stemmed from my lack of self-awareness rather than structural reality. My fingers floated over the keyboard, ready to reply, though I forced myself to keep reading.

Jorge suggested I reach out to teachers at his previous school for support with meeting the needs of children with Individual Education Programs. A few teachers, he noted, had experience in both special education and early childhood education. With a little more effort, I should be able to teach the curriculum.

The suggestion felt dismissive. He knew I had been teaching for twelve years. He was aware I had spent countless hours trying to adapt the curriculum to meet the needs of children who did not speak English. Jorge's response didn't acknowledge any of this. His encouragement to just "teach the curriculum" brought back memories of our long, circular conversations in his office that left me feeling powerless.

He referenced my frustrations during my first year with the previous curriculum, implying this was just another adjustment period.

Heat rose in my face, and my neck stiffened. He was suggesting I was resistant to change, not recognizing the immense challenges of my circumstance.

Then came the paragraph that hit the hardest.

He encouraged me to reach out to the Explorer teachers at Vista who could help me develop classroom management strategies.

It felt like a slap in the face. I had been doing everything he suggested all year. I had sought out advice from the early childhood education team, asked Tom and the other special education support staff for resources, and collaborated with peers who completed the English Language Development Department courses with me. None of it had been enough.

Then came the final blow.

Jorge reminded me that I had already used my personal leave time on professional development. He wrote that the budget did not allow for additional subs. *Most times I'm out, there isn't a sub. My students are just divided between Explorer classrooms. Where did that money go?* I thought disdainfully to myself. He offered to help me reorganize my schedule to better "utilize" my planning periods.

The proposition was cruel. Those planning periods were already consumed by paperwork, parent communication, and an endless curriculum to-do list. This wasn't a solution. It was a reminder of how little support I had.

Jorge closed by offering to meet in person to discuss other potential solutions. He wished me well and encouraged me to enjoy the rest of my weekend.

Enjoy my weekend? The words felt empty.

I sat back, staring at the screen. My jaw, shoulders, and hands clenched. Exhaustion and frustration surged to the surface. His email, wrapped in civility, stripped away any illusion that help was coming. The events of the year replayed in my mind: the broken promises, the endless hurdles, the moments when I gave everything I had, only to be told it wasn't enough.

His response suggested the problem was me. That I wasn't resourceful enough, adaptable enough, or simply strong enough to make it work.

I took a deep breath and thought of the children in my classroom, the families who had placed their trust in me, and the colleagues who had become my lifeline. They were the reason I hadn't applied for the associate professor position at Rocky Mountain Community College. They were the motivation for my doctoral work. Adapting and being resourceful were the cornerstones of my teaching approach for the past eleven years.

I grabbed my journal and a pen. The words spilled out in a torrent. I wrote about the events that led to this moment, the fragmented communication, and the expectations that ignored every aspect of relationships. I wrote about the dreams I had for the itinerant position and the crushing realization that they had slipped away.

Somewhere in the early hours of the morning, I began to write about what I could do next.

You can only control what you can control. Letting go isn't giving up. It's survival, I wrote, pressing the pen hard against the paper.

I can control how I respond. I can focus on my classroom, on the children and families who need me. I can end this year strong, for the children and families, not for the district and not for Jorge. I must forgive and forget.

I repeated the last sentence three times. It was an honorable ideal. Deep down, I knew the relapse was inevitable. That was the story of my school year.

The only comfort I had was Diana's promise from just days before that the itinerant job would be mine next year.

By 1:30 a.m., my hand ached, and seven pages in my journal were full. My mind felt clearer, though the skepticism in my own handwriting made it plain: I didn't know if I could really let go.

***

The sun hovered just above the horizon as I pulled into the Vista parking lot the morning of February 18. I walked toward room 122, still thinking about the journal entry I had written six hours earlier. Jorge's email had cracked something open in me, exposing a truth I could no longer ignore. Virginia's words came to mind. *Leadership may not look exactly how you pictured it, but start with the people and build from there.* Leadership wasn't about titles or positions. It wasn't about escaping room 122 or finding the perfect job. Leadership was about showing up, having the courage to act with integrity, and valuing the authentic relationships around me—Lillie and Cecilia, the families, the children. It was about finding strength in the face of adversity and continuing forward, not because the path was easy, but because it was the only one that felt honest.

The morning passed in a fog. After the last child left, the classroom fell silent. The quiet didn't soothe me. It pressed in like a low ceiling, heavy and unyielding. I sat at my desk eating the peanut butter sandwich I had thrown together that morning, my body going through motions my heart could not define.

An email appeared in my inbox. It was from Diana. The subject referenced the message I had sent Jorge.

I stared at the screen. How had it even reached her? The thought of Jorge forwarding it twisted in my gut. He had promised to support me. He had asked for honesty. Now it felt like I had handed him my heart, only to watch him deliver it to someone else without warning.

The words in Diana's message only deepened the ache Jorge had started.

She opened by acknowledging the year's challenges, agreeing with Jorge's take on the situation. She wrote that although things had been difficult, there were valuable lessons to be learned.

Valuable lessons? Was that what this year had been reduced to?

Her tone was composed, professional, and unshakably distant.

She referenced the Every Early Learner Succeeds curriculum, explaining that other teachers in similar positions had managed to implement it successfully. She offered to connect me with them for conversation and guidance.

A conversation? A week earlier, she had warned me Jorge didn't value my leadership. Now she was siding with him, pretending that none of that had been said. Why would I seek insight from people with no connection to my students or their families?

Then came the deeper cut. Diana wrote that, given my credentials, I should be able to adapt any curriculum to meet special education requirements. She acknowledged it would require significant thinking but assured me she believed my mind was capable.

My mind?

Was this supposed to be encouragement?

It sounded like blame. As if the problem wasn't systemic but personal. As if the reason I was struggling was because I hadn't tried hard enough. There was no mention of Jorge's misinterpretation of the Binding Compliance Order or his failure to support inclusive practices. No acknowledgment of how impossible the situation had become.

She referenced the tears. She mentioned my doctoral program, suggesting it might be contributing to my stress. There was no mention of any of her past praise for my academic work. Then she reminded me that success in this role required wearing many hats and that not everyone was suited for the task. My reflection, she concluded, would help me find the right path forward, which may not be as a teacher.

May not be as a teacher!

She signed off wishing me the best of luck.

Without thinking, I reached for the "Best Teacher Ever" mug on my desk, the one I had carried with me since my first year in Tucson. I hurled it across the room. Ceramic exploded against the wall with a sickening crack, leaving a jagged hole in the drywall.

The silence that followed was deafening.

I stood frozen, chest heaving, adrenaline coursing through me like fire. The mug lay in shards on the floor. The words once printed across it were now splintered and meaningless.

For months, I had clung to professionalism and ethics. I had written reflections instead of raising my voice. I had cried in my car and scribbled notes at midnight. This moment felt different. The rupture was real and raw. In the violence of the act, something inside me surfaced, something honest. I could no longer pretend everything was fine.

Ana appeared in the doorway. Her eyes moved from the broken wall to the mug's shattered remains, then to me.

"Andrew," she said softly, stepping inside, "what happened?"

I didn't speak. I couldn't. She walked forward and wrapped me in a tight hug. My body trembled. I whispered, "I'm so sorry. I don't know what came over me."

She held me quietly, then gently pulled back. Her eyes searched mine with concern.

"Do you want to talk about it?"

I shook my head. "No. Thank you."

Ana didn't push. She nodded and glanced once more at the wall. "Well," she said, her voice calm, "when you're ready, you know where to find me."

She left without another word.

I remained in the silence, alone with my thoughts and the mess I had made. I crouched down, gathering the shards of ceramic into my hands. Each piece cut into memories of classrooms, children, families, and years spent believing I could make a difference. The mug had been a symbol of my ideals as a teacher. Now it lay broken, like the year, like the path I thought I was walking.

That afternoon, after the last child had gone home, Beatriz lingered in the classroom with Jimmy and Ellie. Lillie and Cecilia were quietly tidying the shelves. I knew they had seen the hole in the wall. I could feel their concern in the air, though no one spoke of it.

Beatriz turned to me, her eyes soft. "Are you okay, Mr. Andrew?"

I tried to smile. "I'm good. Just a little stressed, that's all."

She didn't buy it. "You don't seem like yourself," she said gently.

Her kindness broke something loose. I began sharing bits and pieces. Six months of tension and disappointment unraveled. I didn't tell her everything. I didn't want to burden her, the same way I had held back with Mr. Tom. I simply admitted that I no longer felt like the teacher I wanted to be.

Beatriz listened closely. "Mr. Andrew," she said, "you're an amazing teacher. Jimmy loves coming to school because of you. You've created something special here. I couldn't have asked for a better start to his education."

The words caught me off guard, and a lump rose in my throat.

"Thank you," I said, my voice thick. "That means more than you know."

She smiled. "We love you, Mr. Andrew. You, Cecilia, Lillie . . . all of you. Don't forget that."

She gathered her children and waved goodbye. Lillie and Cecilia continued working in near silence. I could feel their care, even if no one said anything aloud.

Later, I stared at the hole in the wall. The mug's pieces sat in a small box on my desk. I couldn't bring myself to throw them away.

The hole and the mug were more than damaged. They were evidence of a career splintering under the strain of everything I had tried to hold together. My year would not be the same after Diana's email. The version of me who believed professionalism, integrity, and inclusion could coexist without cost had cracked. Yet Beatriz's words lingered. Maybe not everything was broken. Maybe, even now, I mattered.

I couldn't glue the mug back together, not really. It would never be whole. But I could finish the year. Not for the district. Not for Jorge. For the children and families who trusted me. For Lillie and Cecilia. For the work we had built together in room 122. And for myself. What shifted was not relief but resolve. I stopped waiting to make things right and began choosing what I would carry forward and what I would no longer try to hold together alone. *Forgive and forget.* This time, I meant it. No relapses.

CHAPTER 12

SWISS CHEESE

The twenty-foot walk from the car to McDonald's was as cold as cold gets in Denver. Passing through the foyer, I felt the rush of warmth from the grills. Virginia was already seated at our usual table, a stack of papers resting beside her laptop.

"Hey, Andrew," she said, smiling warmly as I slid into the seat across from her. "How's it going?"

I sighed, removing my winter outerwear. "It's been a lot."

She leaned forward. "Want to talk about it?"

I hesitated, but the events of February 18 were still sharp in my mind: Diana's email, the mug shattering against the wall, the stunned silence from Ana, Lillie, and Cecilia, and Beatriz's kind words afterward. If there was anyone I could unpack this with, it was Virginia. I began to tell her the whole story.

She listened without interrupting, her presence steady. When I finished, she said, "You are being too hard on yourself. You're human, and you're working in a system that doesn't leave space for that humanity."

I shook my head. "It's not just the system. If I want to be a leader through all this and beyond, I need to be able to hold it together."

"You have been holding too much for too long. You're navigating an environment that pulls you in opposing directions, constantly making you question your value. Try not to let what's happening in room 122 tarnish your vision."

She slid an academic article across the table and pointed at the title, "The Fail-Safe Schools Challenge: Leadership Possibilities from High Reliability Organizations." She said, "You're caught between competing expectations: the district, the administration, your team, and your own ethics. The authors of this article use the Swiss Cheese Model to describe how cultures work in an organization. Each one is a layer of the system. Every layer has holes, gaps, limitations, and blind spots, but when the layers overlap, the holes do not always line up. That is how systems stay functional. Problems arise when too many holes align and something falls through" (Bellamy et al. 2005).

I nodded slowly, skimming the section. "That's exactly how it feels. Every layer I'm part of—the classroom, the early childhood education team, the district—has gaps. Some days, it feels like they all line up."

"That's the challenge," she said. "You can't fix all the layers at once. Your classroom is one layer of the system. The others— the administration, the district, even the neighborhood—have their own structures and weaknesses. The best you can do is strengthen your layer. When you keep your section strong, you prevent the holes from aligning. That is leadership."

"Ana, Lillie, Cecilia, Mr. Tom . . . together, we maintain a balance."

"They matter," she agreed. "They are part of your layer. But remember, balance also depends on what you can't see from within. You need outside perspectives, people who aren't immersed in early childhood education or the daily rhythm of the classroom. They can help you notice patterns you might miss because you're too close to the work."

She gestured to our booth. "Look at us. How do you feel right now?"

I paused, noticing that the tightness in my shoulders had eased. "Better."

"Exactly. Stepping away helps you see the system differently. It reminds you that your worth isn't confined to one space. You are part of a network of layers, and the health of one affects the others."

Her words stayed with me. She was right. I had been so focused on what was breaking apart that I hadn't noticed what still held together. I kept searching for a culture that prioritized inclusion. Subcultures that overlapped, exposing no holes. That wasn't my current reality, but the conversation reminded me that leadership didn't have to start with staggering all the holes. It could start with reinforcing my own layer. Leadership meant showing up, acting with integrity, and maintaining balance through the relationships that sustained me.

I let out a breath. "I forgot how much I need reminders like this. It starts with room 122."

Virginia smiled softly. "That's why you're not alone in this work. Sometimes the reminder comes from others. You just have to let people in."

***

The library study room was silent. I leaned closer to the screen and reread the reflection prompt: *Reflect on how you, as a leader, navigate differences in roles, priorities, and perspectives to build alignment within your organization.*

The question brought me back to my recent conversation with Virginia and the article she shared about the Swiss Cheese Model. What stayed with me wasn't the metaphor itself but the responsibility it implied. Leadership wasn't about repairing every layer or closing every gap. It was about tending to the one I inhabited and recognizing how my choices affected the stability of the whole.

I stared at the blinking cursor, trying to find words that would capture that truth. After several stagnant minutes, I opened the paper I had written months earlier about how I, as a leader, would support professionals in my organization to work toward a shared vision. In that earlier paper, crafted here in this same room, I had laid out the Four Core Elements for Effective Inclusion: leadership, collaboration, training, and peer models.

The framework still shaped my thinking, yet the months since had tested every principle. As I worked to strengthen my connections in room 122 and at Vista, I was sharpening my understanding of how the layers needed to create high-quality, meaningful inclusive environments that could fit together. Each element in the culture was in the slices of cheese. None of the pieces were perfect, but together, with the same ingredients, they formed something strong enough to keep children and families from falling through the gaps.

I had known for years that inclusion was never something one teacher could hold alone. It had to be collective, built on relationships, and allowed to take shape organically. Now I was beginning to understand how leadership within and beyond affected the other three core elements. Leadership was no longer an abstract ideal. It had become a daily choice to act with consistency and integrity. Leadership was the ingredient that gave the cheese its form in every culture and subculture.

I sat back, staring at the wall-to-wall whiteboard in front of me as though it were a canvas and my thoughts the paint. Collaboration was about building trust that creates consistency despite competing priorities. Mr. Tom modeled this by spending full days in room 122. He joined our play and routines instead of following the common practice of pulling children out for isolated sessions. His presence blurred the lines between "specialist" and "classroom teacher," showing what real shared ownership could look like. I embraced his philosophy. Lillie and Cecilia did the same in their own way. Rather than seeing myself as the expert in everything, I trusted them to lead activities and guide interactions with families in ways that reflected their strengths, not just my directions. That kind of trust created a classroom where everyone's expertise was valued.

Training needed to match the lived realities of classrooms like ours, not just the formalities of the Every Early Learner Succeeds curriculum. Opportunities for training were constant if we stayed open to them. The day we transformed dramatic play into a winter market after Thanksgiving came to mind. I didn't do it because it was in the curriculum; I did it because it reflected the children's own experiences and sparked their engagement in ways scripted lessons never could. I stayed connected to families even when they could not volunteer in the classroom and despite Jorge's refusal to allow more home visits. I found other ways to keep them involved in their child's learning. Lillie's decision to leave when her contracted hours ended, rather than cave to the pressure of staying late, was another kind of training. It reminded me that no matter how long I stayed in the classroom, no one could ever be fully prepared for a day in an early childhood education classroom. Pacing ourselves was part of sustaining our work.

Peer models only thrived when adults modeled the same sense of community we hoped to see in the children. Cecilia and Lillie demonstrated that sense of community when they welcomed new students and families with warmth. Collectively, we nurtured each student in room 122 and made space for them to be who they were, even when the schedule pushed us toward the next part of our routine. When I took Lillie's advice to advocate more for our classroom or when she asked questions about my teaching that made me see my work differently, we both learned. Those exchanges were as much a part of building community as the way we guided the children. All of these were daily examples of showing up, acting with integrity, and valuing relationships built on listening. They created the classroom culture. They were the ingredients for resilient Swiss cheese.

Through all this, though, the future still felt uncertain. The system around me looked less like a straight path and more like a series of overlapping layers, each with its own gaps and weaknesses. I was beginning to see that progress depended on how those layers connected, not on how perfectly they were built. My place was somewhere within them, steadying what I could so that less would fall through.

I leaned back in my chair, looking out the study room window to my right. My thoughts became motionless, orderly, like the framework guiding my academic work. The blank screen in front of me waited, so I began to write. The reflection paper became a reminder that systems did not have to be perfect for inclusion to live. Even with gaps, it was the ingredients and the connections between the layers that made it whole.

At last, I was reframing my experiences in room 122, the powerlessness, the frustration, the shame, and the emotions I still could not name. I did not have all the answers, but I was beginning to understand that inclusion has no destination, only direction. For now, that was enough.

***

Ana leaned back in her adult-sized chair, her hands resting on her swollen belly. The small metal frame creaked as she shifted, trying to find a moment of comfort. Her face, usually lit with humor, was tight with frustration and fatigue. Her lunch sat untouched.

"I swear, Andrew," she muttered, "if I could leave right now, I would. But Sergio and I, we can't afford it. And Jorge"— she gave a bitter laugh—"he won't let me take one more day off. I don't think he even cares what this is doing to me."

My heart clenched. I sat beside her, unwrapping my sandwich. "I'm so sorry. It's not right. You shouldn't have to keep pushing like this."

She pressed her hand to her lower back, eyes glassy with weariness. "I just need to make it through the next few weeks. But every day feels harder. It's worse knowing no one in leadership even notices."

I reached across the table and squeezed her hand. "You're incredible. Truly. You shouldn't have to do this alone."

Her eyes softened. "Thanks, Andrew."

We sat in silence for a moment, the soft murmur of children down the hallway filling the space between us.

"You just made me think of something," I said quietly. "I wrote this paper last weekend. The prompt asked how leaders navigate differences in roles, priorities, and perspectives to build alignment within their organizations. It's got me thinking about our early childhood education team."

Ana glanced at me, curious. "Like what?"

"Like how we started," I said. "Five strangers, placed on a team based on our professional titles. No clear roles, no shared direction. Then Sharon and the challenges with her actions . . . everything changed."

Ana's expression tightened, but she nodded. "That was awful. But it forced us to grow."

"It did," I agreed. "It taught us how to trust one another. Even now, with the Every Early Learner Succeeds curriculum, no subs, and split classes, I see how those lessons matter. We learned to work around the issues, to build something steady even when the school isn't."

She smirked faintly. "Sometimes it feels like we're not working around issues or steady."

"Maybe," I said, smiling. "But the ideas I wrote about in the paper help me see it differently. So, I'm going to use another metaphor. Sorry. The cardiovascular system won't work well."

"I like your metaphors. What is it?"

"Well, it's not my metaphor. I'm just using it. It's called the Swiss Cheese Model. It's the idea that every system, every team, has holes, like slices of cheese. None of us can fill every space, but when the layers overlap, the holes don't line up. The connections between us keep things from falling through."

As I spoke, my mind drifted to the Four Core Elements I had written about in the paper: leadership, collaboration, training, and peer models. They were the ingredients that gave classrooms their strength, the substance that made the slices hold together. I didn't say this to Ana, though, as it felt too abstract for the moment. What mattered now was the reminder that our team, imperfect as it was, still had the power to steady itself.

"That's what I need to remember this year," I continued. "It's not about pretending the holes don't exist. It's about building enough connection and trust to strengthen each layer. We need to support one another's needs with our strengths."

Ana smiled faintly. "So, we just have to keep the cheese stacked?"

I laughed. "And strengthening. Every time we show up for each other or adapt when something falls apart, we're making our layer more resilient. We can't control the system, but we can make our classrooms and team stronger."

Her smile softened, though her eyes stayed serious. "But what happens when one of us is gone? Like when you're pulled to another room, or I'm out sick? Then it feels like all the holes line up . . . y todo se viene abajo."

I exhaled. "That's what keeps me up at night. The system's fragile. Too fragile. That's part of why I wanted the itinerant role this year and why I still hope to move into it next school year. Not because I want to leave this, but because I want to help other teams build stronger layers. I want to help create systems that don't collapse every time something shifts."

Ana looked at me with quiet intensity. "Andrew, you'd be good at that. But you can't trust Diana. I don't want her to hurt you again. Your health and happiness matter too much." She paused, letting her words settle. "Do what's right for you, Natalie, and the girls."

Her concern sank deeper than she knew. "I get it," I said. "I want to do what's best for my family. But I also know I can make a difference for more classrooms in that role."

She smiled again, this time softer. "I know. Just promise you'll keep the focus on Natalie and the girls." Ana leaned forward and whispered, "She told me to say that, but it's true."

We both laughed, the tension loosening just enough to finish our lunches.

***

The short walk through the passageway to room 122 felt longer than usual, my mind churning with the conversation I'd just had with Ana and the countless tasks awaiting me before the afternoon group arrived. The room was quiet. The thumping of my own ruminations filled the space as I stepped inside.

Everything looked familiar, but after my conversation about Swiss cheese with Ana, something in me felt different. Sitting at my desk, I thought about the concept and how it applied to the room 122 culture. I visualized the new learners who had recently joined our afternoon class, especially those with Individual Education Programs. Balancing a developmentally appropriate environment with the individualized supports these children needed felt increasingly complex. It was a hole in the curriculum that lined up with a hole in special education, which lined up with a hole in Jorge's interpretations of the Binding Compliance Order.

My thoughts wandered to the morning's activities. Group time had gone more smoothly than usual, though I'd had to pivot midway. There were holes. The first book I had chosen didn't engage the children, especially those less familiar with English. I covered the hole with my ability to modify my teaching. I switched to a story that had stronger visuals, and everyone participated. It was a small win, but the lesson's intended objective was lost. It was a living example of the Swiss Cheese Model in my teaching approach.

Then there was Lobo, the stuffed wolf puppet. For years, he had helped me model conversations and social interactions. With the Every Early Learner Succeeds curriculum, puppets and stuffed animals were no longer allowed to "talk," a policy that felt counter to everything I knew about child engagement. I introduced Lobo during the story, animating him gently. As soon as the story ended, I placed him back in the cabinet, out of sight.

Lillie and Cecilia returned from lunch. They moved through the room with practiced ease, preparing materials and laying out the routine for our afternoon learners.

As I sat at my computer making revisions to my plans for the following morning, I thought about the transition song we had used that morning. We had struggled for weeks to get the new children calmly into group time. The song helped a little. Timing, tone, and patience did the rest. It wasn't perfect, but it was something.

"Hey, I was thinking about the morning group," I said, projecting my voice across the room so it would reach Lillie and Cecilia at the kidney table. "The story switch helped with engagement, but it disrupted the lesson objective. I'm wondering if there's a way we can—"

Lillie cut me off. "Andrew, I need to tell you something." Her voice was deliberate. Then she stood up and walked in my direction. Cecilia followed.

I stopped mid-sentence, startled by her tone. She glanced at Cecilia, who nodded.

"I've accepted a new job," Lillie said. "I'll be starting next week. March 23."

The room went still. "You're leaving?" The words escaped before I could soften them.

She nodded, her eyes apologetic. "I wasn't planning to. The opportunity came up, and it felt right. It's something I need . . . for my growth."

I swallowed hard, my mind racing. *Is it because of me? Should I have seen this coming?*

"I understand," I said finally, though the words were meaningless.

"I'm sorry to spring this on you. I care about this classroom. About you and Cecilia. The kids. The families. This decision wasn't easy."

Cecilia stepped in, calm and steady. "We'll figure it out, Andrew. We always do."

I nodded, managing a small smile. "Of course." But my thoughts fell silent. The lesson ideas, the curriculum planning, the song—everything faded beneath the wake of her words.

For a year and a half, Lillie's reflective questions, unwavering fairness, and calm presence had been essential. Her departure felt like losing part of our classroom identity. Yet part of me resisted the emotion. After everything I had put this team through, who was I to be disappointed?

"Lillie, can I ask something personal? . . . And you don't have to answer . . ." She nodded as Cecilia quietly moved to the back of the room.

"I'm sorry, but I have to ask. Has my behavior . . ." I reconsidered how to phrase my question. "Was there something I could have done differently?"

She gave a soft, knowing smile. "Andrew, it's not because of you. I mean, it is . . . but in a good way. You've helped me see beyond these walls. The way you stand up for kids, for families, for us . . . that's what I want to do too." Then she smirked. "The only difference is, I'm doing it outside the district. Because let's be real, you have to be a masochist to try that inside one."

"You're not wrong," I said, sighing.

"It's just too much, Andrew. The policies, the restrictions. It's too much."

I stood up. "I get it. I really do. I've always admired how you show up. You're fully yourself, no matter what."

"Thank you," Lillie replied, humbly.

Our words grew sparse, but meaning lingered in the silence.

Lillie joined Cecilia in prepping the classroom. Their quiet conversation became background noise as my thoughts drifted. English Language Development, Early Childhood Special Education, Early Childhood Education, Student Services, Teaching Observation Protocol, Vista . . . the political contradictions were endless. Facing them without Lillie felt impossible.

I thought about the morning circle, the curriculum shifts, the way we adjusted the room to support engagement. Every small act was part of something bigger, a constant effort to build safety and support for every learner. With Lillie and Cecilia, it felt like we were holding it all together.

What I had told Ana echoed back to me. Inclusion wasn't just about the kids. It was about the team. I hadn't just learned the Swiss Cheese Model from an article, conversation, or reflection paper. I had lived it. Together, Cecilia, Lillie, and I upheld the Four Core Elements for Effective Inclusion: leadership, collaboration, training, and peer models. Losing Lillie would reveal holes, but holes could be covered. Each layer was resilient and could still protect us.

The chorus of voices outside grew loud. Cecilia, Lillie, and I convened at the back door. "Would you like to tell the families, or should I?" I asked gently.

Lillie zipped up her coat. "Please let me. I'll prepare something for tomorrow." She paused. "Andrew, don't worry about me leaving. I know you'll be okay. You always are."

Her voice was kind but final. I pushed the door lever, welcoming the children and families that made our layers of cheese possible.

Lillie's departure would leave a hole, but Cecilia was still there. Mr. Tom. The kids. The families. Maybe a strong substitute. These were the layers in our classroom. Our Swiss cheese stack wasn't perfect, but it was real.

We would keep going. Because that's what the work demanded.

CHAPTER 13

VALUES

The familiar smell of McDonald's fries and burgers filled the air as Virginia and I settled into our weekly tradition. These Wednesday lunches were more than a brief escape. Virginia was the one person I could speak to without filtering my thoughts.

I unwrapped the deli sandwich I brought from home and took a bite, already thinking of how to begin.

"What's on your mind?" she asked before taking a sip of her coffee.

I looked down at my sandwich. "Too many holes in the cheese," I said, smirking. "It's been a lot again. The classroom keeps shifting: Lillie leaving, Ana preparing for maternity leave, and new children with significant support needs. I'm trying to keep the kids engaged with the Every Early Learner Succeeds curriculum, but it feels like everything is in flux."

Virginia nodded, her expression calm and curious. "And how are you handling it?"

"Well, I'm trying to make sense of the complexity through this paper I'm writing on structural leadership," I said. "I'm analyzing how different systems interact and affect one another. Living it, though, doesn't feel like clean layers or clearly defined roles at all. It feels more like a circulatory system where the blood flow is uneven, where some parts are thriving while others are barely getting oxygen. Room 122 is just one chamber of the heart, pumping as best it can, but the arteries and veins that connect us to families, administrators, and district offices twist and constrict. Sometimes the pulse reaches where it should. Most of the time, it doesn't."

Virginia tilted her head. "Yeah, I see what you're saying. How does that show up at Vista?"

"Take Jorge," I said. "He's part of the immediate circulation. Instead of keeping the blood moving evenly, he pushes with a pressure that doesn't match the rhythm of the rest of the system. His vision doesn't fit, and it strains the whole network. Then there's the Binding Compliance Order. It's a policy decision made far beyond the classroom, but it hit room 122 like a blockage in an artery. We have the skills, the relationships, and the language resources, but the flow keeps getting restricted."

Virginia leaned in. "So, what you're describing isn't just circulation. It's control, who regulates the flow and who doesn't."

Her words caught me off guard. I set down my sandwich, realizing how much I had been trying to force lived experiences into neat theoretical patterns. "Exactly," I said. "Room 122 feels like the heart, constantly working to keep things moving. But no heart can compensate forever when the system around it is constricted. The oxygen never reaches where it's needed most."

Virginia smiled slightly. "That's clearer. But remember, the heart doesn't control how much oxygen it receives. That's the respiratory system. That's where power sits."

Her words lingered in the quiet between us, tightening something in my chest.

After a pause, she added, "But you're still trying to make it work, even when the flow is limited. Why?"

"Because I have to," I said. "For the kids. For the families. For Lillie and Cecilia. For Tom. And for myself." I looked down at my half-eaten sandwich. "It's like the Swiss Cheese Model. No system is perfect. There are always holes. But if we work as a team with integrity . . . We have enough skills and strategies. We can be resilient and catch one another before we fall through."

Virginia leaned in. "Here's the common thread between the Swiss Cheese Model and the cardiovascular system metaphor: You're looking at what's happening in a single moment. What if you stepped back and looked at how the system was shaped over time? How multiple systems had to engage to create the moment you're experiencing. What if it was designed in a way that made it difficult for teachers to support one another's holes? To make teachers dependent . . . at the mercy of administrators and regulators? That kind of structure grants more power to people in roles like Diana's and Jorge's."

Her words were a shock of anger. "What the f—" I caught my words.

"I agree," she said, calm and steady. "The misuse of power can lead to significant harm, as you've witnessed."

I shook my head, contemplating the connections between Virginia's ideas and my experiences. "I think I've only seen it as what my colleagues and administrators do during specific events," I said. "I've thought many times about power as it relates to gender, race, economic class, et cetera, but I never consider how a school system could be built to consistently give some people more power than others."

"That is the difference between your academic views and what you're living," she said. "Support from your colleagues is essential, but if it relies on chance, it is fickle. When the structure itself provides those supports through mentorship, collaboration, real planning time, shared resources, people feel a sense of purpose and stability. There's shared power. But those need to be baked into the values of a team . . . of a school . . . of a district. I don't think connection and genuine support are widely held values anywhere."

It was a new way of looking at systems I thought I already understood. I had been focusing on individual actions, on my own leadership behaviors, on whether I was doing enough or speaking clearly enough. I hadn't been asking why the conditions required constant effort just to hold things together or why some voices were heard, while others were silenced. I hadn't been looking closely at how power was structured, only at how I moved within it.

As I walked back to my car, I returned to the paper on structural leadership and my definition of leadership: showing up, acting with integrity, valuing relationships—all predicated on listening. But I saw something I hadn't seen before. Whether I imagined it as a cardiovascular system or slices of Swiss cheese, the truth was the same: behind it all was power shaped over time. Leadership wasn't only about integrity, relationships, and listening. It was about who held power, how it was distributed, and whether the system itself allowed the heart to keep beating or the holes to reliably cover one another. That begins with an organization's values around power.

***

The hallway felt quieter than usual. The distant melody of children's voices and the shuffle of papers were the only sounds breaking the stillness. I arrived at the table where Ana, Sharon, Cindy, and Esmeralda were already seated, their expressions ranging from tired to cautiously curious.

Stephanie Peters had returned to our team meetings shortly after my Valentine's Day collapse. She wasn't so much an instructional coach as a steady, humorous presence—more mediator than manager. She sat at the head of the table, her calm demeanor balancing what we all knew would be another delicate conversation.

After lunch with Virginia, I had a clearer sense of how I wanted to show up. As frustrating as these team meetings could be, I needed to believe in the potential of our shared values as the ingredient for more resilient slices of Swiss cheese. I had emailed Stephanie beforehand with a few suggestions. I didn't want to present them myself, not in front of everyone. She responded with appreciation and followed up with a group email requesting we bring the values forms we had completed at the start of the year as part of the process for revising the team norms.

Stephanie began with her usual warmth. "Today, we're going to take a step back from instructional stuff. I want us to focus on values, both as individuals and as a team. This year has been difficult, but I believe reconnecting with what brought us to this work can guide us forward."

"We have the norms," Sharon interjected. "Why do we need to talk about values again?"

Stephanie gestured toward the poster on the wall and pointed to the third norm. "Sharon, we collaborate with openness and flexibility. This is a chance to practice. Let's begin." She motioned to the sheets in front of us.

"Let's start by reflecting on how these values play out in our work," Stephanie continued. "Andrew?"

I nodded. "Fostering collaboration has been a survival mechanism this year. With Lillie leaving and Ana preparing for maternity leave, it feels like the only way we're going to finish strong is by leaning on each other, not just professionally, but as people."

Cindy's voice followed. "That's true. But it's hard to build those connections when we're all stretched thin. It feels like we're just surviving, not really functioning as a team."

"That's exactly why values matter," Stephanie said. "When things get tough, they can ground us."

Ana shifted in her seat, clearly uncomfortable but determined. "Every Early Learner Succeeds doesn't align with how I was trained. It's like I've had to choose between what I know works and what we're told to do."

Sharon added, "This year feels like a reset. We were starting to get somewhere last year, and now it's like we've been thrown backward."

I thought of Virginia's words. "Someone reminded me recently that even when things feel out of our control, we can still choose how we show up. Maybe values like trust, flexibility, and support are the only real anchors we have."

Stephanie nodded. "Exactly. These values aren't just about aspirations. They're about what we practice every day. How do they show up in our team meetings, classrooms, and personal interactions? And how do they align with Vista's current values: collaboration, innovation, and equity?"

I thought about the previous values: perseverance, respect, integrity, diversity, and excellence. They weren't perfect, but they felt more like a distribution rather than an overreach of power. The new values felt disconnected. They didn't speak for us. They spoke for Jorge.

Then Ana surprised me, saying, "What about the values from before Jorge? P.R.I.D.E. That's what we used when Kris was principal."

Stephanie's face lit up. For the first time in months, it felt like someone from outside the classroom was genuinely listening.

The conversation flowed. Esmeralda admitted the curriculum initially stifled her creativity, but she had found ways to adapt. Cindy spoke about the need for more organization. Ana, exhausted but passionate, thanked the team for their support as she prepared for maternity leave.

Stephanie closed the meeting. "No one expects perfection. If we commit to our values, not just in theory but in practice, we can finish the year with purpose. Together."

After she left, the atmosphere shifted. We lingered in the atrium, more candid now that the formal meeting had ended.

"I don't know if I buy all this talk about shared values," Sharon said, arms crossed. "It sounds nice, but most of us don't even want to be here anymore."

She wasn't dismissive, just tired. Beneath the frustration was a fierce loyalty to something we feared we had already lost. Faith that our skills, knowledge, and passion still mattered.

Cindy sighed. "What's the alternative? We check out and leave the kids to fend for themselves? I can't do that."

Ana looked at me. "Andrew, what do you think?"

I paused. "This year has been harder than any of us expected. The values talk can feel hollow, but it's also all we've got. If we don't lean on those, on each other, then what's left? Jorge has all the power, and we're left to fend for ourselves. Alone."

Ana nodded. "I feel that's been our whole year. We can't change anything now. It's too late. I just hope we can hold it together for the kids. They deserve that much."

As we parted ways, I thought again about Virginia's words, that power is intentionally constructed over time to benefit some and marginalize others. The idea echoed the conversations I'd had in past college classes about power and privilege in society. Maybe the answer wasn't in trying to change the entire system or even the team. It lived in our collective values, daily acts of showing up, honoring one another's contributions, and standing together against the forces designed to pull us apart. We had to keep supporting each other, for the kids and the families.

***

The late March afternoon light filtered through the windows of room 122. Cecilia and I cleaned up the last of Lillie's farewell party before joining Lillie, who was standing with Beatriz and Kelly, Ricky's mom, near the back door.

"I still can't believe you're leaving," Beatriz was saying.

Lillie smiled. "I'll miss everyone so much. This was a hard decision."

Kelly nodded. "You've been so good with the kids. They'll miss you."

Lillie gave a small laugh. "I'll miss them too."

They said their goodbyes, and Lillie gathered her things. Cecilia and I stood watching.

"I'm going to stop by the office to finish paperwork before I go," Lillie said.

"Okay," I replied, walking in her direction with my arms open. "Thank you for everything," I said while we hugged.

After she left, Cecilia and I exchanged words of optimism. She gathered her items, and I walked to my desk. The room was quiet again. A notification chimed on my laptop. The subject line caught my eye: *David Alvarez*.

The message was from a case manager at Defending Rights Colorado. Eight people, including Jorge and Esmeralda, were woven into the unfamiliar conversation. As I read the thread that started weeks earlier, frustration rose in my chest. David had been transferred to Esmeralda's classroom in January to support his social, academic, and Spanish language development in an English Language Development–Spanish setting. We had believed the transition would benefit him, and he had been thriving in our classroom. Now something had gone wrong, and no one had told me.

I had seen it too many times before. When classrooms failed to adapt, they blamed the child instead of examining the environment and beliefs.

The email exchanges revealed more than a miscommunication. The itinerant teacher for Esmeralda's class had suggested a specialized classroom placement. Jorge's follow-up email was worse.

My program had fewer students and two full-time paraprofessionals to address David's needs, he alluded, as if staffing ratios were the key issue, but I knew it wasn't just about numbers. It was about the environment. David had shown he could thrive in a general education setting with the right supports. Now it felt like his new team was giving up on him.

Reading Jorge's words, my chest tightened. It wasn't just about David. It was about the leadership I had experienced all year: decisions made without collaboration, feedback dismissed, and values serving as slogans more than unifying elements. Jorge often invoked Vista's values of collaboration, innovation, and equity, but he rarely modeled them. His tone in meetings, his disregard for progress, and his constant deference to bureaucratic ease over real inclusion had worn me down.

I recalled the mug I had shattered in February. I thought I had moved past that anger, but this email brought it all back. Jorge's leadership didn't reflect his stated values. It reflected avoidance. My memory drifted to the P.R.I.D.E. poster. I couldn't help but consider how different the school year would have been if Kris were still the principal.

In the early months, I had raised concerns about how Every Early Learner Succeeds impacted children with developmental delays, especially when we couldn't speak their home language. I had hoped for dialogue and shared problem-solving. Instead, Jorge gave me neutral nods and vague promises to support me. Even when Cindy tried to facilitate honest discussion, Jorge shaped what we could say.

David's struggles in Esmeralda's room made one thing clear: The curriculum wasn't failing just one classroom; it was failing children in every early childhood classroom. David A.'s behaviors weren't evidence of his inability. They were a reflection of an environment that didn't fit him, and if it didn't fit him, there was no question there were other children that the curriculum excluded. Jorge's response only reinforced what I knew my entire twelve-year career in classrooms: Children are only as disabled as the context around them.

This wasn't just about one decision or one child. It was the accumulation of dismissal, rigidity, and silence all year long. David's case was the spark that reignited my distrust for special education. It reminded me why I had wanted the itinerant role, as well as why I wanted to stay in the classroom. Why I still cared.

Jorge's suggestion that David couldn't succeed in a general education classroom felt like a betrayal. David hadn't failed. The classroom and the system had failed him. Inclusion wasn't about placement. It was about leadership, collaboration, training, and peer models.

I closed my laptop and leaned back in my chair. Virginia's voice echoed in my mind. I could hear her reminders about relationships and power. At that moment, those concepts felt too far and, at the same time, too close to the email exchanges.

As I packed up to leave, the anger remained. I thought about the next early childhood education team meeting, our talk about values, and how I would show up. I couldn't stay silent: not for David, not for the other students, and not for my love for the children and families at Vista.

***

Like a thirsty plant in need of rain, spring break was a blessing. Natalie and I sat at the kitchen table, listening to the girls rolling on the living room carpet, their laughter tumbling across the vinyl flooring.

"It's like every time I think I've hit my limit with Jorge, he finds a way to make it worse," I said, poking at the food on my plate. "His email about David A. brought back everything I've been trying to let go of: the itinerant position, the curriculum, and the constant dismissiveness in our meetings. It's like he's allergic to listening."

Natalie leaned her elbows on the table, her gaze steady. "You need to let it go. You're leaving Vista after this year, right? Don't give him any more of your energy. He doesn't deserve it."

"I know." I sighed, setting down my fork. "It's just hard when it keeps piling on. And the thing with David A. is that he was doing fine in our room. Now he's struggling in Esmeralda's, and no one asked for the input of the people who worked with him in our classroom. From the sound of the email, David's inclusion in her class has been difficult since January. Not once did she talk to me. Not once did the itinerant talk to me. It feels like no one values his inclusion."

"I get it, but you've done everything you could. It's not on you anymore. Don't bring David A. up with Esmeralda. It's not your thing to worry about. You need to stop making things personal and start putting yourself, your mental health, and your peace of mind before anything in the classroom."

I gave a dry laugh. "Easier said than done when I'm stuck in that building all day."

"That's why you need to get out during your lunch breaks," Natalie said firmly. "The weather's warming up. Go for a walk. Clear your head."

I raised an eyebrow. "Sure, until the next spring snowstorm. You know how Colorado is: sunshine and shorts one day, a foot of snow the next."

"No excuses," Natalie shot back, smirking. "You're going to drive yourself crazy if you don't find a way to step away from all this: room 122, the university, and even us. You need space to breathe."

I leaned back in my chair, letting her words sink in. "You're probably right. Now that Ana is on maternity leave, things are going to get even more chaotic. I should use that time to just get outside."

"You should," she said, her voice softening. "It's not fair what they've put her through. Making her stay until she goes into labor? That's cruel."

I nodded, the tension in my shoulders tightening. "Yeah. She wanted her last day to be two weeks before spring break, but she had to wait until now. She's shown up every day, uncomfortable and in pain. She deserves so much better."

"She does," Natalie said gently. "And you're going to miss her."

"I will," I admitted. "She's been such a good friend. It's going to feel emptier without her."

Natalie smiled faintly. "Well, then honor that friendship by taking care of yourself. It's what she would want you to do. Go outside during lunch. Relax. And no, Vista Park doesn't count."

I scoffed, shaking my head. "Vista Park? That's like sitting in the school's backyard. If I really want to relax, I need to get farther away."

"How far is Clear Creek Hill from the school?" she asked.

"About six blocks. I've never been there," I said. "I'll look into it."

"You should," she said, encouraging. "Lunch with Virginia is great, but you need to get out of your head a couple times a week. Stop thinking about the classroom, stop worrying about your work, stop trying to solve everything for everyone."

I let out a long breath, a small smile tugging at the corner of my mouth. "All right, I'll give it a shot when I return."

Our animated three-year-old rushed to my side, with Itzel crawling close behind, both absorbed in the joy of childhood.

"Daddy, I'm Elsa, and sister is Ana. You're a dragon. Come get us!"

"I'm going to char you with my fiery rage! Go find safety in your castle while I finish talking with mommy dragon," I roared, scrunching my face into a scowl. Citlali ran back to the living room, Itzel trailing behind.

"Good," Natalie said, rising from the table. "It's your spring break. You've got a week to give it a rest . . . and capture princesses."

As the conversation shifted and the girls' laughter echoed through the duplex, I found myself holding on to Natalie's words. She might be right. I needed to stop making things personal and start putting mental health before anything in the classroom. Maybe it was time to step outside of all of it, even for a few minutes.

***

The end of the day was always a mix of joy and relief. Parents trickled up the ramp to the back door, eager to gather their children and head home. It was Monday, April 6, the first day back after spring break. As the class dispersed, I stood by the door, thanking each parent as they left, scanning for signs of connection or concern.

Then I saw her, one of our learner's moms. My stomach dropped as she wobbled up the ramp, her steps uneven and slow. The sharp smell of alcohol drifted through the air before she even reached the door.

The child had already told us about the needles at home, domestic abuse, and other dangers. We had called child protective services twice. Both times, we believed our reports went unanswered, as there was no change.

I looked at the child, who stood near the coat rack with his backpack hanging over one shoulder. His eyes flicked toward his mom, then back to me.

"Let's go," she slurred, her voice too loud for the playground.

I stepped forward, instinctively positioning myself between them. My ethical commitment to do no harm to children pressed hard in my chest. The last time she came like this, I told Jorge.

He reminded me I had no legal standing to intervene unless there was immediate evidence of harm. She wasn't driving, so I had to let the child go.

Beatriz stepped forward. Jimmy was already beside her, holding her hand. She read my face, then turned to the child's mom with a steady calm.

"Your son can come play at our house for a bit," she said, warm but pointed. "I'll drop him off later."

The child's mom blinked, confused. Then she shrugged. "Sure, okay. If that's okay with you."

The child didn't hesitate. He hurried over to Beatriz and stood beside Jimmy. The boys shifted into a playful conversation, as if it were any other afternoon. Beatriz gave me a small nod as they walked away together.

The door closed, and silence settled. I slumped into a chair, overwhelmed by the sense of powerlessness. Despite everything I had tried, I couldn't shield our learner from what awaited him at home. My ethical commitments felt hollow when systems designed to protect children remained paralyzed by similar policies to those that paralyzed public education, when leadership, training, collaboration, and peer models focused on compliance rather than people.

Still, I was grateful for Beatriz. Her compassion extended far beyond Jimmy. That day, it extended to our learner in danger. Her offer wasn't just kindness. It was a lifeline.

I thought about the relationships I had tried to nurture. Jimmy, Ricky, and Eric—three English-speaking boys—had built something strong. They trusted each other, shared jokes, and played with ease. Their friendship was built on a network of authentic relationships.

Then I thought of the morning class. Ernesto, Brandon, and Mateo had the potential for that same bond, but their connection never quite clicked. Their interactions felt scattered, like puzzle pieces that didn't quite fit.

Would it have been different if we had shared a common language? If Cecilia, Lillie, and I had been able to connect with Ernesto, Brandon, and Mateo in Spanish the way I connected with Eric, Jimmy, and Ricky in English?

I thought of Ernesto's energy, Brandon's curiosity, and Mateo's charisma. Each of them had something to offer, something I struggled to fully reach. Their behavior didn't create the barriers. The barriers were part of an unjust system that prioritized compliance.

As I locked up the classroom, I couldn't shake the image of our learner in danger walking off with Beatriz. I hoped his evening would be filled with warmth instead of harm.

That day was the last time I saw his mom come to pick him up. After that, it was always his brothers or grandmother. Part of me felt relieved. The other part knew it didn't mean anything had truly changed. Just like David A.'s transition, this was another example of a system that refused to listen. Another story of decisions made without insight or care.

I left carrying that weight. Without Lillie and without a substitute, Cecilia and I were exhausted. I heard echoes of Ana's and Natalie's voices in my mind. *You need to stop making things personal and start putting your mental health and peace of mind before anything in the classroom.* I wondered whether what I had been calling personal was simply the cost of paying attention and whether protecting my peace might require carrying less of what was never mine to hold.

CHAPTER 14

CLEAR CREEK HILL

———

The library was quieter than usual. With all the study rooms taken, I claimed a corner table with my laptop and a stack of journal articles, determined to make progress on the paper that was due Tuesday. My fingers hovered over the keyboard, typing and backspacing as I tried to formulate cohesive thoughts.

I paused over a line I had just written: *An effective leader understands the culture of the organization they are stepping into.* The words made me think about my own work. I had learned, often the hard way, that leadership in schools was not just about policies or plans. I had to read the culture in real time, see where it could grow, and choose how to respond based on my knowledge of Metro Denver Unified School District and Vista's culture.

Diana's promise to hire me for the itinerant position had been made months ago, and the long silence since then still lingered in the background. I only now realize the uncertainty was similar to my years of experience with special education administrators in the school district. The stretches of waiting, messages of reassurance, and the gaps that followed. Too often, administrators didn't understand school or classroom cultures. I knew I could not control Diana's timeline, but the question of what came next still edged into my thoughts.

I returned to the paper in front of me. *A leader must reflect on their passions, abilities, and resources to leverage capacity for organizational success.* I thought about my first year at Vista, when Jovan's IEP meeting left me frustrated by the lack of follow-through. Back then, I had learned that leadership sometimes meant creating culture from inside the classroom, even when the system failed to support it. That was the same approach I was now taking in room 122, trusting the culture we built together more than the structures imposed from above.

I continued: *New leadership clinging to an old system can permit stagnation or degradation to endure.* I could see it clearly in the ways district priorities often veered away from the children and families we were supposed to serve. They didn't adapt as the inclusion of children with disabilities in the district evolved. But the opposite was also true. Leadership could be a catalyst for growth. I had seen it when Ana reshaped family events to make them more welcoming, when Lillie encouraged me to advocate more boldly, and when Cecilia modeled inclusion in the smallest interactions.

My gaze moved to the stack of journal articles, then back to the computer screen. *The balance a school leader must create to thrive is difficult.* That sentence felt deeply personal. I was not a principal, yet I had spent years balancing leadership and bureaucracy in my own classroom, navigating policy demands without losing sight of what mattered most in the classroom.

I glanced at the clock, feeling a pull for fresh air. Natalie's suggestion of Clear Creek Hill came to mind. I had brushed it off before, but now the idea of walking away from the noise of the week felt worth penciling in. I needed balance.

I packed my things and closed my laptop. Whether in an itinerant role or back in a classroom, I would continue to cultivate classroom cultures that centered children and families, the way I always had. The thought of going to Clear Creek Hill during my lunch break steadied me as I stepped into the train, ready to keep moving forward.

***

As soon as the last child left the morning class on Monday, April 13, I grabbed my lunch and walked quickly to the parking lot. The noise from the classrooms seeped into the hallway at Vista. My bag felt heavy against my shoulder, but not from the weight of what was inside, rather from the morning I'd just had.

For weeks, I had been preparing for Individual Education Program transition meetings. Each required me to assess progress and decide on next steps for pre-kindergarten or kindergarten. Since the January meeting for David A., those decisions had felt more consequential. I had been debating whether Antonio and other children with significant support needs should remain in another Foundations classroom or move to a specialized classroom, such as one for children with autism. My mind told me to weigh their growth carefully. My heart told me it might not matter. Too often, the district placed children in specialized classrooms regardless of one teacher's recommendation or a family's initial desire. The thought was hard to carry.

Once in the car, I shut the door and tried to let the sensory stimulation of Vista settle. The drive to Clear Creek Hill took only a few minutes, but with every block, the school's demands seemed to loosen their hold. By the time I turned onto the narrow, winding road, the air through the open window was cooler. It carried the faint smell of damp earth.

The parking lot was nearly empty. I stepped out and started the climb. The first steps were steep, making me shift my bag higher on my shoulder. Small patches of snow lingered in shaded spots, while elsewhere the ground was soft, the grass flattened from winter and just starting to green. With each step, the view opened a little more, giving me a glimpse of the city through the bare branches.

At the top, I found a dry patch of earth and set my bag beside me. The trees stood leafless, their branches stretched against the sky. Birds called from somewhere above, their notes clear and distinct. The brown shrubs bent in the breeze, thin and scattered.

I leaned back, feeling the breeze pass over my face. My shoulders loosened as I took a slow, cool breath. I told myself, *Let go of what I cannot control.* I repeated it until my chest felt lighter.

I unwrapped my lunch and ate slowly, watching clouds drift and reshape themselves. They moved without hurry, without needing a direction.

When I stood to leave, the challenges at Vista were still there, but the space between them and my thoughts had widened just enough to carry me through the rest of the day. Relief had not come from research articles or relationships, but from the open air showing me what it meant to slow down and breathe.

***

I swung the glass door of McDonald's open. The familiar scent of fries, burgers, and coffee mingled with the coordinated banter of patrons. Virginia waved from her usual spot by the window.

"Hey, Andrew," she said, smiling.

"Hey," I replied, sliding into the seat across from her. I unpacked the lunch I brought and took a deep breath. "It's been a week."

She raised an eyebrow. "Do tell."

I told her about my reflections at Clear Creek Hill, how the quiet there had given me a moment to breathe, even as my thoughts kept drifting back to work. I admitted the paper I was struggling to finish for a class felt more difficult than it should. Then I shared the worry that had been gnawing at me since the last round of Individual Education Program transition meetings. I had wrestled with whether to recommend that children with significant support needs stay in a Foundations classroom for another year. My head and heart were overwhelmed by paradoxes.

Virginia listened quietly, her gaze steady. "That is a lot to carry."

"It is. And it's connected to everything else," I said. "The leadership gaps, the lack of trust, the endless confusion about roles and vision. It all ends up in the same place, the kids and the families paying the price."

I told her how six different departments swayed decisions for my classroom. None seemed to share the same vision for children and families. Inclusion felt more like a game of tug-of-war than a value

Virginia tilted her head. "That is not just vision you're talking about. It's the value of belonging."

I looked at her.

"Belonging is what gives a vision its power," she said. "People need to feel they are part of something that matters. That sense of belonging is what sustains commitment when the work is hard. Belonging is not the outcome. It's the value underneath it all."

Her words triggered a cascade of memories. I thought about how my first two years at Vista had been different under Kris. The vision had been clearer. The values of perseverance, respect, integrity, diversity, and excellence were central to the work at the school and guided the progress of the early childhood education team. Within those values, belonging was an unspoken priority. We had worked with the same system, but we had done it together. All those concepts around inclusion and leadership I had been writing about in class boiled down to a vision that made everyone feel like they were part of something that mattered—both the stack of Swiss cheese and the cardiovascular system.

"Okay, help me out. For me, the issue right now is transitioning children into their classroom next school year and whether the teacher has the right preparation," I said. "We can't share a vision of inclusion where everyone feels like they're part of something that matters if they haven't been trained effectively. Not just for special education practitioners, but for general education teachers too. They are expected to include children with disabilities without being given the resources or training to do it well. It is not fair to them or to the kids."

"So, the way we train teachers needs an overhaul?" She said.

I nodded. "Yes, but I know it is easier said than done. I recognize it might seem naïve from a teacher's perspective, but they are still the right things to do."

"Naïve or not, you have thought it through," Virginia said. "And you care about the people, the kids, the families, and your colleagues. That is where real leadership starts. You have to care about your relationships."

Her encouragement sparked a familiar flicker of hope, but didn't ease my concerns with the Individual Education Program transitions. As we wrapped up lunch, she said, "You are not just trying to change a system. You are trying to change lives through relationships. Keep your focus there, and the rest will follow."

I left McDonald's thinking that maybe leadership was less about a teacher's professional training and more about building trust with the teachers who would work with the students transitioning to their classrooms. Relationship by relationship, I needed to care for the people. That would be more possible as an itinerant teacher than as a classroom teacher.

***

The morning light streamed through the window of room 122 as I prepared the community center. Tom sat at the table in the literacy center, working on special education paperwork. Cecilia was cleaning the kidney tables and putting the question of the day on the whiteboard. Children and families could be heard outside on the playground, but they had not yet grouped to come into the classroom. That meant we had at least ten more minutes to find out if we had a substitute for Lillie or if we'd be running the room in survival mode.

"What do you think, Cecilia? It's 7:35. Sub or no sub?"

She smiled an ironic smile. "I don't know. We'll be fine. Right, Mr. Tom?"

Tom tapped his pen in a peppy rhythm against the table. He looked up, face set in a thoughtful grin. "Sorry, what was the question?"

"Nothing. We're happy to have you with us today. We haven't had a regular sub in our class since Lillie left. We get someone two, maybe three days per week," I said, walking casually in his direction. "The office doesn't tell us anything. We'll just have to wait and see if anyone walks through the door between now and 7:45."

Cecilia sighed heavily, folding her arms. "It's been ridiculous. Since Lillie left, it's like they don't even care if we have enough support in here. Every day it's a guessing game."

The message was clear: Our work didn't matter enough to warrant consistency.

"I'm sorry," Tom said, giving us a compassionate frown.

"It's not just us," I said. "Cindy, Sharon, and Esmeralda have been scrambling too. The subs they get aren't trained for early childhood education. Half the time, they're more work than help."

Cecilia shook her head. "You know what it's like when you're gone? They split the class between Cindy's and Ana's rooms, and it's chaos. The kids don't know where they belong, the teachers are stretched too thin, and nothing gets done. It's a mess."

I nodded, the frustration simmering just beneath the surface. "I know. I've heard the stories. And now with Ana gone on maternity leave, it's only getting worse."

Cecilia glanced at Tom, then back at me. "Tom, you were here that one day when Andrew was out for a training. Remember how crazy it got in Cindy's classroom?"

Tom nodded. "That was difficult. By the way, how's David A. doing in Esmeralda's class?"

I rubbed my hand over my scalp, exhaling slowly. "Didn't I tell you? His new team determined he would do better in an autism classroom for kindergarten. There's so much I could say about that, but it's out of my control, and I decided to let it go," I said, my voice tinged with sadness. "Once a child is in a self-contained classroom, they rarely, if ever, make it back to true inclusion. And I don't just mean being physically present in a general education classroom. Truly included means having access to all the learning opportunities, the necessary supports, and a sense of belonging."

Tom nodded thoughtfully. "Yeah, that's tough."

Cecilia chimed in. "I'm sad for his mother. It's like he moved to that classroom and wasn't looked at in the same way. They see him as a child with autism, rather than as David A. Even if he is technically in the same room as everyone else, he isn't included. It's like you say, Andrew, labels narrow possibilities. Once defined by autism, children like David A. are seen as their disability rather than possibility."

"Exactly," I said despairingly. "And for kids like David A., that's heartbreaking. David A.'s mom has always had such high hopes for him. She believes in his potential, and we saw it when he was here. But now . . ." I trailed off, unable to finish the thought.

"You did everything you could for him, Andrew. We all did," Cecilia said.

"I know," I said, my throat tightening. "But it doesn't make it any easier. These kids deserve so much more than what the district, or maybe just Vista, is giving them. And their families do too."

The three of us sat in silence for a moment. I thought about the dysfunction and whether I would ever be comfortable in a classroom again. Seeing children and families I cared for being wronged and not speaking up felt unethical. Resistance from inside a classroom could only go so far. All I could do was hope that I would have a chance to make a difference as an itinerant next year. I wanted to make a difference not just for the kids, but for the system that kept failing them.

The sound of footsteps approaching room 122 from the hallway pulled us out of our thoughts. We looked toward the door, waiting to see if it was a substitute. The uncertainty of the day and the future was deep in my being. I heard Natalie's words. *You can only control what you can control. Letting go isn't giving up. It's survival.*

***

The elevator doors opened, revealing the roof terrace of Ana, Sergio, and their newborn daughter, Lucia's apartment. It was a beautiful late-April Saturday afternoon, perfect for the delayed baby shower. Natalie stepped out first, holding Citlali's hand. Citlali, in turn, held Itzel's. Natalie let Citlali's hand drop, and the two girls moved carefully, full of anticipation.

I smiled, watching Itzel toddle confidently alongside her sister. "She's finally walking," I whispered to Natalie.

Natalie nodded, her voice warm. "Everything happens at its own pace."

Her words landed deeply in me. I glanced at the girls ahead of us and felt my thoughts drift. Not just to Itzel's first steps, but to my own in recent weeks. The visits to Clear Creek Hill, stepping away from the noise to sit still and breathe, were exactly what I needed. It was only now, in this setting, that I could feel how far I had come.

The terrace was sleek and modern, with trendy earth-tone furniture accented with bold cushions, hanging plants catching the breeze, and a plexiglass parapet wall opening to a panoramic view of the downtown skyline. At the far end, Sergio stood behind a white bar counter serving sangria and offering plates of paella with the practiced ease of someone who enjoyed hosting.

Citlali and Itzel had found the baby shower cake on a nearby table and were inching closer than they should have.

"Girls," I called out gently, "take our gift bag over to the table . . . yes, that one . . . and don't touch the cake, okay?"

Citlali gave me an exasperated look and nodded. "Sister, don't touch the cake. That's for later," she lectured. The two of them ambled off in the direction I pointed. The gift bag bounced off the tile.

Natalie and I crossed the room toward Ana, who sat in a scarlet plush lounge chair, nursing baby Lucia in her arms. Ana's hair was swept back casually, and her expression had that mix of exhaustion and awe only new parents seem to carry. Maya and Cecilia sat beside her, cooing over the baby. They were certainly avoiding any mention of Vista and reminders that Ana would not return for the rest of the school year. The silence about our daily circumstances wasn't just polite. It was deliberate. Protective, even.

Ana looked up as we approached. Her eyes lit up. "Andrew, Natalie, I'm so glad you came." She and Natalie exchanged words of affection in Spanish.

"We wouldn't miss it," I said, leaning down to gently kiss her on each cheek. "Congratulations. She's beautiful."

"Of course she is," Ana joked, brushing a finger over Lucia's tiny hand. "Even with the sleepless nights."

I hesitated only a moment before sitting beside her. "I've been meaning to tell you . . . I've missed our lunches, but I've found this spot to go during lunch. Clear Creek Hill."

Ana looked up, curious. "The one near Vista?"

"Yeah. It's quiet and simple. I've started going there to sit. Think. Being there . . . it helped me see things a little more clearly."

Ana smiled, nodding slowly. Her eyes were soft with understanding. "That sounds like what you needed."

"It really is," I said. "I think I'm finally figuring out how to create space for myself."

Cecilia looked up from the baby. "You've seemed more relaxed the past few weeks."

"When am I not relaxed?" I said glibly.

We laughed, all of us knowing that I hadn't been able to breathe for since August.

I sat back in the chair, letting the voices and laughter swirl around me. I didn't feel like a teacher battling the tide of dysfunction. I was a human among others being their true selves, a feeling far from the dynamics at Vista.

Later that afternoon, I found myself sitting with Sergio and a few fellow Spaniards he and Ana had met during their time in Denver. They were kind, thoughtful, and easy to talk to. We shared stories over a few rounds of sangria. The afternoon sun softened as it slipped toward the western skyline. At one point, Sergio leaned over and told me quietly, "We've decided to move back to Spain. Ana can't imagine going back to a school with Jorge, and we want to be with family."

I nodded. I wasn't surprised.

After an hour or so, with equal parts joy and sorrow, I stepped to the edge of the terrace and looked out at the cityscape. The sounds of laughter echoed behind me. Ana was leaving. She meant more to me than I could put into words. Her ability to endure the challenges she faced with patience and resolve was uncanny. The balance and stability she maintained was like no one else I had ever met. A chapter was closing.

I took a slow breath and repeated a truth I had come to understand clearly but often ignored: It doesn't matter what the future holds for a job. My family is what matters most. That seemed more real than before my visits to Clear Creek Hill. It was long overdue and settled into me like the last light of the April evening.

***

Dark clouds filled the sky the day before my fourth visit to Clear Creek Hill. Their presence mirrored the heaviness I carried inside. The previous week, the child, whose mother was drunk and belligerent when she came to pick him up, had been removed from his home. We didn't know why, only that a court order now required his child protective case manager to bring him to and from school to his foster home. In class, the child carried on as though nothing had changed.

The day before, his grandmother came to pick him up, even though she had no legal right to do so. As soon as she saw me, her voice turned sharp. She shouted profanity and threatened to hurt me and my family because it was my fault that child protective services had taken her grandson from her home. Cecilia was frozen with fear, her eyes wide. Beatriz asked if I wanted her to call the police. I shook my head, trusting that everything would be fine. For several minutes, our learner's grandmother's voice filled the playground, heavy and unrelenting, before others convinced her to leave. The air stayed tense long after she was gone. When I told Jorge, he apologized and told me I could file a restraining order. Beyond that, there was little we could do.

Since Ana's departure, there was no one in the classroom who could fully understand my fear of both our learner's grandmother and Jorge.

By the time I turned onto the winding road at Clear Creek Hill, the air through the open window seemed to alleviate some of the heaviness I harbored.

I stepped out and started up the slope. The ground was soft, the grass thicker than it had been on my first visit. Small patches of yellow and purple flowers broke through the gray light. The damp smell of earth and rain lingered in the air as I climbed. My breathing slowed.

At the top, I sat where I could see the hill curve toward the horizon. The clouds blurred the distance into shades of gray. Birds perched on branches, their calls overlapping into a single, steady sound. The breeze carried a chill, rippling through leaves and grass until everything around me seemed to blend together under the shadow of the dark sky.

My mind wandered back to room 122. The children had adapted to every disruption, but their resilience was no sign that all was well. It only underscored how much they deserved stability, safety, and room to grow without fear. Even Cecilia, who had kept the classroom steady, carried a fear that mirrored my own. At Vista, nothing fit together. Policies, threats, and uncertainty pulled us apart instead of drawing us closer.

Here, though, the world maintained a balance. Despite the weather and clouds, the birds kept calling, the grass kept growing, the trees kept swaying together. I realized the disharmony at school was not the whole story. Clouds come and go. What remains is the sky itself—vast and steady—like the connections with Cecilia, the children, and my colleagues. Those ties were always there, even when storms tried to cover them.

When I walked down Clear Creek Hill, that sense of harmony stayed with me. The darkness inside me was still there, but I saw it differently now. In the parking lot, I glanced upward and caught a break in the clouds, a strip of quiet blue reminding me of what endures.

CHAPTER 15

THE EVALUATION

Natalie's tender voice carried through the thin walls of our duplex, a soothing rhythm as she read the girls their bedtime story. Citlali's voice chimed in, pleading to read a book to Itzel. I smiled to myself, picturing Natalie's approving nod and Itzel's confusing giggles. Their moment was perfect, a testament to the love and connection that bonded our family together, even as I wrestled with my thoughts in the solitude of the closet-office.

Natalie stepped in a few minutes later, leaning on the doorframe. "Still writing?"

I gestured to the screen. "A reflection paper. It feels like everything from this year is spilling into it."

She moved closer. "That's not a bad thing."

"It feels like I'm trying too hard to make sense of things." My thoughts drifted momentarily. "I should email Diana about the job next year, but . . ." My words trailed off.

"But you haven't," she said, finishing for me.

I met her eyes. "What if she tells me it's not happening? What if I've been reading too much into everything she's said?"

Natalie pressed her hands on my shoulders, firm but gentle. "Then at least you'll know. You've done enough waiting. You can't let fear hold you in place."

Her certainty steadied me. "You're right. Tomorrow I'll send it."

She kissed my temple. "Good. Now come to bed."

I lingered a moment longer, the glow of the screen reflecting back at me. I visualized Clear Creek Hill and told myself what Virginia had said many times in many ways: Whatever happens, it's an opportunity. The waiting would be hard, but not as hard as holding on to doubt. It was time to let go.

***

By my seventh visit over the past few weeks, spring had taken hold of Clear Creek Hill. The week at Vista had been bleak from the start. Without a sub for Ana, her class had been divided among the other Explorer rooms most days. Earlier this week, both Esmeralda and Cindy were out, and only one sub could be found. Their students were split between my room and Sharon's, thirty-two children for two straight days. Because the Explorer students had full-day schedules, they stayed through both our morning and afternoon sessions. The room never quieted. Routines broke down under the sheer number of children. Sharon took her concerns to Jorge and made sure everyone else in the school knew. I chose not to join that battle, but the noise and disruption still settled into me.

Esmeralda and Cindy returned on Friday. When the morning ended, I stepped into the hallway and felt the stale air of the building sitting heavy in my lungs. I moved quickly to the parking lot, glad to shut the car door behind me. The short drive to Clear Creek Hill was enough for the school's sounds to fade from my mind. By the time I turned onto the road that curved upward toward the parking lot, I could feel my shoulders start to loosen.

The air was warm when I stepped out of the car, scented with recently pruned tree branches. Along the climb, blossoms brightened the path while bees moved methodically from flower to flower. At the top, I sat where the city was framed between the trees. The wind bent the ornamental grass in soft waves. Birds crossed the branches without colliding. Above me, shifting leaves cast slow-moving shadows across the ground. Nothing here had rushed into being. Leaves had opened in their own time, flowers had bloomed when ready, and the hill had filled with grass without instruction. Everything grew at its own pace, yet still fit together.

An indistinguishable amount of time passed. Thoughts about the week at Vista, and Itzel learning how to walk quietly surfaced. My instinct was always to push, to solve each problem as quickly as it came. Here, it was obvious: Not everything could be forced into place. Some things needed time, space, and the right conditions.

The answer about the itinerant position still hadn't come, but I could wait.

When I left, the bleakness from earlier in the week had lifted. The steadiness of Clear Creek Hill stayed with me, and I knew it would be enough for whatever came next. Change would come when it was ready, not when I forced it.

***

Virginia leaned back in the booth at McDonald's, her coffee steaming in front of her. I glanced at my list of interview questions for an assignment in my leadership class. Diana had been my original choice, but with my professor's approval, I decided to talk with Virginia instead. I knew it would be more than just an interview.

"Ready?" I asked, lifting my notebook.

"Always," she said with a smile. "Hit me with your best shot."

I read the first question aloud. "How do you see your role as a leader in your organization?"

"I see myself as a bridge builder," she said without hesitation. "Leadership is about connecting people to each other, to their goals, and to the bigger picture. It is not about having control and telling people what to do. It is about making sure they have what they need to succeed."

I nodded, writing quickly. "That is something I have struggled with at Vista this year. The disconnect between what we need and what we are given is constant. Leadership often feels like checking boxes instead of building bridges."

"That is a common challenge for teachers," she said. "A good leader knows how to navigate those constraints. You do not ignore the system, but you do not let it define you either. You focus on the people and use your power to empower others."

Her words made me think of the past few weeks. "Before we go on, a few really difficult events happened last week. Do you mind if I share them?"

Her expression tightened with worry.

I went on to tell her about the incident with the grandmother of the child whose mother showed up to our classroom drunk. "She berated me and threatened to hurt my family." I paused, recognizing the fear and pain that was rising. Virginia stayed silent. "Jorge apologized but said there was not much we could do."

The look in Virginia's eyes showed that she longed for the right words.

"And then, last week, Ana and Esmeralda's classes had to be split for two days due to a lack of substitutes. It's been hard."

Virginia held space for a few seconds before responding. "Those are both examples of why leadership matters. In moments like that, people need to know someone has their back. It is not just about problem-solving. It is about creating emotional and physical safety so people can keep doing the work, even when it is hard."

I nodded. Hearing her talk about the fundamentals of relationships briefly brought me back to the dark clouds and effortless growth at Clear Creek Hill. "Okay, enough about my troubles." I read the second question. "What are the biggest obstacles you have faced as a leader?"

"Two things," she said, "funding and resistance to change. Funding is obvious. You cannot do much without resources. Resistance to change is more complicated. People hold on to what they know, even if it is not working, because change feels risky."

"Do you think that is what happened at Vista?" I asked. "With the early childhood team and me?"

"Yes and no," she said. "What you experienced was not true resistance. It was change imposed without relationships. You were expected to adapt, and there was no trust. That is self-protection, not resistance."

Her words stayed with me. I thought about the moments when speaking up had felt necessary, and the moments when it had also been a way to protect myself from being run over.

A follow-up question arose from uncertainty. "How do you handle it when it is true resistance?"

"Patience and persistence. You listen to their joys and their concerns. You help people see why the change matters and how it benefits them. You give them time to adjust, stay open to modifications, and hold firm to a shared vision. With time, there will be success . . . Maybe not the success you expected, but there will be success."

Virginia's response reminded me of the words she shared that helped me reframe leadership and inclusion: *It may not look exactly how you pictured it. Start with the people and build from there.*

"That's where leadership at Vista faltered. There was no consideration for us teachers. We never saw the need for change, we didn't share Jorge's vision, and he expects his version of success."

As she spoke about patience and persistence, I thought about the language Natalie often used. Survival. I wondered whether what I had once considered resistance had, at times, been something closer to endurance than change.

She laughed and turned the question back on me. "What does success look like for you?"

I paused. "Goodness. That's deep." I thought back to the papers I'd written for my classes and the numerous conversations we had at McDonald's. "I think it's when everyone has trust, feels valued, and has a sense of belonging. When inclusion is not just a policy but a collective expectation. It's not about a benchmark or isolated event."

"That is the kind of vision that inspires people," she said.

Her own vision was specific, bold, and straightforward: provide every early childhood professional with affordable access to a bachelor's degree. She aimed for an early childhood education program at Rocky Mountain Community College that responded to the desires and needs of the community. She proposed a bachelor's degree program in early childhood education at the community college, removing barriers for students who could not transfer to a university. "It would keep them learning and growing without having to leave the community. It is something the community wants. What they value and want is what I value and want," she explained.

"That is similar to what I wrote about in a recent paper," I said. "A shared vision is a way to create a mission of ownership and belonging."

"Exactly. Without a shared vision rooted in collective values that guide a mission and goals, an organization is just a group of people working in isolation."

When I asked about her biggest professional regret, she hesitated. "Not speaking up sooner when I knew something was wrong. Silence is complacency. If you see something that needs to change, you have to say something."

"Even if it costs you?"

"Yes. Even if it costs you. That's integrity."

Her words sat heavily with me. "Are you saying my choice to speak up this year was integrity?"

"Yes. It may have cost you, but it was the right thing."

I let that settle. What I had been struggling to name all year was not defiance or self-protection. It was the willingness to speak when silence would have been easier, even without guarantees of safety or success. Hearing her name, it brought me back to the dark clouds and effortless growth at Clear Creek Hill. It was the story of my school year.

We finished the interview discussing boundaries and balance. She reminded me to protect time for myself and my family and to make space for what kept me physically and mentally healthy.

Before we left, she asked, "Any word on the itinerant position?"

I shook my head.

"Then reach out to Diana. If you do not hear back, start exploring other options. And happy birthday, in case we don't talk before Friday."

As I walked out into the parking lot, I felt both comforted and challenged. The events of the past few weeks had tested me in ways that went beyond the classroom and reshaped how I understood leadership. Leadership, I realized, is never a title. It lives in the responsibility to act when safety, dignity, or belonging are at stake. That was not the reality at Vista, but I did what I could within it. I spoke when silence would have been easier, and I learned what it costs to lead with integrity.

***

The playground outside room 122 was gradually getting louder, the way it always did before the afternoon children arrived. I sat at my desk, staring at the vacated space where my coffee mug used to rest. My eyes drifted to the hole in the wall. The laptop was open, the cursor blinking in the email draft I had been avoiding. It was an urgent task I had to complete that day.

I had told myself to be patient, but Natalie and Virginia convinced me that enough was enough. Diana had promised during our phone call on February 13 that I wouldn't need to reapply. My candidacy for the itinerant position was already secure for next year. I had believed her then, clinging to her words like a raft in the wreckage of the school year. Now, with the final weeks of the year approaching, her silence spoke louder than any of her reassurances.

I exhaled slowly and typed:

Howdy Diana,

I am wondering if my candidacy for an itinerant or a similar position in Metro Denver Unified School District's Early Childhood Special Education program is as desirable as it was earlier this school year?

Andrew

The message read like a text, but texting was no longer how Diana and I communicated. I didn't know how else to phrase it. Anything more casual would sound desperate. Anything more assertive would sound desperate. I hit send before I could overthink it and stared at the screen, wondering how long it would take for her to respond.

After a few minutes, I stepped away to begin the afternoon routine. Diana no longer held control over my thoughts in the classroom. My focus shifted to Jimmy, Ricky, and Eric. Their questions, sparked by what they noticed outside, reminded me why I was still there. The compassion of Sofia, Ernesto, Brandon, Mateo, and Nelia validated the power of peer models. My priority was fostering authentic, meaningful connections within the rigid structure of the Every Early Learner Succeeds curriculum. The unit on neighborhoods gave us some flexibility, which was especially needed when we didn't have a substitute.

Room 122 was tidy. The overhead lights were off, and the chairs rested on top of the tables. As I packed up for the day, my laptop pinged. My heart leapt. I clicked Diana's name and read the message slowly. The tone felt distant, carefully crafted.

She thanked me for my interest in the itinerant position, acknowledged my commitment to early childhood education and early childhood special education, and explained that the district had chosen other candidates. "Individuals who had a stronger alignment with the collaborative leadership qualities required for the role."

She continued. While my enthusiasm and experience were evident, there were areas where further alignment with district expectations would be beneficial. The position required managing multiple classrooms and teams, demanding adaptability and strategic leadership across diverse settings.

She stressed that the decision was not a reflection of my value but rather an assessment of readiness. With time and further development in system-level collaboration, she believed I could become a stronger candidate for similar roles. She closed by offering to provide feedback and thanked me for my work with students and families.

My whole body tensed. Filled all the positions? I read the paragraph again. The words didn't change.

As much as I had tried to prepare for any answer, the spell was stronger than my resolve. My thoughts returned to every conversation I had shared with Diana: her encouragement, her assurances, her praise for my commitment to inclusion. How had it come to this?

I wasn't angry. I wasn't even disappointed. I was ashamed. Ashamed that I had believed her, that I had let her words carry me through this year, and that I had trusted someone inside a system that had failed me over and over, because blaming myself felt easier than sitting with the loss.

I closed my laptop and pushed my chair back from the desk. My thoughts scattered, pulled in every direction by the weight of what the year had been. Frustration. Disillusionment. Resilience I hadn't known I carried. Diana's silence and now her polished dismissal felt like personal betrayals. They were symptoms of a system where leadership deferred to policy, professionalism was reduced to compliance, and responsibility for inclusion dissolved once it became inconvenient.

Clear Creek Hill came to mind, and I took a deep breath. Her response only confirmed what I had sensed for months. If I wanted a future rooted in integrity and inclusion, I needed to stay steady, control what I could control, and let the next opportunity come to me in its own time.

"Forgive and forget," I muttered aloud.

It wasn't Diana's fault. It wasn't entirely anyone's fault. Power was concentrated in a few places, probably less with Diana and Jorge than I wanted to believe. In a district as large as Metro Denver Unified, there were three or four layers of administrators above them. They were navigating their first years in demanding roles, trying to hold things together and cover gaps they did not create, within a system that incentivizes isolation.

****

The meeting started like any other. I had done this twice before under Kris's leadership. Both times, I walked in with confidence and left feeling validated. Last year, I was rated "commendable." The year before, "exemplar." My routine was the same: a friendly greeting, shake hands, sit down, and talk through the highs and lows of the year.

This time, I sat across from Jorge. He glanced down at his notes, and my torso stiffened.

He smiled, although it didn't quite reach his eyes. "Andrew, thank you for coming in. I know how busy things are, especially at this time of year."

I nodded, anticipating the usual flow: highlights, areas to improve, an overall rating, and then back to the classroom to wrap up the year.

"This has been quite a year," he began, his tone measured, "for all of us."

I nodded again, sensing the conversation might veer in a different direction.

"I want to start by saying how much I appreciate your dedication to the children and families in your classroom. You've done a lot to support them, even in difficult circumstances." His words were warm, although there was a cautiousness behind them that made me sit up straighter.

"Thank you," I said, managing a small smile.

He continued. "I've been reflecting on our conversations this year, your Teaching Observation Protocol feedback, and the broader challenges you've faced with the early childhood education team. It's clear how deeply you care about your work. That's evident in everything you do."

I felt a flicker of relief, but it didn't last.

"That said"—he paused—"there are areas where I believe there's room for growth. This year, we've seen some successes as well as some missed opportunities to align fully with expectations."

My neck and shoulder muscles tightened.

"Specifically in the areas of instructional effectiveness and collaboration," Jorge said. He listed examples of times I had come up short. Most were reasonably accurate, although they misrepresented the context. He offered no acknowledgment of how I had responded or grown. Then he delivered his conclusion.

"I've rated your overall performance as . . . 'approaching.'"

The word knocked the air out of my lungs. I sat frozen, trying to process what he had just said.

"Approaching?" I repeated, barely above a whisper.

"Yes," he said. "This rating reflects potential. There are strengths to build on as well as areas that need further development."

Potential. I let the word sit, cold and clinical.

On the surface, I had no grounds to contest his judgment. Yet I understood the gravity of a teacher rating. The implications extended far beyond a moment of reflection. My mind flashed back to the HR email I'd received earlier in the year: "Great teaching is the single most important factor in driving improved student outcomes. It takes time to develop the skills to be effective in the classroom and to demonstrate consistent levels of high performance," It had read.

This was the year I was eligible for non-probationary status. After twelve years in classrooms and three in the district, it was the moment meant to bring stability.

Jorge kept talking, mentioning specifics from his observations. Nested within them were moments I was proud of, but he only mentioned the areas for improvement. He referenced my midyear feedback, twisting what I had perceived as constructive into a justification for his decision.

"Ultimately," he said, "this rating means you'll remain on probationary status for another year."

I stared at him, struggling to hold back tears. The word "approaching" felt like a brand, searing into my identity as a teacher.

He leaned forward slightly. "I know this isn't the outcome you were hoping for. I believe this is an opportunity for growth. You have a lot to offer, and I know you'll use this as a chance to reflect and strengthen your practice."

I nodded stiffly, unable to find a response.

I began to stand when Jorge's voice stopped me.

"Andrew, one more thing."

I paused and sat back down. His tone was softer now, hesitant.

"I want to acknowledge something before you leave."

I held the arms of the chair, bracing myself.

"I heard," he began carefully, "about the itinerant position."

I stopped breathing for a moment. The rejection wasn't news, but hearing him mention it reopened the wound.

"I talked with Diana. She mentioned," he continued, "that ultimately, she questioned your ability to balance your passion for early childhood special education with collaboration across a larger team. She felt . . . uncertain about how clearly that passion could be harnessed."

He paused. I sat there, numb to the emotions brewing in my chest.

"She also expressed reservations about your approach to leadership. She wondered if, at times, you might prioritize the children in the classroom over the broader vision of the itinerant role."

I clenched my jaw. The words I wanted to say dissolved into the torrent of emotion beginning to surface: shame, anger, disbelief. Seven months had passed since the interview. Diana had never mentioned any of this to me.

"I'm sorry to hear you didn't get it," Jorge said. "We also talked about the future of the Foundations classroom at Vista, and I think it's important for you to know our decision for the future of the program."

I blinked. "The future of the program?"

"We decided it would be best to close the classroom after this year."

His words hit me hard. I couldn't speak. I couldn't move. I couldn't yell the words I needed to yell. They were shutting down the program. My program. Our program. The classroom we had built with compassion, intention, and dedication. The place where children saw themselves as part of a community. Where families had learned to expect trust and belonging. He wasn't just pushing me out. He was erasing it all.

What made it worse was Diana's role in it. She had been part of the decision, or at least part of how it was carried out. Had she always been? Had she seen me as a liability rather than a strength? The thought lodged in my throat. I didn't want to believe it, but the timeline, the distance, the interview, the silence all began to blur together.

I couldn't tell whether Diana and Jorge had acted together or whether the system, HR procedures, Office of Civil Rights requirements, and upper-administration oversight had simply closed around them. Either way, the outcome was the same. I felt myself pushed out, with nowhere left to stand. The possibility was unbearable.

Jorge leaned back. "I wanted you to hear this from me. I think it's important for your future plans in the district."

"Thank you for letting me know," I said, my voice clipped from my emotional state.

He hesitated. "I hope this doesn't discourage you. You have so much potential. I'm confident you'll find a teaching position next year where you can thrive."

His words were meant to soften the blow, but they deepened the sting.

"If it's not in this district," he added, rising, "then I wish you the best of luck finding something that's the right fit somewhere else."

Even as he pushed me out, Jorge's tone remained smooth. He had said everything right, but he had done everything wrong for the people most affected.

I nodded. "Thank you. Have a good weekend."

It was a gut punch. Everything my teaching assistants and I had built for children and families was being erased. I was at a loss for words. My face remained frozen as I stood and walked out of his office.

Down the corridor to the early childhood wing, everything I had been handed in one conversation collapsed in on itself. Diana's comments echoed in my mind, layered with Jorge's polished delivery.

In that moment, it did not feel structural. It felt personal. I could hear myself sliding back into familiar thinking, turning systemic harm inward, because that was what I had learned to do when things fell apart. The performance review, the rejection of the itinerant role, the subtle implication that I never fully belonged, and the decision to close the classroom churned together, threatening to suffocate me.

This was the end. My job at Vista—and likely in the Metro Denver Unified School District—was over.

The thought was terrifying. I could not yet make sense of what it meant.

My phone buzzed. A text from Natalie: *Daddy come home. We're singing happy birthday and eating cake.*

The system had decided what it would not make room for. I didn't yet know what that would cost me.

CHAPTER 16

INNER DOUBT

———

The birthday candles had long since been blown out, and the duplex was silent. Natalie had gone to bed hours earlier, but I couldn't sleep. The celebration had been wonderful, filled with laughter and warmth. Yet in the quiet of the night, my thoughts were anything but celebratory.

I sat at my desk in the closet-office. My thoughts swirled. Every word from Diana, every silence, every email exchange, and every promise left unfulfilled pressed down on my shoulders. The email I wanted to write was the culmination of everything that had been building since the start of the year. It held what I hadn't said, didn't want to say, but could no longer keep contained after my meeting with Jorge.

I opened her response to my inquiry about the itinerant position for the next school year. Then I got started:

*Dear **Diana**,*

The cursor blinked, waiting for me to find the words. My thoughts were tangled between anger, sadness, frustration, and fear.

I spoke with Jorge this afternoon. He shared comments he heard from you regarding my candidacy for the itinerant position. To hear that I did not get a job because I have failed to express my passion for working in early childhood special education and my priority for collaboration is heartbreaking.

I paused, staring at the screen. Was this too direct? Too harsh? Was Jorge being honest? My internal voice wavered. It echoed the anger and pain I experienced on February 18, the day I promised myself to forgive and forget. That promise had long felt futile. Every moment of the year had revealed how disconnected leadership had become from the people it was meant to serve. Those failures were not just for me, but for the children and families I served. Whether or not Jorge was telling the truth, I needed to speak up.

I continued typing, my fingers moving faster as I poured out everything I had held back for months:

> *As I search for a new job, I know that regardless of what comes my way, I cannot allow it to shake my core values around the inclusion of children with disabilities.*

I paused again as the importance of the words settled in. The core values that had driven me to this work had been battered this year. The access, participation, support, and belonging I had fought to create for my students had been undermined, not because they were wrong, but because they were treated as classroom concerns rather than leadership responsibilities. Those principles did not stop at the classroom door. They applied to adults too.

Administrators needed the same things children and teachers did: a sense of belonging rooted in shared values, opportunities to listen and be heard, meaningful connections with peers, and the space to learn and grow together. Instead, collaboration was framed through compliance, and decisions were made in isolation. The result was not inclusion. It was endurance.

As I wrote, memories of Vista flashed through my mind: the meeting about Jovan's placement my first year at Vista, the heartbreaking outcome of moving David A. to Esmeralda's classroom, the reprimands for trying to connect with my students. I remembered the countless moments of exhaustion after Lillie left, Ana's struggles to stay until her maternity leave, and the early childhood education team's disconnection and mistrust.

The words on the screen became a kind of catharsis.

Because of my passion for working directly with children and my yearning for continued growth as a collaborative team member, I chose to stay in the classroom rather than pursue the associate professor position at Rocky Mountain Community College before this school year began. When being a collaborative team member was compromised at Vista, I listened to your praise for my work and followed your encouragement to pursue the itinerant position. It has been made clear that trusting you was a poor choice.

My chest tightened. It wasn't just a poor choice. I had trusted her, and she had betrayed that trust. Jorge, too, had failed to honor the values he claimed to hold—collaboration, innovation, and equity—for children, families, and Vista employees.

I kept writing, my internal dialogue shifting between resignation and defiance.

What is unfathomable and crushing is the closure of the program I teach in. That program was becoming a touchstone for Vista and the community.

The memories came flooding back. I thought of parents telling me how much they valued the program, how it gave them hope for their children. Their voices echoed in my mind as I typed:

The past three years, families have come into my classroom, and they had a voice, they belonged, and they trusted us. They knew we, as a team, worked to give their child the start to early education that they had never considered.

I stopped typing. My eyes welled up. The thought of twenty-five families standing up for us in Jorge's office back in September, David A.'s mother, Beatriz's and Gabriela's engagement despite the limitations made the words poignant. How could I expect Diana to understand the impact we had and the pain caused by her and Jorge's decision to close the Foundations class?

The email grew longer, my emotions spilling over.

It is hard for me to say, but I have been demoralized this year. Everything I believe in has been chewed up and spit out in my face. The teaching challenge that I decided to take on ended up being more of a one-sided boxing match, where I was repeatedly bullied and manipulated.

I leaned back in my chair, letting the words settle. *Do I sound too bitter? Too emotional?* My internal voice whispered again, *Forgive and forget.*

But forgiveness felt miles away. By the time I reached the end, the clock read 3:43 a.m. My hands hovered over the keyboard. My heart pounded. Would sending this change anything? Probably not, at least not in a positive way. It wasn't about Diana. It was about speaking up and refusing to be complicit. It was about saying what needed to be said, even if no one listened. I clicked send.

For a moment, I just sat there, staring at the screen. The silence of the duplex stretched around me, as if releasing the email had exposed the enormity of my emptiness. I thought about Natalie, still asleep in the other room, and the girls, who would wake up soon, ready to fill the day with their endless energy. Their love kept me tethered to gratitude.

Forgive and forget, I told myself again, this time with a little more conviction. I wasn't there yet, but maybe this was the first step.

Those were the last words I ever sent to or received from Diana.

***

As the potluck for the afternoon class wound down, I dimmed the lights in room 122 and invited everyone to gather around the screen. The children wiggled in their parents' laps. Their fingers clutched remnants of enchiladas, pan dulces, and ice cream. I connected my laptop to the Promethean board, and the title screen of the year-end slideshow filled the screen: *Room 122: Our Year Together.*

"Are you ready to see all the amazing things we did this year?" My voice was animated. The children cheered, and the parents smiled, their expressions bittersweet. I pressed play, and the gentle strumming of Jack Johnson's version of "Friends" filled the room.

The first photos were from our restaurant unit in the Every Early Learner Succeeds curriculum. Images of the children dressed as bakers and chefs flashed on the screen. Eric, Jimmy, and Ricky wore white aprons and chef's hats, each holding a pretend pizza as they grinned for the camera. Another shot showed Sofia taking orders on a notepad with a determined look.

The pictures were sweet. They didn't spark the inspiration I had felt in previous years. These weren't candid moments I had rushed to capture because they brimmed with wonder. These were staged for documentation. At the time, they were a requirement to show children's developmental progress, not memories I had wanted to hold on to forever. Watching, my heart broke, discovering those moments of belonging and authentic, meaningful connections that I couldn't see when the picture was taken. I cherished each slide.

The slideshow moved on to the children building structures with blocks. They were stacking and balancing, their faces intent as they worked together. The music transitioned to "Bare Necessities" from *The Jungle Book*. Parents chuckled at the images.

Next came photos from art projects. Messy hands coated in paint, children concentrating on their brushstrokes, and a group shot of everyone holding their finished masterpieces. Then a video clip of the playground. Children chased each other, shrieking with laughter, their hair flying in the wind. Watching, it was evident that I had gradually let the children take the lead rather than forcing them into developmentally inappropriate curriculum activities.

The slideshow for the end-of-year routine was shorter than all but my first year at Vista. There were fewer spontaneous moments I felt compelled to photograph or record. Minimal bursts of creativity emerged during free play since those moments were often interrupted to stay on schedule or in fear of someone walking in to observe. In past years, these slideshows had been overflowing with joy. The hardest part had always been deciding what to cut.

As the final image of the children sitting in front of the literacy center faded to black, I turned to the parents and children. The room was quiet except for a few sniffles.

"Thank you," I said softly, my voice catching. "Thank you for sharing your children with us this year. It's been an honor to be their teacher."

I invited the children to the circle on the carpet for one last goodbye. The children settled down, their parents kneeling or sitting on the floor behind them. I looked around at their eager faces.

"This is our last day of this school year," I said, my voice steady but soft. "It has been such a very special year. Each of you has brought something unique and wonderful to our class, and I am so proud of all of you. You're all ready to go to pre-kindergarten in an Explorer classroom."

Eric, sitting cross-legged by my left side, raised his hand. "Are you gonna be my teacher in the Explorer classroom?"

I felt the pull of tears as I turned to him. "No, Eric," I said gently, my throat tightening. I looked up, trying to compose myself. My eyes connected with the hole in the drywall near the front door. The shame I had felt on February 18 was rising. "I won't be your teacher. I won't be a teacher at Vista. I might not be a teacher anywhere."

His brows shifted in confusion, and I heard a parent gasp softly. Everyone looked at me. I feared they could see the broken heart on my sleeve.

After the families had left, I lingered in the spacious classroom filled with the solitude caused by the goodbyes I had just said. I sat down at my desk, staring at the white Promethean board and bare walls. The slideshow wasn't just a reflection of the children's year. It was a reflection of mine. It had been a year where joy was overshadowed by struggle and inspiration was buried under frustration. It had been a year where I documented progress instead of celebrating moments. Still, that final day was mine. I had chosen to show up fully. I had chosen to connect with the children, families, and Cecilia in a way that felt true. As I sat there, I reminded myself of something I had told parents for years. I had told this to Esmeralda and David A.'s mom at his Individual Education Program meeting in January. Every step forward, no matter how small, is worth celebrating.

✳✳✳

Gabriela walked into room 122 with Ernesto at her side. Her eyes swept the space as if she were capturing a panoramic photo.

"I wanted to see you before we left for the summer," she said softly, "to tell you how much I've appreciated your work at Vista these past three years. I can't count the number of times parents whose children were in your class have told me what a difference you made."

I started to respond, but movement caught my eye. Ernesto was slowly drifting toward the community center. He paused in the corner, his gaze landing on three thirty-gallon storage buckets stacked beside a blue felt board with a deep pocket sewn into the back.

He tilted his head. "What's this?"

The felt board had been a gift from my mentor during my first year in public schools. It had been the centerpiece of our circle time every year, a way for every child, including those with disabilities or learning English, to join in a story. This year, though, it had stayed hidden in the closet, along with the buckets. The Every Early Learner Succeeds curriculum left no room for them.

Ernesto slipped his small hand into the back pocket of the felt board and pulled out a Ziploc bag stuffed with felt pieces. Then another. He turned to his mom. "Mira, Mamá."

Gabriela stepped closer, her fingers brushing the fabric. "I've never seen this before," she said. "This would have been wonderful for the kids."

"It was," I said quietly. "Since I began teaching, it has been one of the best tools I had for building a community. This year, I was told I could not use it." The words caught in my throat, the loss pressing in.

Ernesto fished out a bag with a cloth glove and five little monkeys. "¿Podemos cantar la canción?" His eyes lit with hope.

"Of course," I answered in Spanish, motioning for him to sit down in front of me.

We sang together, his voice rising above mine, his body swaying and bouncing with each verse. When the last monkey fell off the bed, he laughed so hard he had to catch his breath.

I noticed another bag lying on the floor. It held the felt pieces for *Brown Bear, Brown Bear, What Do You See?* "Do you want to read this one?" I asked.

He nodded. We spread the felt animals across the carpet, opened the board, and began. Ernesto had never read the story, yet the English words flowed from him as if he had always known them. He placed each animal on the board, sometimes upside down, sometimes sideways, and soon they were dancing with one another, ignoring the sequence entirely.

I joined him in the play. The last page of the story revealed it was the zookeeper telling the story. The children in his company were the animals. At that moment, I saw the whole year reflected back to me. It was a story told the way children needed it, not the way it was scripted. I thought about how I could never leave the classroom. This year was an aberration.

My eyes drifted to the hole in the drywall. It pulled me back to the policies and practices that I felt had done more harm than good. They dictated how we were expected to serve children who were dual-language learners, children who had disabilities, and children who were three years old. Vista had not created these problems; it had only revealed them. Once the hole appeared, I could no longer pretend I hadn't seen what it exposed. As much as I loved teaching, I knew I could use what I had learned here to better support others in another district as an itinerant or in another support role.

When I looked up, Gabriela was standing over us with a smile unlike any I had seen from her before. I rose to my feet, and she pulled me into a tight embrace.

"I don't have the words to express how much I appreciate your work," she whispered, reaching out to me as I stood up.

I wanted to freeze the moment. Ernesto slipped into our hug, his arms stretching around both of us.

As they stepped toward the door, Gabriela turned back. "I'll keep fighting for these children and families while you're gone," she said, her voice steady. "Even if it has to be quiet, like I told you before."

Her words brought me back to our hallway conversation months earlier. Her eyes had scanned for anyone who might have overheard. Her voice had been low as she admitted she had to be careful about what she said because of her job. Even then, her conviction had been clear.

"I know you will," I said.

It was the last goodbye I gave a parent at Vista Elementary.

***

The laughter and shrieks of children echoed through the indoor pool, creating a humid cacophony that made it difficult to stay focused on the phone call. Itzel toddled toward the water playground, her legs moving with determined wobbles. I followed closely, phone pressed to my ear, while keeping an eye on Citlali, who splashed happily by the water slide.

"Virginia? Can you hear me?" I asked, raising my voice over the background noise. The reception was weak, and her voice crackled on the other end.

"Barely. Try again," she said, her words breaking up.

"I said I had a job interview with the Denver 44 School District last month," I repeated, weaving around other parents as I stayed close to Itzel. She had discovered a waterspout and was trying to cut through it with her hand.

"You got an interview? That's great!" Virginia said, though her tone was cautious.

"Yeah, I was hired a couple of weeks ago. I got assigned a school last week," I said, glancing down to make sure Itzel wasn't about to lose her balance and fall into the waterspout. "In Denver 44, all the early childhood special education teachers are itinerants, but it's different from Metro Denver Unified. They're assigned to two to four classrooms, usually in one or two schools. It's more like being a co-teacher than a traditional itinerant."

"Congratulations. That's great! It sounds . . . different," Virginia replied.

"It is," I said, leaning down to steady Itzel as she tried to plug the spout with her foot. "I like the idea of working more closely with the teachers and kids. It's not the whirlwind of eight schools and twenty classrooms like it is in Metro Denver Unified. Still . . ."

"What's the hesitation?"

"I don't know how I'll feel about not leading my own classroom," I admitted. I stood up and scanned the pool for Citlali. She was playing a game with another child. Their laughter blended with the roar of water dumping from buckets above. "That's the part I keep thinking about. I've always been the one setting the tone, building the relationships, and co-creating a classroom with my teaching assistants. It's hard to imagine stepping back from that. In Metro Denver Unified, I saw the itinerant role as a chance to grow as a leader. I wanted to support other teachers and model inclusive practices beyond a single classroom. Now I'm not so sure. I mean, I know Vista. I know Metro Denver Unified's Early Childhood Special Education Department. In a new district, I'd be starting over. If I want to do it right, it could take years just to understand the culture. It could take even longer to influence it. Maybe Jorge and Diana were right. Maybe I'm not ready for this."

There was a long pause, or maybe the reception cut out. My mind began to wander. I thought about Jorge, how he had arrived at Vista with a vision and forced it on us before taking the time to learn who we were. He hadn't immersed himself in our community, and that disconnect had caused real harm. I didn't want to make the same mistake. As an itinerant, I would be moving between classrooms, each with its own culture, its own dynamics. If I wasn't careful—if I tried to lead before I listened—

I might repeat the very missteps I'd spent the past year trying to survive.

Virginia spoke tenderly, interrupting my insecurity. "I get that. You've always been about setting the tone. Co-teaching might feel like giving up some of that control, but it's another opportunity for growth. I don't think it will be much different from how you approached teaching with your teaching assistants. Even the service providers."

"I know. That was my thinking," I said, adjusting my grip on the phone as I trailed Itzel to the water slide. "I went to the district orientation yesterday. The superintendent spoke and said a lot of nice things about innovation and equity, but the words and the culture felt just like what I heard in Metro Denver Unified. It made me realize it's not about the district or even the administrators. It's the system. Like you suggested way back in March, the system is designed to put teachers at the mercy of administrators. I could hear it behind all their slogans and initiatives."

"That sounds frustrating."

"It is. I don't have many options, though. I need to figure something out. Summer's going to fly by."

Virginia hesitated before saying, "Well, I heard there's an associate professor position opening at Eastern Community College. Their early childhood program is apparently a mess, but it could be a great opportunity for you."

I laughed dryly. "A mess, huh? That's tempting."

"No, really," she said, her tone brightening, "you'd be perfect for it. They need someone with experience in early childhood and special education. Someone who understands inclusion and can build something out of nothing."

"I can't," I said quickly, shaking my head even though she couldn't see me. "There's the grant for the university. It requires me to work directly with children."

"How much longer do you need to do that?"

"Four more years, I think. But I may be able to get approved to do indirect work with children," I said, guiding Itzel away from the water slide toward water toys. "I'm not too interested in walking into a mess without support."

Virginia chuckled. "You've always got my support, Andrew."

I glanced at Itzel, now giggling as the fountain coming out of a water toy sprayed her face, and Citlali, who waved at me from across the pool. "I don't know, Virginia. Maybe I'll give it some thought. Right now, I just need to figure out what's next with the Denver 44 School District."

"Whatever you choose, it will all work out," she said confidently. "You've got to take that first step, even if it's scary."

The call dropped before I could respond, but her words percolated as I watched my daughters. As Itzel toddled toward the playground structure, her determination unwavering, I followed behind.

"Maybe," I mumbled, pocketing the phone and letting the splashes and laughter of the pool wash over me.

My phone vibrated again. "Hi, Virginia. Sorry about that. You've got a point," I said, adjusting Itzel's swim diaper after her enthusiastic splash sent water flying. She continued toddling toward the water playground, relentless in her pursuit. "If I were at Eastern Community College, I could make inclusion a real focus in the courses I teach. You know I'd advocate for kids with disabilities and their families no matter what."

"Of course you would," Virginia said, her voice warm with encouragement. "You were already doing that in your Exceptional Child class last summer. I learned so much from you about making inclusion real in the classroom."

I smiled, remembering the lively discussions from that course. "Yeah, that was a great group of students. You all were so passionate about early childhood. Still, I felt like we barely scratched the surface."

"Exactly! That's why it's such a bummer you're not teaching it this summer."

"I know. I'm sorry," I said, keeping my eyes on Citlali, who was now showing Itzel how to splash the water just right to make a big wave. "I just needed to take a step back this summer. Spend more time with the girls, get settled into whatever job I land, and focus on my own classes. But I miss it. I really do."

"Well, if you apply, get the interview, receive an offer, and take the job at Eastern, you'll be right back in it. And you'll get to help shape the program. That's huge."

Her words stayed with me after the call ended. As the girls played, I sat down at the edge of the pool, letting the warm water lap against my legs while I thought about what she'd said.

Later that evening, after dinner and baths, I read bedtime stories to the girls. As I turned the pages, I kept thinking about teaching literacy in an inclusive classroom. The felt board, finger plays, puppets, and big books. After tucking them in, I went to the living room. I needed to find out whether the associate professor position at Eastern Community College would fulfill the scholarship requirements.

I hesitated before opening my email, my fingers hovering over the keys. Could I really make this work?

I drafted a message to the lead of the early childhood special education doctoral program:

Dear Annika,

I hope this message finds you well. I have a hypothetical question regarding the scholarship requirements. If I were an associate professor at a community college, teaching courses that focus on advocating for inclusion and supporting children with disabilities, would that fulfill the scholarship's requirements?

Thank you for your guidance!

Best,
Andrew

The response came the next day after I finished making breakfast. I opened my phone and read the email aloud to Natalie, who was feeding Itzel a banana.

"Dear Andrew," I began, "Yes, other students in similar positions have been able to fulfill the scholarship requirements in this way. As long as the courses you teach maintain a focus on inclusion and advocacy for children with disabilities, it is absolutely fine. Good luck!"

"Well, there's your answer," Natalie said, smiling.

"Yeah," I said, a blend of uncertainty and gratitude stirring in my gut.

As soon as the girls were down for their afternoon naps, I sat back at the laptop and found the associate professor position posting for Eastern Community College. My hands shook slightly as I uploaded my résumé and cover letter, then double-checked every detail of the application.

Hesitation gripped me. I stared at the "submit" button. All the self-doubt and second-guessing bubbled up again. But then I thought about the potential: what I could build, who I could inspire, and the impact I could have on future teachers and children.

I clicked submit.

***

The Colorado sun was blinding as I stepped out of my car and stared at the two-story, rectangular administration building at Eastern Community College. It was modern but unassuming. While it didn't scream opportunity, it didn't push me away either. Virginia's words echoed in my mind. *You don't have to decide before you get the offer.* I adjusted my tie, smoothed my shirt, and took a deep breath. *Why am I even here? I have a job with the Denver 44 School District.* The answer wasn't clear, but the weight of my experience and the relentless cycle of the same policies and barriers I had fought through in public schools had pushed me to consider something new.

I hesitated in the parking lot, recalling flashes of the previous school year. I replayed Diana's email from February 18 and Jorge's words during my final evaluation meeting. *I'm not capable of a leadership position. I'm not good at collaborating*, my inner voice pleaded, trying to send me back to my car.

The automatic doors slid open, and I stepped into a vast, open lobby. Students of all ages and demographics with backpacks lounged in clusters. Their laughter and chatter filled the space. I found my way to the reception desk and gave my name.

"The early childhood education associate professor interview . . . let me see?" the woman behind the counter said, smiling warmly. "Okay. I found you in Dr. Moore's calendar. Just head down that hallway and take the elevator to the second floor. I'll let her know you're here." I nodded and started walking, the notepad and flash drive in my hand feeling slipperier with every step.

Dr. Amanda Moore greeted me warmly as she led me off the elevator. She introduced herself as the chair of the Early Childhood Education Department. She was a Black woman who looked like she was in her late twenties. Her appearance caught me off guard, immediately drawing my awareness to my biases. I had imagined a White woman behind the name. I briefly questioned whether I was prepared to meet her expectations. I had never had a Black woman as a supervisor, and I found myself holding a quiet awareness of what that might mean. As I followed her down the hallway, something opened in me. It occurred to me that this might be the kind of leadership I had been craving. She might be someone who saw the full scope of inclusion, around all my blind spots.

We walked into the classroom for the interview, and I tried to quiet the self-critical thoughts that followed. My consciousness of internalized bias felt like a double-edged sword. It kept me accountable, but it also sometimes paralyzed me. *Today,* I told myself as I breathed in deeply, *I will be intentional. Mindful. Open.* I already had a job for the next school year. This interview wasn't about leaving the classroom. It was about the potential opportunity to claim a new path, moving in the same direction.

The other interviewers—a middle-aged White woman, man in his early fifties, and a younger White woman—smiled and welcomed me as I took my seat at the long table.

"Thank you for coming, Andrew," Dr. Moore began, her tone warm but professional. "We're really looking forward to learning about your experiences and how they might fit with the goals of this position."

I nodded, my nerves masked with a polite smile. The first few questions were straightforward. They asked about my experience in early childhood education, my work at Rocky Mountain Community College, and my philosophy on inclusion. Unlike the final evaluation meeting at Vista, where inclusion felt more like a compliance box, this interview felt like an unwritten story. It was still uncertain, yet it felt real. I spoke about my years in the classroom, the lessons I had learned from children and families, and the ways I had adapted my teaching practices to ensure every child felt a sense of belonging.

Then it was time for my teaching demonstration. Dr. Moore introduced it, explaining that they wanted to see how I engaged others in learning. I had prepared a mini-lecture on Urie Bronfenbrenner's Ecological Systems Model, weaving in ideas that had evolved since the conversation about the cardiovascular system and Swiss cheese with Virginia and Ana. I stood and began, careful to balance the theoretical framework with real-life application.

"With Bronfenbrenner's model," I explained, gesturing to a diagram with four concentric circles I had sketched on the whiteboard, "we understand that a child's development is influenced not just by their immediate surroundings, or what he called the microsystem, but also by the larger, interconnected systems that shape their lives. For example, in my work, I've seen how policies set by the macrosystem, like district mandates, can create barriers or opportunities in a child's microsystem, like their classroom or family."

The interviewers nodded, their pens moving quickly across their sheets of paper. As I spoke, I remained mindful of identity and race. I drew on examples from diverse classrooms, highlighting the importance of cultural responsiveness with children and adults and the need for teachers to reflect on their own biases.

"Inclusion," I said, looking directly at Dr. Moore, "is not just about physical presence in a classroom. It's about ensuring that children and families feel a sense of belonging, have access to opportunities, and have the necessary supports to participate in ways that are meaningful and authentic to their identities."

Her expression gave little away, but I noticed a slight nod of approval. The questions that followed were more pointed.

"How do you see your role as an associate professor being different from your role as a classroom teacher?" asked the older White man.

I paused and allowed the question to wander around me as I considered my answer.

"My role would shift," I began slowly. "In the classroom, I have been focused on direct relationships with children and families, building trust and creating environments where they can thrive. As an associate professor, my focus would broaden. I would be preparing future teachers to do that work, ensuring they have the skills, knowledge, and tools to create inclusive classrooms." I gestured back to the whiteboard. My conversations with Virginia and Ana, comparing a high-quality inclusive environment to the cardiovascular system, coaxed an unassuming smile from my face.

"Looking at the ecological model"—I pointed to the whiteboard—"we can see that as a classroom teacher, I have been at the microsystem level, directly influencing children. As a professor, I would be part of the exosystem of a child who is in the care of one of the adult learners. I would influence the environments they will create for children and families. Furthermore, the adult learners' experiences with children would influence the content we discuss in class. It is a different role with the same goal. I want to make sure children are at the center." That ripple effect, impacting not just one class but many, felt like a new kind of inclusion, one rooted in systems change, like a healthy cardiovascular system.

The interview wrapped up with more questions about my leadership philosophy, my approach to collaboration, and how I would handle resistance to change. I drew from the ideas Virginia and I had discussed during our lunches at McDonald's: trust, patience, and listening.

As I walked out of the building, my mind was tangled. I replayed the teaching demonstration, scrutinizing every word I had said. *Was I clear enough? Did I connect the theory to practice effectively?*

Another part of me felt hopeful. Nervous, but hopeful. This was a different kind of classroom door I'd be stepping through, and maybe it was the right one.

CHAPTER 17

THE DISSERTATION

———

It had been nearly a year since I began my role as an associate professor in the Early Childhood Education Department at Eastern Community College. Dr. Amanda Moore, now both a colleague and a mentor, had quickly become an integral part of my professional and academic life. She was sharp, direct, and refreshingly insightful. By the end of our first semester together, our conversations had become daily rituals. We exchanged ideas in her office and built a camaraderie rooted in our shared commitment to inclusion.

The first conversation about my dissertation happened on an unusually cold afternoon in early April. I was bundled up against the chill, my mind racing as I walked directly into her office. Her workspace reflected her personality, practical yet welcoming. Her desk was cluttered, but every item seemed to have a purpose. The whiteboard to her right displayed a chaotic mix of notes, arrows, and diagrams, adding to the room's charm.

I draped my winter wear over the back of the chair and sat down, my hands clutching a yellow legal notepad. Dr. Moore turned to face me.

"So," she began, breaking the silence, "you've talked about inclusion, systems, and families in just about every conversation we've had since you got here. If this dissertation is going to matter, you need to focus. What's the scope?"

I hesitated, trying to organize my thoughts. "I'm thinking of examining how community colleges prepare early childhood educators for inclusive practices, especially in settings with dual-language learners and children with disabilities."

She nodded, though her expression didn't shift. "Good. Let me push you a bit. Are you talking about teacher preparation broadly, or are you zooming in on specific strategies? For example, how do faculty model inclusion in their own instruction?"

I took a deep breath, feeling the importance of her question. Memories of my time at Vista Elementary surfaced. "Honestly, I think it has to be both preparation broadly and specific strategies. At Vista, I saw firsthand how gaps in teacher preparation affected children. There were moments, like with these two students, David and Antonio, when I struggled to engage them meaningfully because the curriculum didn't permit me to use effective practices and strategies. Granted, they spoke Spanish, and I didn't . . . or wasn't allowed, but even if I was, I watched other teachers struggle. They weren't taught how to create meaningful, inclusive classrooms."

Her gaze sharpened. "So, you're saying it's about bridging theory and practice? That's fine, but you have to be clear about how you're defining success. Is it about student outcomes? Faculty development? Program structures? You can't measure everything."

I paused, replaying conversations I'd had with Virginia over lunch at McDonald's about power and belonging. Reflections about resilience and patience during quiet moments on Clear Creek Hill emerged. "What if I start by documenting the authentic approaches each instructor in the Early Childhood Education Department here at Eastern Community College uses to teach about inclusion? I can compare them to prescribed state standards. I'll interview graduates of the classes and see if it was their instructors' authentic approach or state standards that had the greatest impact. I could also look at how students apply what they learn during their practicum experiences."

She tapped her pen against the desk, her expression softening. "Now we're getting somewhere. But you still need to narrow your attention. Let me ask you this: how do your experiences at Vista shape what you want to find?"

I leaned forward, energized by the question. "During my three years at Vista, I learned that inclusion isn't just about placing kids in the same room. Inclusion is about creating a sense of belonging for every child, family, and professional. I learned that to connect, we must start with authentic relationships. That's what I want future educators to understand. It's not enough to follow a checklist or implement a curriculum. We must have authentic relationships between teachers, teaching assistants, support staff, children, and families. Like Ricky helping David R., or Sofia and Ernesto helping Antonio join their play. The connections provide access to meaningful learning opportunities, participation in the activities, and support for engagement. Those experiences in the classroom weren't just a moment of inclusion. They were a reflection of the environment we'd built."

Dr. Moore smiled. "And how do you teach that? Because it's one thing to say inclusion is about authentic, meaningful connections. It's another to show teachers how to foster it."

Her question struck me, and I felt the familiar tug of self-doubt. "That's what I'm trying to figure out," I admitted. "I know it starts with understanding the barriers. At Vista, the curriculum we used during my last year was supposed to be inclusive, but it often felt rigid. Teachers weren't given the autonomy to adapt it for dual-language learners or kids with disabilities, not because of the curriculum itself, but due to district policies. Or rather, one administrator's interpretation of those policies. Maybe part of the answer is showing future educators how to navigate those constraints."

She scribbled something on a sticky note and handed it to me. "Start there. Barriers are part of the story, but they're not the whole story. Frame them as opportunities for innovation. What are the unique challenges here at the college, and how are instructors responding? Don't forget the voices of students and instructors. This isn't just about policies. It's about people."

Her words settled over me, both comforting and challenging. I jotted down notes, feeling the pieces of my dissertation beginning to take shape. As I left her office, I realized how much this process mirrored my time at Vista. Just as I had navigated the complexities of inclusion in room 125, and then room 122, I now had the chance to reimagine what inclusion could mean in higher education. The setting had changed, but the questions and my commitment remained the same.

***

The evening twilight painted the living room windows of our 1972 split-level house tucked into a Denver suburb. Natalie sat on the couch, her posture relaxed but attentive, as she listened to me recount the latest developments in my dissertation journey from a chair across the room.

In the basement, Citlali, now five, was orchestrating a play with her dolls while Itzel, just two years old, obediently followed her sister's lead. Their giggles filtered up through the air vents, filling the house with a soundtrack of innocence and joy.

"It will be such a relief when I'm done with the coursework," I said, leaning back into the cushions.

Natalie smiled. "It will be a relief for all of us, trust me. You've been so much more present lately. It's nice . . . and probably more about being out of the classroom than classes at the university."

I chuckled, though her words stirred something bittersweet in me. She was right. I was more present. Still, I couldn't deny that I missed the classroom deeply. The energy of working directly with children, the connection with families, it was a void nothing else could quite fill.

As if reading my thoughts, Natalie asked, "Do you miss it? The classroom, I mean."

"Every day," I admitted, "but I feel like I can start channeling that energy into something meaningful with this research. It's not the same, but it's important."

Natalie nodded thoughtfully. "You've been talking a lot about leadership ever since you started your doctorate. Are you incorporating that into your dissertation research?"

I leaned forward, animated now. "It's something I have been reflecting on a lot, especially after everything I experienced at Vista. Leadership in education is often seen as something for administrators or policymakers. Classroom teachers, especially early childhood educators, need leadership skills just as much. It is like that framework I created long ago, the Four Core Elements for Effective Inclusion. It all starts with leadership. Teachers are the ones implementing inclusive practices, navigating language barriers, and building relationships with families. They are the front line. Yet there is so little focus on empowering them as leaders."

She tilted her head, considering my words. "Do you think any of the situations at Vista will make it into your research?"

I hesitated, a familiar knot forming in my chest. "No. As much as I want to move on, it's still really hard for me to look back on that year without feeling . . . raw. There's too much pain there. I think I need more time and distance before I can make sense of it in a way that's useful."

"That makes sense. You went through a lot."

Her support was soothing, and I found myself smiling. "Thanks. I think this path has potential. Focusing on leadership skills could make a real difference. Not just for teachers, but for kids and families too. I just need to figure out who, how, and what to analyze."

The laughter from downstairs had turned into youthful bickering, signaling the end of the girls' harmonious play session. I glanced at the clock on my phone and then at Natalie.

"It's about that time," I said, rising from the chair.

"Good luck," she teased.

I called down the stairs, "Citlali! Itzel! Time to get ready for bed!"

The sound of tiny feet thundering up the stairs followed, and I knelt to greet them, scooping Itzel into my arms as Citlali chattered about her dolls' latest adventures. Their energy was boundless.

As I led them through their bedtime routine, I felt quietly content. The stress of my final year at Vista was still there, but so was the promise of what lay ahead. For tonight, that was enough.

***

It was a quiet afternoon in my lamp-lit office at Eastern Community College. My L-shaped desk was covered by a patchwork of course materials, Post-it notes, and a small pot with a six-inch ZZ plant. I was trying to connect the dots between the concepts I was teaching and the ideas emerging from research and conversations when my phone lit up with Virginia's name. I smiled. Her calls always seemed to come at just the right moment.

"Hey, Virginia," I said, leaning back in my chair.

"Hi, Andrew! How's the dissertation coming along?"

I sighed, half-laughing. "It's coming, slowly. Dr. Moore and I have had some great conversations, but pulling all these ideas together into something cohesive is a challenge."

"That's the way it goes," she said knowingly. "But from what you've shared before, it sounds like you're on the right track. Have you thought more about looking at interpersonal leadership? I was reading through the Division for Early Childhood of the Council for Exceptional Children's Position Statement on Leadership (2015) this morning, and I thought of you. It struck me how well the framework aligned with our conversations over the years and could align with your work."

"The five forms of leadership?" I asked, pulling a notebook closer to me.

"Exactly," she said. "Advocacy, pedagogy, administrative . . . Let me see. What are the other two?" I heard clicking on the other end. "Conceptual and community. It would be fascinating to see how students in your director's certificate program understand those forms or whether they're being taught at all. It could reveal a lot about how we're preparing early childhood professionals to lead. I've heard you talk about the need to rethink teacher preparation periodically and leadership regularly. Maybe this is the intersection you needed."

I nodded, jotting down a note. "That's a great point. Dr. Moore and I talked a little about barriers for teaching about inclusion and the need for innovative ideas. This might be the starting point. I'm not sure if you remember the Four Core Elements for Effective Inclusion framework I shared with you during one of our McDonald's lunches, but thinking back, working with that helped me see how inclusion always starts with leadership."

Silence rested between us for a moment. I continued. "Okay. So, in regard to that Position Statement on Leadership, it's about influencing and empowering others within a system shaped by constant, unpredictable dynamics. Schools and programs exist within communities, surrounded by spoken and unspoken policies. Curriculum is never neutral, and change happens every minute. These are all manifestations of power. We either respond to them intentionally or let them act on us."

"Exactly," Virginia said. "The five forms of leadership aren't about style or personality. They're not transactional. They show how layered leadership can be, especially in inclusive environments. Advocacy and conceptual forms of leadership are essential, but they're often missing from training. We talk about adapting to changes in society and how to speak up for our values, but we don't name that as leadership. If we don't teach it explicitly, how can we expect our teachers in training to see themselves as leaders?"

I thought of my students in the director's certificate program. "You know, it reminds me of the Swiss Cheese Model we've talked about. There will always be holes, but when we layer the cheese, meaning everyone is a leader, someone will catch what falls through."

"I remember that," she said, laughing. "It's a helpful image. I do think there's overlap, but the forms give us a wider lens."

"Maybe we've touched on some of this in the classes I teach, but we've never framed it using those five forms of leadership. It could be really interesting to survey the students and see how they define leadership. Do they feel prepared to take on those roles and responsibilities?"

"That could be such powerful data, Andrew." Virginia's energy carried through the line. "And it ties perfectly into your themes of inclusion and leadership. How do we prepare leaders who can build authentic relationships, collaborate, and advocate for inclusion at every level in the profession?"

"Exactly," I said, the pieces beginning to fall into place. "This research could uncover real gaps, but also opportunities. If we shift how we prepare early childhood professionals, if we give them the tools and language of leadership, we're supporting not just the adults, but the children and families they serve."

Virginia laughed softly. "That's the Andrew I know. Always considering the micro and macro. The cheese and the cardiovascular system. I have no doubt this dissertation is going to be something special."

"Thanks, Virginia," I said, smiling. "It really helps to have you and Dr. Moore in my corner. The conversations we've had about Vista, about leadership, about what inclusion really takes have shaped this more than you know."

"Well, you've come a long way," she said. "I can't wait to read the final product. As soon as you schedule your defense, you'd better invite me."

"Of course," I said, laughing. "I wouldn't dream of doing it without you there."

As we ended the call, I felt more at ease with my direction. I looked at the ZZ plant on my desk, growing slowly, at its own pace. The path ahead still felt daunting, but with the support of mentors like Virginia and Dr. Moore, I knew I could keep moving forward. This dissertation wasn't just a degree requirement. It was a way to give voice to a profession I loved. It was a continuation of what had started in room 125, then in room 122, and was now growing steadily in the community college.

***

It was a sunny afternoon in late January. Dr. Moore's office felt especially inviting, with its space heater, a wall-length window overlooking an open field, and a whiteboard decorated with ideas we had shared. I sat leaning forward in the chair opposite hers, feeling a mix of exhaustion and exhilaration. I was so close to finishing my dissertation research that I could practically see the finish line.

"You've been deep in this work for so long," Dr. Moore said, leaning back with her usual welcoming demeanor. "How are you feeling about everything now that the research is almost done?"

I sighed, running a hand around my scalp. "Honestly, it's been eye-opening and a little disheartening. The interviews with the faculty and the graduates of the director's certificate program have made one thing painfully clear: We're not preparing teachers and directors to be leaders in inclusive classrooms."

Dr. Moore nodded, her expression thoughtful. "What are you hearing in the interviews?"

"Well," I began, flipping open my notebook to my latest set of findings, "students who graduated from the program feel like they have been taught the basics. They know how to manage a classroom, meet licensing requirements, and plan curriculum. Yet they do not see these practices as leadership, even though, in many respects, they are. Leadership, especially in inclusive settings, feels undefined and out of reach for them. More than once, I have heard, 'I know inclusion is important, yet I do not know how to make it happen without more support.' But they don't know what kind of support they need."

Dr. Moore raised an eyebrow. "And what about the faculty?"

"They're trying," I said. "But the interviews show they focus on leadership as an administrative responsibility. A couple admitted they're not equipped to teach leadership for inclusion because it wasn't part of their own training, and they've never experienced it. One professor told me, 'I can teach students about inclusion, but leadership for inclusion? That's a whole other beast.' It's like we're all stuck in a cycle of perpetuating the same gaps in knowledge and skills."

She nodded slowly. "And these gaps, are you finding connections to your experiences at Vista?"

I exhaled sharply. "Absolutely. Every barrier I faced in my classrooms—whether it was a lack of support, communication breakdowns, or administrators who didn't understand inclusion—can be traced back to leadership. And I'm seeing why inclusion worked well for me in my first two years at Vista. Teachers and directors aren't being prepared to lead in inclusive settings. It's not that they don't care or don't want to. They just don't know how or where to start. And it's the children and families who suffer for it."

Dr. Moore leaned back in her chair. "So, what's the takeaway? What are you hoping your research will accomplish?"

I paused, choosing my words carefully. "I want this dissertation to be a catalyst for change. If we want inclusive classrooms to succeed, we have to start with the people leading them. That means rethinking how we train teachers and directors, not just at this college, but across the board. We need to embed leadership for inclusion into every level of education and professional development."

She smiled slightly. "And you think you can change the world with this research?"

I laughed, feeling a bit self-conscious. "I don't know about that. But if I can shine a light on the problem and start a conversation about solutions here at Eastern Community College, then maybe I can help move the needle, even just a little, in the Colorado Community College System."

Dr. Moore sat quietly for a moment, then said, "When's the big day?"

I grinned. "March 19. That's my defense date."

Her smile widened. "You'd better believe I'll be there. Front row."

"Thanks, Dr. M.," I said, feeling a swell of gratitude. "Your support has meant so much to me throughout this process."

"And your work means a lot to this field," she replied firmly. "Don't forget that, Andrew. What you're doing here matters, even if it's just your classes. It matters."

As I left her office, her words echoed in my mind. *It matters.* I felt a deep sense of purpose, unlike my last year at Vista. The finish line was in sight, and I knew I could cross it.

***

The canyon walls of downtown Denver stretched in front of me as I walked toward the towering Lawrence Building at the university. Mid-March morning sunlight bounced off the western skyline, glinting across the highest windows. I entered the elevator and rode to the eleventh floor, where years of learning, unlearning, reflection, and growth were about to culminate.

The room was small. A dozen people—some in person, some online—attended. My dissertation committee sat in the front row, four individuals who had rigorously challenged my thinking and shaped the work I was about to defend. Among them was the professor who had guided me through my early leadership courses, now watching with an encouraging smile.

Scattered throughout the room were people who had walked beside me, embodied reminders of the journey. On the right, near the door, sat Natalie, Citlali, and Itzel. Citlali was coloring in her *Moana*-themed coloring book humming the lyrics of "How Far I'll Go" from the *Moana* movie. Itzel played with Natalie's fingers on her lap. I glanced at them with love and hope. I wanted this research to shape the way future teachers and directors in Colorado would co-create inclusive spaces for children like my daughters.

In the left corner sat Virginia, quiet and steady. She had been my stabilizing force for years. In front of her were Mr. Tom, Cecilia, and Beatriz.

Mr. Tom, who was nearing retirement, and I had shared occasional breakfasts. His collaborative approach to early intervention still echoed in my thinking. Cecilia and I had stayed connected in a number of ways. When Vista's status as a "good" school was threatened the year after I left because it lacked opportunities for children with disabilities, a new Foundations classroom opened, and she stepped in as the Spanish-speaking paraprofessional for an early childhood special education teacher who did not speak Spanish. She only told me days before the defense.

Beatriz, Jimmy's mom, whom I had bumped into weeks earlier at a conference, was working on a master's degree in social work, inspired by our work and experiences she had in room 122. I was stunned. I hadn't realized how deeply our time together had affected her. In that moment, I felt a powerful rush of gratitude for the mutuality of learning that had happened in room 122.

Others from my twelfth year of teaching young children were there in spirit. A few months prior, Cecilia had texted me about David A. and David R., who were both now in specialized classrooms for children with autism.

The only time they see kids without disabilities is lunch, she wrote.

I knew this would happen. How do they expect the Davids to thrive if they never experience inclusion? It's heartbreaking, I replied.

Who's responsible for getting them into the regular classrooms? Cecilia questioned.

The Individual Education Program team. Say, have you heard anything about Diana? I asked.

Cecilia responded instantly. *The lady from the Early Childhood Special Education Department?*

Yeah, is she still in Metro Denver Unified School District? It was an itch I needed to scratch.

I heard from someone that she resigned earlier this year. I don't know. Why?

I didn't know how to feel about her departure. *Just curious.*

Ana joined from Spain, her camera off as she nursed her youngest daughter. She and Sergio now had two girls. During a recent WhatsApp chat, she reminded me of how Maya, her former teaching assistant, and Lillie, mine, had taught me something unforgettable about relationships. Their abilities to develop and maintain meaningful relationships without carrying them beyond the classroom were indelible. It was something Ana and I committed to work on.

Dr. Moore, who had hoped to attend, called that morning to say she couldn't make it. But before hanging up, she left me with words I would carry into the room: "You've done the work, Andrew. Your research is going to matter in ways you can't yet foresee."

As the conversations in the room quieted, the chair of my committee nodded to Natalie to begin introductions. Everyone shared who they were and their connection to me or the research. Then, it was Virginia's turn.

"My name is Virginia," she said to the audience, "and I'm Andrew's mentor."

Her voice was steady but full of emotion. I had always called her my mentor, but I had never heard her use the word herself. It landed like a gift, a confirmation of something sacred between us. She was a steady presence who believed in me before I could believe in myself.

Then it was my turn. I stepped forward, heart pounding but not from fear. I was ready, and behind me was the PowerPoint I had been working on for weeks.

I introduced my study, "Preparing Early Childhood Professionals to be Directors in High-Quality Inclusive Programs: A Case Study of One Community College." Each slide was built upon the last, grounded in both research and lived experience.

When I reached the slide about the significance of my research, I spoke plainly. "The barriers I faced creating inclusive classrooms weren't just about curriculum or training. They were systemic and deeply tied to the absence of leadership development in early childhood education."

I advanced to a quote from my dissertation. "The quality of leadership directly impacts the ability to create and sustain inclusive environments where all children, regardless of abilities, feel a sense of belonging."

The committee nodded, and Virginia took notes.

I shared findings from faculty and student interviews, which underscored the leadership gaps in community college course content. I offered four key findings and three recommendations, then I arrived at the final slide.

I paused, noticing Natalie slip out with the girls. She blew me a kiss and mouthed, "You got this." My face perked up, and I stood tall to say what I had come to say.

"Inclusion doesn't rest on one teacher or one classroom. It's a system. And systems only change when we lead together—directors, educators, families, assistants, policymakers, all working from shared values and senses of belonging, being welcomed as they are."

I looked around the room at the people who had shaped me personally and professionally, then I continued. "This work was inspired by them. For the children who deserve to belong. For the teachers still trying. And for the leaders not yet discovered, who will carry this work forward."

I glanced at Virginia, who was beaming.

"Inclusion begins with leadership," I said. "If we fail to build and nurture leadership, we will continue to fail our children. My professional mission is to change that."

Applause followed, then came the questions. They were deep, curious, and validating. When the committee stepped out to deliberate, the silence that remained was reverent, not empty.

They returned minutes later. My dissertation committee chair stood and said, "Congratulations, Dr. Goff."

The words wrapped around me like a blanket warmed by loved ones. Virginia hugged me first. "You did it," she whispered. "I always knew you would."

Cecilia, Mr. Tom, and Beatriz embraced me one by one, sharing celebratory words of encouragement. Ana messaged before signing off. *¡Felicidades! You don't need a coffee cup to tell you you're the best teacher ever. You are,* she quipped, referring to the shattered mug that once lay on the carpet of room 122. *No sería quien soy sin ti. Estoy muy orgullosa, Dr. Goff.*

I finished my goodbyes and began packing up. While waiting for the computer to shut down, I thought of Dr. Moore's words. She believed my work carried more significance than I realized. She was right, though not in the way I first understood. The significance was not only in what the research might offer others. It was how the research helped me understand the purpose beneath my work. I could see how much I had changed from the beginning of my doctorate to that very moment.

As I stood there, I finally understood what I had long been trying to name. My leadership is not confined to one classroom, one job title, or one formal role. It is the work of creating conditions where high-quality, meaningful inclusion is the expectation in every classroom, school, and community. It is shaped over time through relationships, integrity, shared responsibility, and the strain of working within imperfect systems. Reflecting on my classroom experiences and completing this research did not fix the system, but it helped me understand my role. My purpose was to help others lead high-quality, meaningful, inclusive classrooms, programs, communities, and beyond. That purpose would guide me, even when the policies and systems around me echoed the broken trust, the shattered mug, and the children whose inclusion I had fought so hard to protect for twelve years.

EPILOGUE

In March, almost two years after I left Vista, I defended my dissertation. I believed I had reached a clear understanding of teaching and leadership, enough to guide the next stage of my career. That sense of certainty did not last long.

In the months that followed, I realized that what I thought was an ending was only a beginning. The questions I carried from Vista continued to reshape how I approached teaching, leadership, and research. My understanding of the work kept evolving, often in ways I did not anticipate.

Looking back, the moment that signaled this shift came the afternoon the Best Teacher Ever mug shattered on the carpet of room 122. I had defined myself by being capable, steady, and in control. That year forced me to reconsider everything I thought I knew about teaching and leadership. The break was painful, yet it opened a path for the growth that followed.

This perspective became clearer after graduation. Dr. Moore assigned me to teach the leadership courses at Eastern Community College, and those classrooms became a place to rebuild. I brought in guest speakers, experimented with new ideas, and worked with part-time instructors to strengthen how we prepared early childhood professionals to lead in their programs. The work was steady and practical. It helped me refine ideas that had taken shape during my time at Vista.

A few years later, I accepted a position at Western Valley Community College, a significantly smaller institution for higher education. I continue to serve as the coordinator and lead instructor. The size of the program allows me to be more intentional. Part-time faculty request guidance. Students are more open to change because their programs, located in remote rural communities, are far more under-resourced than those near Denver. The work feels grounded and aligned with my values.

Early in my tenure, I joined an Office of Special Education Programs in the United States Department of Education grant-funded research partnership between the Colorado Community College System, the University of Colorado Denver, and the University of Denver. The project aimed to prepare college faculty to teach their students how to create inclusive classrooms. Strategies were embedded across the eleven courses taught at all thirteen community colleges in the state, but there was still no explicit focus on leadership in inclusive programs, the center of my work.

That focus emerged when one of the lead researchers from the University of Denver asked to study Western Valley Community College more closely. We had embedded leadership for inclusive programs into every course, following the recommendations from my dissertation. The early results were promising. When the grant was renewed, the research team expanded the scope and placed specific emphasis on leadership, shaped in part by the work we had already completed.

For the first time, it felt like the questions that began in room 122 were influencing practice on a larger scale. The project became the closest I had come to seeing my dissertation research fully realized.

A year into the expanded work, the Office of Special Education Programs in the United States Department of Education canceled the grant. The decision arrived without warning, and the justification was even harder to absorb. The project used the words inclusion, equity, and diversity, terms that had been required and praised by federal reviewers when the grant was renewed. The research team was heartbroken. The primary investigator mounted a determined defense, emphasizing that the project centered on children with disabilities, not the broader political issues those words had become associated with. The distinction did not matter. The decision stood. The work stopped.

As I write this, an email canceling all remaining research team meetings sits in my inbox. The abrupt end felt like another shattering, echoing the same systemic failures I witnessed at Vista, the ones that first pushed me to question how institutions shape the experiences of teachers, families, and young children. Systems often incentivize isolation. Teachers are expected to navigate impossible expectations quietly, vulnerable to the decisions of administrators and policymakers, and often discouraged from taking initiative on behalf of inclusion. The cancellation of the grant was another reminder of how deeply those patterns run. I began to see that my work would always live in the space between policy and purpose, between what institutions require and what children deserve.

Even so, the work has not ended. It is simply shifting. The momentum slowed, the scope may have narrowed, and the timeline changed, yet the commitment remained. I have come to understand this through the same lessons I learned at Vista and on Clear Creek Hill. Progress unfolds in its own time, and the work that endures depends on presence.

The connections I once wrote about still matter, though now I see connection as something broader. It is not only about people. It is also about time, growth, and the relationship I have with my own becoming. The connection I value most now is the one between who I was, who I am, and who I am becoming.

This is what I meant in the introduction when I said this story is one of becoming. It took ten years for me to understand that the stories I shared in *Love Is a Classroom*, and now in *Shattered and Becoming*, were not just memories. They became mirrors that revealed how imperfect, painful, and meaningful moments shaped who I am today and windows that helped me see who I was still becoming. Those early responses were not always right. They were honest, they were human, and they created the conditions for better ones.

Shattered and Becoming is not a conclusion. It is a continuation. It reminds me that teaching does not come from what we master but from what we notice. Leadership is still central, yet it no longer looks like a set of strategies or a defined role. It begins within us. The centerpiece is leadership grounded in presence. Our responsibility as leaders is to meet each opportunity with an open heart and an open mind, in service of others. My dissertation taught me this in theory. My years since Vista taught me this in practice.

So, thank you for reading this book. Thank you for stepping into my journey. Thank you for loving children and yourself enough to keep growing. We never stop becoming, not as long as we stay present and receive each moment with an open heart and open mind, in service of others. The weight, the shattering, and the becoming are all part of the journey between policy and purpose.

ACKNOWLEDGMENTS

I want to thank my editor, Chrissy, cover designer, Sam, and beta readers Terri, Brittany, Katy, Jenna, Dorothy, and Kyla. Your thoughtful feedback throughout the two-year journey of writing this book helped me see both the story and my own experience with greater clarity. Thank you, Janiece and Ashley, for always being there when I've needed an eye, ear, or a shoulder.

I am also deeply grateful to my wife and daughters for keeping me grounded. You reminded me to stay disciplined, to step away from "the book," and to be present with our family. Your love, patience, and interruptions mattered more than you know. You continually remind me that while I may be well-versed in my profession, I am still learning how to be a father. Each day, you invite me to reflect more deeply on what it means to carry a father's heart. I love you three immensely.

REFERENCES

Bellamy, G. Thomas, Lindy Crawford, Laura Huber Marshall, and Gail A. Coulter. 2005. "The Fail-Safe Schools Challenge: Leadership Possibilities from High Reliability Organizations." *Educational Administration Quarterly* 41 (3): 383–412.

Cashman, Kevin. 2008. *Leadership from the Inside Out: Becoming a Leader for Life*. Berrett-Koehler Publishers.

Division for Early Childhood. 2015. "DEC Position Statement: Leadership in Early Intervention and Early Childhood Special Education." Council for Exceptional Children.

National Association for the Education of Young Children and Division for Early Childhood. 2009. "Early Childhood Inclusion: A Joint Position Statement of the Division for Early Childhood (DEC) and the National Association for the Education of Young Children (NAEYC)." The University of North Carolina, FPG Child Development Institute.

www.ingramcontent.com/pod-product-compliance
Lightning Source LLC
Chambersburg PA
CBHW071542120726

48009CB00002B/63